GABLE & LOMBARD & POWELL & HARLOW

BY THE SAME AUTHORS:

LUCY:
The Bittersweet Life of Lucille Ball

LANA:
The Public and Private Lives of Miss Turner

BRANDO:
The Unauthorised Biography

REBELS:
The Rebel Hero in Films

JUDY:
The Films and Career of Judy Garland

The Amazing Careers of Bob Hope
(with Eleanor Clark)

Those Great Movie Ads
(with Eleanor Clark)

The Films of World War II
(with John Griggs)

Gable & Lombard & Powell & Harlow

Joe Morella & Edward Z. Epstein

W. H. ALLEN · LONDON
A Howard & Wyndham Company
1976

PRINTED IN GREAT BRITAIN BY
FLETCHER & SON LTD, NORWICH
FOR THE PUBLISHERS, W. H. ALLEN & CO. LTD,
44 HILL STREET, LONDON W1X 8LB
BOUND BY RICHARD CLAY (THE CHAUCER PRESS) LTD,
BUNGAY, SUFFOLK

ISBN 0 491 01975 0

To Our Families
and to our good friend,
Maddy Solter

The authors gratefully acknowledge the co-operation of the many individuals who granted interviews for this book. In some instances names have been withheld at their request.

A special Thank You to:
Gabe Essoe, Tom Jones, David C. L'Heureux, Kay Mulvey, Lou Valentino, and Madelaine Solter.

A WORD ABOUT 'GABLE AND LOMBARD' –
THE MOVIE

Clark Gable and Carole Lombard were fascinating, controversial personalities, and it was to be expected that the new Universal film, *Gable and Lombard*, would be a fascinating project.

The idea was director Sidney Furie's. After helming the highly acclaimed *Lady Sings The Blues*, the story of singer Billie Holiday, Furie had the inspiration to make a film about the most famous lovers Hollywood has yet produced – Gable and Lombard.

Furie's timing was perfect. Today the film industry is able to present realistic portrayals of legendary personalities. However, the major problem in making a film like *Gable and Lombard* was, of course, the casting.

Many top stars coveted the leads. After extensive screen testing the parts were awarded to James Brolin and Jill Clayburgh. Sidney Furie says: 'I wanted to cast Brolin from the start. He has what I wanted. A basic resemblance to Gable, and a lot of talent, guts and the quality of a gentleman.'

Jill Clayburgh, a noted young Broadway actress, won the role of Lombard because of her remarkable ability to merge facets of her own personality with those of Lombard's. She captures the *essence* of Lombard.

Producer Harry Korshak and director Furie made the final casting decision because Brolin and Clayburgh could project the personalities of the stars and most importantly there was that necessary 'star chemistry' between them.

This book reveals the love story of Clark Gable and Carole Lombard and details their relationship with many other stars of their era. The final chapter brings Clark and Carole back to the screen and explores the making of Universal's *Gable and Lombard*.

CHAPTER ONE

'Step back. Step back, *please*.' The MGM studio police force, along with local authorities, was on hand to help control the crowds. Hordes of gawkers were gathered at the main gate.

Another black limousine drove up.

'I'm sorry, Mr Gable,' said one of the cops. 'I'll have to ask your chauffeur to open the trunk. We're checking for stowaways.'

It was a beautiful, balmy June day in 1937. The cinema great and near great had congregated at the vast green Valhalla known as Forest Lawn Memorial Park to bury one of their own. Box-office sex goddess Jean Harlow had died at the incredibly young age of twenty-six. Not since the demise of Rudolph Valentino, eleven years earlier, had a star of such current popularity passed into another world.

The solemnity of the occasion didn't muffle the squeals and gasps of delight from onlookers as they caught a glimpse of Clark Gable and Carole Lombard, Hollywood's most famous lovers. Clark and Carole, both in black and wearing dark glasses. But still strikingly recognizable. They were not married yet, and rarely made public appearances together. In fact, Gable was still married to his second wife. But everyone had known that today Gable and Lombard would be there.

William Powell, grief-stricken, was at least accorded some dignity by the gaping crowd as it pressed forward toward each new arrival; the fans had to know what autographs they might garner afterward.

It was a scene that could have been out of *A Star Is Born*, and Gable and Lombard, both Hollywood veterans by now, were disgusted at the spectacle.

'Don't let this happen when I go, Pa,' Carole whispered to Clark. He was visibly shaken, and clasped Carole's hand tightly.

Gable had loved Jean Harlow both on and off screen. They were in the midst of making the film *Saratoga* when Jean was stricken with what developed into her fatal illness. It seemed inconceivable to Clark that now, barely a week later, he was one of the pallbearers at her funeral.

Though it was only a twenty-minute ceremony, to those present it seemed like hours. The air was heavy with the sweet smell of the thousands of floral tributes.

As Gable helped lift the bronze coffin and carry it to the hearse, he was again struck by the spectacle of the stargazers crowding the entrance to the church. Lombard, walking somberly behind, in black turban, dress, and Persian lamb cape, was tense and distraught. Her heart went out to Bill Powell, who was trembling from the ordeal. Carole had, after all, been married to 'Pop', and they had remained intimate friends after their divorce. She would have to help him though.

How could Carole Lombard have suspected that personal catastrophes yet to strike hovered menacingly over her and Gable and Powell even as Jean Harlow was being laid to rest?

Gable. Lombard. Powell. Harlow. The all-consuming love affairs of these vital, pampered, passionate human beings had captured and held the imaginations of moviegoers throughout the world. They were sex symbols of their time, lovers and mates in the fabulous world of genuine make-believe that was Hollywood in the 1930s.

An emotional distance of almost four decades tends to soft-focus memories, to romanticize events. The good is remembered; the bad is forgiven or forgotten.

Objectively weighing all facts and new information: Would the fabled Gable–Lombard marriage have survived, had Lombard lived? Would tormented young Jean Harlow, victim of three disastrous marriages, have found 'true happiness' with her final lover, William Powell, Lombard's ex-husband? Had Jean Harlow and Clark Gable been bedmates as well as soulmates?

Are any of the fantastic rumors true? For many years there was talk that Gable was impotent, even sterile. Or did he, in the mid-1930s, have an illegitimate child by a leading Hollywood star?

What of the lurid stories of Harlow's sex life? Did William Powell walk out on her when she needed him most? Has Powell, who triumphed over cancer, ever recovered from the anguish of losing Jean?

And was Gable's overwhelming guilt over Lombard's death because of his continual and flagrant infidelities during their marriage?

9

Many cold, harsh facts about the private lives and loves of these four were clouded in an era when press agents directed considerable energies toward manufacturing fantastic fictions about idols of the day.

In the off-the-record comments of a former top film writer-producer and one-time chief of a major studio: 'A liberated approach to life – sex, drugs, alcohol – is not indigenous to the current generation, you know. We did everything you kids do today, only we didn't talk about it, and newspapers didn't dare print it.'

Gable and Lombard and Powell and Harlow were liberated even by today's standards. They were unique, ambitious individuals who thrust their way to movie stardom. All Midwesterners, they were as American as apple pie – but definitely not the folks next door.

Clark and Carole and Bill and Jean. Their lives were indelibly intertwined, and each had a direct effect upon the others. Who were these four? What brought them together? How did they come to be legends in their own time?

CHAPTER TWO

'I don't love you any more,' Billy Gable snarled curtly at his tearful sweetheart, Frances Doerfler. 'I never believed this could happen to me, but I'm going to study with Miss Dillon for the next few years. Without her help, I'll never get anywhere. Working with her has come to mean everything to me.'

It was not a film, and the dialogue wasn't invented by a writer.

Frances was crushed. But it didn't stop twenty-two-year-old Billy Gable and thirty-five-year-old Josephine Dillon from leaving for Hollywood soon afterward. Billy didn't look back. The world would come to know this ambitious youth as Clark Gable. But he didn't as yet remotely resemble the handsome, suave, debonair, swash-buckling screen hero he would become. It would take nearly ten more years, two wives, and an expert dentist to transform Billy, the boy from the little town of Cadiz, Ohio, into the leading male sex symbol – and one of the most beloved screen idols – in the history of films.

It had been a tough journey.

Adela Hershelman Gable was a frail woman, and during her pregnancy she was warned there would be complications. But on February 1, 1901, she gave birth to her only child, William Clark Gable. All seemed well, but post-natal complications set in, and Mrs Gable died when her son was ten months old.

The baby's father, William Gable, Sr, was an itinerant oilman. He left the rearing of his son to his parents, his wife's parents, and his brother-in-law and sister-in-law, Tom and Josie Hershelman.

'Your boy will be raised as a Catholic,' Gable, a staunch Protestant, was told. He didn't like that idea. When Billy reached two, William, Sr, married 'a plain Methodist woman', Jenny Dunlap, an ex-librarian. The marriage was completely ordinary, but it was love at first sight between Jennie and little Billy. She had never had children, and raised Billy as though he were her own.

She spoiled him thoroughly, and the boy adored her. 'The best day of my life,' recalled the adult Clark Gable, 'was the day I met my stepmother. She was a wonderful woman, although I didn't realize it then. She must have loved me very much.'

Billy Gable enjoyed a normal upbringing – he went to high school, played basketball, had the usual adolescent love affairs. At sixteen, with the country in the midst of World War I, Billy left home and went to Akron. 'To work for the Firestone Tire and Rubber Company, for ninety-five dollars a month.' It was in Akron that Billy got his first taste of the theater. He went to the Akron Music Hall, saw *Bird of Paradise*, and was so infatuated that he went back every night and began hanging around the stage door, making friends with the actors. He was stage-struck.

The boy was certainly no budding Adonis. He was tall, with unusually large ears, hands, and feet, poor teeth, and a gangling manner. His face was so thin that his protruding ears made his head resemble a sugar bowl. But he was personable, and talked himself into a job as a callboy at the Music Hall: the guy who knocks on dressing-room doors and yells, 'Five minutes!'

11

He also wangled a small walk-on role, with one line of dialogue.

Billy returned home briefly when his beloved stepmother died. His father decided to sell the house and farm and go to the Oklahoma oil fields. 'Come with me,' William, Sr, urged his son.

Billy wouldn't go, and returned to Akron and the theater. Billy's father, en route to Tulsa, stopped off in Akron to see his son. 'We had our picture taken together, and we shot a lot of pool,' the elder Gable recalled many years later. 'That was one game I always beat him at.'

Billy next tried his luck in New York. The only job he could get was another as a callboy. However, the stars of the show were John and Lionel Barrymore. The famous brothers were in the midst of their 179-performance run of *The Jest*. Lionel took a liking to young Gable, but the boy was untrained and had no experience, so there wasn't much Barrymore could do for him at this point. When the play closed, Billy was out of work and out of money in the big city. He decided to join his father.

In Bigheart, Oklahoma, Billy toiled for twelve hours and twelve dollars a day as a tool dresser, an oil-field apprentice. He hated it, and when he turned twenty-one he knew he would return to the theater. His father advised him against it, and the boy's decision caused a rift between father and son that would not heal for years.

After bumming around the country in several stock companies, Billy found himself at liberty in Oregon. Earning some money by working as a lumberjack, he moved to Portland and spent his spare hours around local theatrical people. There he met the first important woman in his life, a young actress, Frances Doerfler.

Theirs was a love affair and friendship that would endure, in an on-and-off-and-on-again fashion, for years. They were even engaged, briefly. When they met, Frances was twenty-three, Gable twenty-one. She was one of the few women Clark was ever involved with who was approximately his own age and not years older.

Miss Doerfler was the first in a string of many women who allowed themselves to be used by Clark Gable. Though he obviously had genuine affection for her, he was aware that she was in a position to help him get a job with the local repertory company, which she did.

Through Frances, Gable met Josephine Dillon, an iron-willed, ambitious acting teacher-director-actress. Miss Dillon, thirteen years Billy's senior, reacted to him as Frances – and most women – had. 'Who could help it?' she confided to screenwriter Ben Hecht years later. 'I was honest with him, and he was honest with me. He was a raw youth, but there was a great potential.'

The fashionable hotel in Portland was the Portland Hotel. Josephine landed Gable a job singing there. Clark wasn't much of a singer, and nobody knew it better than he and Josephine. But the rich old ladies were delighted just to watch him. Josephine had him finish his act with the old chestnut 'Mother Machree', a consistent show stopper.

After working in several theater-group productions under Miss Dillon's direction, they became inseparable. Billy dumped Frances Doerfler, and after Josephine went to Hollywood, Gable joined her there. Some stories would have us believe that Gable, when he got to Hollywood, 'ran into Miss Dillon on a Hollywood street', and since he was down to his last dollar she invited him to stay at her twenty-dollar-a-month apartment while she moved in with a friend.

The truth, of course, is that their relationship had long since progressed to one of intimacy. They had lived together in Portland for a year, and after six months in Hollywood they were married, on December 13, 1924.

The new Mrs Gable was no slouch. She had an impressive background. Her father was a noted California judge who had served as prosecutor. She had been educated abroad and at Stanford University. One of her sisters was an opera singer, the other a composer. Josephine had chosen the theater, and after starring on Broadway she turned her talents to lecturing and teaching. (In addition to Gable, her roster of students later included Gary Cooper and 'Mexican Spitfire' Lupe Velez.)

In Hollywood the newlywed Gables shared a common cause: advancing Billy's career. One of the few jobs Dillon allowed her young husband to take was as an extra in movies. Even though they often needed money desperately, she refused to let him accept any other type of employment.

During 1925 Gable literally scrounged for bit parts. He was an extra in *The Merry Widow*, starring John Gilbert and Mae Murray. Billy was dazzled by the opulence of the MGM

13

production and the royal treatment accorded Gilbert and Murray. It was almost unreal. Every whim of Gilbert's was attended to. Miss Murray had only to ask and her wishes were granted.

When asked, in an interview she gave in the mid-1930s, what she thought of 'the new rage' Clark Gable, by then a top star, Miss Murray, who hadn't made the transition from silent films to talkies, replied: 'He's the poor man's John Gilbert.'

Gable hungered for the success of a John Gilbert. Josephine pushed him without letup. He must be ready when the right opportunity came along. Breathing exercises day and night to make his voice deeper; climbing up and down stairs to give him a less-gawky walk. She sent him off to the movies to study actors he could learn from.

Josephine made Gable educate himself, reading Thackeray and Dickens. She took him to some all-important Hollywood parties where he could be seen, and, while there, educated him in the niceties of the social graces.

Her efforts paid off. He was a good student. 'Too good,' warned her friend William Farnum. Farnum, a great star in silent pictures, told her: 'Josephine, darling, don't you realize what will happen if that big he-man of yours ever makes it big in show business?'

They were at a party, and Gable was not in sight. Josephine motioned for Farnum to continue.

'The first thing,' he went on, 'is that you will lose him to a younger woman.'

She clenched her fists. 'That is not inevitable,' she said, containing her anger.

'Possibly not. But you must know that he is the sort of man all women go crazy about. The moment he becomes important here or on Broadway, rich women, younger women, beautiful women will be after him. Dozens of them. So why don't you stop teaching him how to act? Get him to go into some profession or trade where he won't attract the attention from women an actor does. Why lose him?'

'That,' she stated confidently, 'Is a risk I must take.'

She wouldn't lose him overnight. Gable's career struggled on, but, as Farnum had predicted, his marriage faltered. Gable often sought the comforts of other women.

On a spring day in 1925, Jane Cowl, a leading Broadway star, was along with the husband-and-wife producing team of

Louis MacLoon and Lillian Albertson, casting for small parts in their Los Angeles production of *Romeo and Juliet*. Miss Cowl and Miss Albertson were on stage waiting to inspect the ten 'spear carriers', for which a call had gone out for men 'over six feet'.

Jane Cowl, once married to *The New York Times* drama critic Adolph Klauber, was a highly sexed woman with a penchant for young, attractive men. When she saw Gable, she turned to Lillian and remarked: 'Lillian. Look at that wonderful-looking young man. I want him.'

Miss Albertson shot her a knowing look, and Miss Cowl quickly added, 'I mean, for the show of course.'

'I assumed that's what you meant,' answered Miss Albertson.

Though he seemed ill at ease and awkward, Gable knew the play by heart. 'What are we waiting for?' Miss Cowl asked. 'He's the right size, isn't he?'

After all ten spear carriers had been cast, Miss Albertson went back to her office. Clark stopped by around a half-hour later.

'Miss Cowl asked me to have dinner with her,' he said nerviously. There was a pause.

'Where?' Lillian asked, as if she didn't know.

'In her rooms,' Clark replied, shuffling his feet.

'Why tell me?' she inquired, genuinely interested.

'I wanted to know if it was all right with you if I went.'

'Sure, it's all right with me.'

Miss Albertson later observed, 'At that time, Clark was terribly thin and awkward. But he had a rugged quality of physique and personality that was interesting.'

Shortly after the play opened, Gable was promoted to the role of Mercutio. The actor playing that role had left the company – 'For good!' – and Billy Gable dined nightly with Jane Cowl.

Josephine accepted what she could not change.

Gable's career had finally started to move. The MacLoons gave Clark a role in *The Lullabye* at the Curran Theatre in San Francisco. During the run he was visited backstage by Frances Doerfler. Miss Doerfler was obviously still in love with Gable, and they briefly continued their affair.

The next important woman to give Gable a boost was the

famous stage and screen star Pauline Frederick. She was only forty, a relatively young woman so far as Clark was concerned. One of the great beauties of her time, she was known as 'the girl with the topaz eyes'. Her greatest successes were in the roles of women in trouble, in such vehicles as *Zaza*, *Madame X*, and *Tosca*.

When she met Gable, she had already been married three times and involved in several divorce actions, and a young actor had committed suicide over her.

Pauline was even more demanding than the other women Gable had 'serviced'. Although she furthered his career by casting him in an important role in her production of *Madame X*, Gable did not enjoy being alone with her. She often had music played by violinists to induce the 'proper mood' for lovers. To avoid having to make love to her, Gable often brought along a pal, Eddie Woods. 'Stick around, don't leave me alone with her,' he'd plead with Eddie.

Gable used to complain to members of the cast of *Madame X* that Pauline stuffed him with oysters, since she considered them an aphrodisiac. Gable moaned to friends, 'They talk about Jolson singing every song as though it would be his last. This dame acts like every lay is going to be her last!'

'Gable was spoiled even then,' noted Hedda Hopper, an actress herself in those years. 'Most older women were easily satisfied just by being with him. He had become used to being pursued.'

Though it has been said that when Josephine learned of the Frederick affair it caused the final break in their marriage, this was not true. Their marriage had long since deteriorated, and she was more than aware that he had used *all* his talents in furthering his career. While they were still married, Josephine decided it would be best for him to adopt his middle name professionally. He agreed, and from then on Billy Gable was known as Clark Gable.

Summer, 1926. Lionel Barrymore was directing and starring in a revival of *The Copperhead* in a Los Angeles stage production. He recalled Clark 'Billy' Gable from *The Jest*. The boy had made nice progress. Barrymore gave him the role of the juvenile lead in his new production.

Despite a couple of on-stage mix-ups which prompted Barrymore to bawl Gable out after opening night, things went well, and it seemed that Clark might be on the way to bigger things.

After *Copperhead* came a small role in a film by highly respected director Ernst Lubitsch. Silent-film superstars Pola Negri and Rod LaRocque headed the cast. But Clark didn't respond to Lubitsch's direction, and another bit player was given his role. Gable, not one to gild the lily when referring to his early days, never forgot this. 'I was crushed,' he admitted of the Lubitsch debacle.

Clark had earned less than a thousand dollars over the past two years. But something always turned up. After weeks of inactivity, he landed the role of the reporter in a stock-company production of *Chicago* (later made into the movie *Roxie Hart*, starring Ginger Rogers). There he was spotted by a Houston stock-company talent scout who had come to Hollywood to find new talent for his repertory group. He offered Gable a job.

'Should I take it?' he asked Josephine. He still respected her advice, and consulted her whenever he felt the need. Her unequivocal 'Yes!' prompted him to accept. They would be separated, but the experience would be invaluable and provide a steady income.

Josephine missed him terribly, and later moved to Houston to join Gable with the Gene Lewis Players. But there was too much friction when she again began coaching him. Asked to leave, she returned unhappily to California.

And now came an indication of how the public would react to Clark Gable. The women of Houston were making him their matinee idol. After each performance, squealing females would gather at the stage door, waiting to glimpse their exciting new discovery. As he always would, Clark allowed himself to accept the favors of a few of them. One girl, whose father was a tailor, arranged for Gable to get a whole new wardrobe. Another woman begged him to divorce Josephine and marry her. As a dowry she offered half of her lucrative insurance business.

But Josephine Dillon Gable would not lose Clark to a younger woman. It would be, in fact, to a woman years older than she was.

Ria Franklin Prentiss Lucas Langham was a Houston socialite, and one of the chief backers of the stock company employing Clark. Born Maria Franklin in Kentucky, she was married at an early age to William Prentiss, by whom she had a son. She divorced Prentiss and, a resourceful woman, moved to Houston, where she took a job at a chic jewelry shop, J. J. Sweeney's. There she met her second husband, oil millionaire Alfred T. Lucas. They had two children, and enjoyed a happy and lavish life until his death. When Ria met Gable, she was married to her third husband, wealthy stockbroker Andrew Langham.

Friends of the time say that Clark was not responsible for Ria's breaking with her husband. But there was no doubt that Ria was intensely attracted to the young man with the gray-green bedroom eyes, and her infatuation with him didn't sit well with Mr Langham. They divorced.

Ria was instrumental in having Clark raised from featured player to leading man, with a salary boost from seventy-five to two hundred dollars a week. More important, she took over where Josephine had left off in the development of Clark Gable. She introduced him to a higher style of living, teaching him about fine clothes, good food, vintage wine, social etiquette, the art of conversation. She even instructed him in table manners. He had evolved into a too slick 'actor type', which Ria modified and made into a 'gentleman'.

Whereas official studio publicity in later years claimed that Clark traveled to New York alone, where he first met Ria when she went backstage with her brother after seeing him in a play, what actually happened was that Clark wanted to go to New York, and he had Ria finance his assault on Broadway. She placed her daughter at a finishing school in Westchester County and took an apartment on New York's Fifth Avenue. She furnished it exquisitely, and introduced Clark to a lifestyle of Chippendale and Tiffany. It was a world Gable had never known, but quickly acquired – and kept – a taste for.

He landed one of the leads in a Broadway drama, *Machinal,* but the play folded in twelve weeks. Then he got a role in a George M. Cohan show, *Gambling.* He was fired by Cohan in Philadelphia, and Cohan played the part himself.

Another, more reliable approach to Clark's career – the Gable tried-and-true method – was utilized. An important Broadway star, Alice Brady, became the target of the considerable Gable charm. She quickly hired him to star opposite her and George Brent in *Love, Honor and Betray.* But it ran only forty-five performances.

Just as Josephine had looked the other way when Clark

romanced Jane Cowl and Pauline Frederick, Ria Langham made no scenes over Clark's forced interest in Miss Brady. Brady was 'strictly business'.

While Clark and Ria languished in Fifth Avenue splendor, a somewhat impoverished Josephine Dillon came to town. Miss Dillon had landed a role in a play titled *The Ivory Door*. She tried to reach Clark, who refused to see her or even talk to her on the telephone. Josephine went to Frank Hotaling, a mutual friend. 'Please find out what Clark is going to do,' she implored. 'Find out if he wants a divorce.'

'What the hell do I want a divorce for?' was Gable's laughing reply to Hotaling. 'I never intend to get married again. If she wants a divorce, let her get it.'

Clark was troubled by enough women in his life. The tailor's daughter from Houston, as well as the insurance lady, had trailed him to New York. But Ria easily and quietly out-classed all competition.

Mrs Langham had none of the brash theatricality of a Jane Cowl or a Pauline Frederick. She made no demands. Seventeen years older than Clark, she was petite, regal, and, though not at all a beauty, she was quite striking. She had style, taste, 'class', as Clark would later say. In addition, she could provide him all the financial help he required to launch his Hollywood career.

Gable was finally honest with Josephine. In her words: 'He told me frankly that he wanted to marry Mrs Langham because she could no more for him financially than I could. I kept my word to him ... namely, that if he ever asked me for a divorce and that I felt that he really meant it, I would grant his request.'

Miss Dillon asked for and received no alimony or financial settlement. (Years later, Gable did help her avoid bank-ruptcy.)

The Gable career was shaping up. There was a proven play which had a role that could make Clark a star. Spencer Tracy had played this role, 'Killer Mears', in a Broadway production of *The Last Mile*. It had gotten him a movie contract. Ria Langham figured the role would do the same for her young protégé.

Gable's friend Lewis MacLoon agreed to stage a West Coast production under the sponsorship of Mrs Langham.

'Forget it, Ria,' Clark told her. 'I saw Tracy do it, and

19

I couldn't be as good. I don't want to kill my career now.'

Ria phoned MacLoon and told him Clark was hesitant. MacLoon phoned Gable and assured him, 'You won't have to be that good out here.'

Gable agreed to do it, and returned to Los Angeles in June of 1930. He found the atmosphere much changed. Talkies had taken hold, the studio heads were in a quandary about their expensive rosters of silent stars. Rudimentary sound techniques were not advanced enough to hide the embarrassing falsettos of such actors as John Gilbert and William Haines, who were about to fall from favor in the public eye.

Moviemakers were looking for stars with stage experience. They found that such people came across best on the talking screen. Drama schools were beginning to flourish, and people like Josephine Dillon would find their services very much in demand.

Gable's performance in *The Last Mile* turned out better than he had thought it would, and Lionel Barrymore, who had faith in 'the kid', said: 'I think you'd be good in pictures. I'd like to have a test made of you.'

The test, with Gable costumed as a native boy in *Bird of Paradise,* was a dismal failure.

'Look at those big, batlike ears,' roared MGM production chief Irving Thalberg when he saw the test. 'Forget it, Lionel.'

But on the basis of the test, and Clark's hit in *The Last Mile,* Gable did get an agent. Minna Wallis, sister of producer Hal Wallis, and Ruth Collier, her partner, took over his representation.

After the MGM test, Gable had a job offer for a play in New York. As he was packing, he got a call from Minna.

'Sonny boy – I can get you a movie job in a western.'

'I can't ride – haven't been on a horse since I was a kid.'

'You'd ride a horse for seven hundred fifty bucks a week, wouldn't you?'

'I'd ride anything for that, but I signed a contract for a play in New York.'

'Get out of it,' Minna suggested.

He did. When he and Minna got to Pathé studios, the casting director said, 'Can you ride, Gable?'

'Are you trying to be insulting?' snapped Minna before Clark could say anything. 'This man has the blood of Buffalo Bill in his veins. He comes from General Custer's home town.'

After Minna had firmed the deal for $750 a week, Gable still protested, 'I can't ride.'

'*Take lessons!*'

The part was as a villain opposite William Boyd. While on location in Arizona, Gable was very unhappy. Boyd, trying to encourage him, once took him to Flagstaff to meet some young girls, who said, 'Is *this* the guy you were telling us about? Good Christ!' And when Boyd asked what was wrong with Gable, they said, '*Everything!*'

Although Pathé was impressed with Gable, the studio was on the verge of bankruptcy.

'Just my luck,' Clark complained.

But Gable hadn't gone completely unnoticed by the film colony. Budding young director Mervyn LeRoy tested him for the upcoming *Little Caesar*. Studio chief Jack Warner and his production executive, Darryl F. Zanuck, both reacted as Irving Thalberg had. 'The ears are ridiculous,' they claimed.

All the same, Gable appeared in a Warner Brothers film, *Night Nurse*, in a small role opposite Barbara Stanwyck. The picture didn't create an overwhelming demand for Clark's services. Gable then took – and failed – a screen test at Universal.

Lionel Barrymore wouldn't give up. He arranged a new test at MGM. Gable followed Barrymore's advice: 'Don't smile.' Barrymore knew Clark's bad teeth would photograph poorly. This time, the studio signed him.

Afraid that MGM would drop their option when they found out about his teeth, Gable went for some quick dental work. Always frugal (a trait never to leave him), he went to a second-rate dentist. It was a sloppy job that eventually would necessitate the removal of all his teeth and require a full set of uppers and lowers. But this secret would remain secure, so far as the public was concerned, until after his death.

Meanwhile, it was 1930, and although he didn't realize it at the time, Clark had arrived. He would remain at MGM for twenty-five years.

CHAPTER THREE

'Let me stitch this without using an anesthetic,' urged the surgeon. 'If I use one, your face muscles will relax and you'll never look the same again.'

The young girl gritted her teeth as the surgeon's painful needle moved in and out of her cheek to sew the fourteen stitches across the left side of her face. Tears streamed from her eyes, but she didn't utter a sound.

Then her eyelids were taped down for several hours. 'Don't move a muscle in your face for ten days,' she was instructed.

She followed the doctor's orders and was horrified when, at the end of the prescribed period, when the stitches were removed, there was a disfiguring red scar.

'No, no,' she sobbed. She had been so pretty that night she went out with her boyfriend Harry Cooper in his sports car.

Then the accident. She was thrown against the windshield of the Bugatti roadster, and the broken glass slashed her cheek.

Now, after the bandages were removed, the doctor tried to quiet her, reassuring her that the scar would recede. In time.

'In time?' She was shattered. And angry.

Meanwhile, with the encouragement of her mother, Bessie, and her older brothers, Frederick and Stuart, Carole Lombard, née Jane Peters, decided to make good use of her time. She was only a teen-ager, but had already appeared in movies, and intended to continue doing so. She threw herself into studying photography, make-up, lighting.

Even with the help of plastic surgery, a tiny part of this scar would always remain. But Jane Peters was not one to give up. When she turned her attentions to a goal, there was no rest until she achieved it.

She was of hearty stock. Born in Fort Wayne, Indiana, on October 6, 1908, Jane and her two older brothers were brought to Los Angeles in 1915, when their parents separated. Her name and her birthplace were the only two ordinary things about the girl who was to become Carole Lombard. The Peters family was well-to-do and industrious. Her father remained in Indiana and ran the Horton Company, which had been founded by his father.

Jane's mother, Bessie Chaney Peters, had a grandfather who had established the first electric company in California and helped finance the laying of the Atlantic Cable. He was also a director of the First National City Bank.

Jane was always a tomboy, and loved the company of her older brothers and their friends. She grew up preferring the company of men, a true 'man's woman', and because of her childhood association with the opposite sex, she always had a healthy truckdriver's vocabulary.

In true Hollywood fashion, the fable is that the little girl was 'discovered' over a backyard fence by a movie director. Actually, the Peters' neighbors Al and Rita Kaufman had seen Jane in a school play and introduced her to their director friend, Allan Dwan. Dwan gave the twelve-year-old a fifty-dollar, three-day job as Monte Blue's sister in *A Perfect Crime*. After that, nothing but a film career would do. Jane's mother, however, insisted, 'School comes first.'

When Jane graduated from junior high school, Mama was won over, and helped Jane pursue a career. The girl won several Charleston dance contests and landed a job at Fox as Edmund Lowe's wife in *Marriage in Transit*. She was only sixteen but classically beautiful, with huge blue eyes and light blonde hair, which had to be darkened to make her appear older.

Fox asked Jane to change her name. She picked up the Lombard from a neighbor, a retired Boston banker. It was her mother who selected the name Carol, without an 'e'. The 'e' was added later, by mistake, but Lombard kept the new spelling. Both Carole and Bessie were serious students of numerology and felt the extra letter would bring good luck.

Carole remained at Fox for two years, and worked in westerns opposite popular stars like Buck Jones and Ken Maynard. The salty language she had picked up from her brothers and their friends was enlarged upon, thanks to her contact with cowboys. She made good use of a blue streak of gamy language for shock effect and to ward off unwanted advances.

Lombard also enjoyed using swear words for comic effect. Few people who knew her were shocked by it. She had a marvelous ability, friends recall, to dish out expletives in calm, conversational tones. 'What the fuck do you think you're doing?' the blonde angel would sweetly ask someone who had grabbed her in the wrong spot. 'Hey, someone, get this fucker

23

off the set.'

But Carole never swore in front of her mother or in front of children.

The automobile accident sidelined her for almost a year. But after nine months Carole said, 'To hell with this.'

With her mother's encouragement, and the help of a friend, Lonnie Dorsey, who was employed by Mack Sennett, she got a job at Mack Sennett Studios. There she met the woman who, next to her mother, would be the closest friend she would ever have: Madelynne Fields, a Sennett comedienne. They had known each other only slightly as children, but now they became best friends. Carole later stated, 'Fieldsie and I shared a room, our clothes, an old car, and even our dates through all those hectic days. I love her dearly.' It seems unlikely they shared their clothes, since Fieldsie was many, many pounds heavier than Carole.

When Sennett Studios folded, Fieldsie, as Carole had nicknamed Madelynne, became Lombard's manager. She got Carole a role in *The Divine Sinner*, a silent picture, and then arraged for a contract at Pathé.

The contract paid $150 a week, and Carole was ecstatic. 'I thought I was in the big money,' she noted. Joseph P. Kennedy, father of the Kennedy clan, was the head of the studio. He told Carole, who weighed 120 pounds at the time, 'You're too fat.'

Lombard, eager to keep the contract, immediately agreed to take reducing treatments from Madame Sylvia, the studio's body expert. But, always an independent girl, Carole got in a parting shot at Kennedy before she left his office. 'You're not so skinny yourself,' she quipped, slamming the door behind her.

As it turned out, both Lombard and Kennedy underwent Madame Sylvia's regimen. She lost 10 pounds, and kept her weight at around 112 from then on.

At Pathé, Carole got valuable experience and worked under talented directors like Raoul Walsh and Gregory LaCava. She was very much a part of the social scene of the day. It was the Jazz Era, the time of Flaming Youth. Carole was in the center of it, and if there was a beau that all the girls were after, like Tommy Lee, Don Lee's son, she went after him – and got him.

And she learned her way around the all-important business side of show business. Fieldsie was a shrewd manager, and the two ladies were a formidable duo. Lombard learned early on that there was no room in the business for misplaced sentiment-

24

ality. 'Kiss my ass!' was one of Lombard's favorite retorts to people foolish enough to try to take advantage of her.

But she was fiercely loyal to people she loved, and she and Fieldsie enjoyed a long and profitable friendship. Through Fieldsie's efforts, Lombard landed a contract with Paramount in 1930. The association with that studio would build her into a top star, and there she would meet the two men she was to marry.

CHAPTER FOUR

William Powell was always a ladies' man. In his debonair, suave, sophisticated, quiet way, Powell was a sexier guy than most of his more braggadocio contemporaries. 'It was men like Bill Powell and George Brent who got laid a lot,' remarked the ever-observant Ben Hecht.

By the time Powell made his first movie, in 1920, he was already twenty-eight years old, with years of stage experience behind him. His looks were very much in the mold of leading men popular in the 1920s, such as Edmund Lowe, Warner Baxter, Adolph Menjou. Powell was not particularly handsome, but he was such a stylish, charming actor that audiences of the day were not aware – or didn't care – that he didn't have 'a Barrymore profile'.

The Powell background was, like Carole Lombard's, upper-middle-class. He was born in Pittsburgh, Pennsylvania, on July 29, 1892, to Nettie Manile Brady Powell and Horatio Warren Powell. Baby William was a month premature. It was a family joke that this was the only time Powell was ever early. Like many a potential actor, he was an opinionated, vocal child. According to his mother, he began making speeches as soon as he could talk.

Girls were a Powell preoccupation from the beginning. 'I shall never forget my first love affair. She sat in front of me in the Sixth Ward grade school – a divine blonde. Somehow I seem to forget her name, which was obliterated by a stunning brunette with blue eyes, who in turn fades before the haunting

25

memory of a certain redhead ...'

Puffery, but accurate nonetheless. However, Powell's interests broadened when the family moved to Kansas City, Missouri, in 1907. Bill entered Central Union High School, and it was there that he discovered the world of drama, in addition to his continuing interest in 'beautiful young ladies'. In a Christmas play he got the part of Captain Absolute in Sheridan's *The Rivals*. He was hooked.

Prior to this, at the urging of his conservative father, a staid public accountant, Bill had been planning a career in law. But after *The Rivals*, 'I had fallen in love with my leading lady during rehearsals, junked my law career with the first burst of applause, and started to rewrite Shakespeare the next day.'

A former classmate remembers Bill for the dramatic manner in which he recited entire chapters of the classics, and for 'an almost visible mantle of aloofness which set him apart.' Powell says that at graduation he was given a 'courtesy' diploma. And his ambitions were apparent to his contemporaries. He was co-recipient of his class's 'most likely to succeed' award.

But the elder Powell was angry that his son wanted to be an actor. It was not a most respected profession at the turn of the century. To please his father, Bill enrolled at the University of Kansas in the fall of 1911, to follow a career in law. However, after only one week Powell quit and announced his intention to pursue a career in acting.

To save money to go to New York to study, Powell took a job during the day as a clerk at the Home Telephone Company, at a salary of fifty dollars a month. In the evenings he ushered at the local opera house. Five months later, finding himself no richer and owing his father fifty dollars, the boy made an impassioned plea to a rich aunt in Pennsylvania.

Powell recalls, 'I wrote a twenty-three-page letter to her, explaining why the world, and myself, would be indebted if she loaned me fourteen hundred eleven dollars so that I could go for two terms. I itemized the probable living expenses in New York.'

His generous aunt responded to his request by return mail, enclosing a check for $750 (a considerable amount in those days). Powell eventually paid her back, with 6 percent interest, making the final payment on the loan thirteen years later.

'As a matter of plain truth,' states Powell, 'I didn't quit school for the stage – it was a girl.'

In New York Powell enrolled at the American Academy. His classmates included Edward G. Robinson and Joseph Schildkraut. Within six months all his money was gone. Years later, when the Powell wit had emerged, he recalled: 'Six months in dramatic school convinced me that I knew more than they did, so I set out to get a job, and landed one in Rex Beach's *The Ne'er Do Well*. The starting salary was eighteen dollars, but my "act" and a few white lies got me forty dollars.'

His luck didn't hold out. *The Ne'er Do Well*, which opened in September, 1912, closed after only two weeks, and Powell and his friend Ralph Barton (later to become a successful caricaturist) suffered through what Bill later described as 'the hardest winter I ever spent'.

But then things looked up, and in 1913 he landed a role in a hit, *Within the Law*, and toured with the road company through that year and the following. There was a pretty actress in the troupe, Eileen Wilson, and she and Powell fell in love. In April, 1915, they were married.

For the next several years William Powell worked with stock companies in Pittsburgh, Portland, Detroit, Buffalo, North-ampton, and Worcester. At one period he played a grueling forty weeks of one-night stands. These were the days without air conditioning, microphones, antibiotics. Frequently he acted two parts in one play. But he kept getting progressively better, and his popularity began to grow.

A role in *Spanish Love* on Broadway in 1920 led to the role of Moriarty in the silent film *Sherlock Holmes*. Then in 1922, came a 'big break'. José Ruben, who was to have played the lead in *When Knighthood Was in Flower*, was hit in the eye with a piece of steel and had to be replaced. Powell was signed for the part by newspaper magnate-turned-impresario William Randolph Hearst, who was producing the film as a vehicle for his sweetheart, Marion Davies. Powell recalls, 'No, I wasn't a smashing success. I was impossible. So instead, I was given a terrifically big scene as Francis First, the heavy.'

It was the big league now. Following the film with Marion Davies, he did a movie for Richard Barthelmess, who was to become one of his lifelong friends. *The Bright Shawl* was filmed on location in Cuba. Then came *Under the Red Robe*, again for Hearst, and *Romola*, for Barthelmess. This was a major production, and Powell co-starred with box-office powerhouses Lillian and Dorothy Gish. The movie was filmed

27

on location in Italy.

This extensive traveling broadened Powell and enabled him to develop even further into the epitome of the 'sophisticated gentleman' he would represent on screen in the thirties.

Marion Davies and William Randolph Hearst, who then had their Cosmopolitan pictures released through Paramount, became friends with Powell, and later would befriend Gable, Lombard, and most of the other top stars of the thirties. Unlike Gable, Lombard, and Harlow, Powell had a philosophical outlook. He took the time to ponder that actors inevitably become totally self-involved.

While in Florence he had time to think. 'That beautiful square in front of the Uffizi Gallery was my favorite haunt. I felt that I *belonged*. I realized that here at home we become frightfully important to ourselves. I do, I know; my troubles are magnified, difficulties within myself are hard to overcome. But there – well, I was lifted out of that.

'I realized how a man is limited by his point of view, how it shapes his whole life. But there – well, I had time to think, and try to figure things out a bit. I could lose sight of myself.'

When *Romola* was completed, he took the opportunity to do something he had always wanted to do: tour the Continent. Then, as a result of his soul-searching in Florence, he made the decision to leave the stage for good and go to Hollywood.

Paramount, which had used him briefly in 1922 in *Outcast*, was so impressed by his performance as the villain in *Romola* – the character who marries Lillian and seduces Dorothy – that he was signed in 1924 to a seven-year contract.

Powell and Eileen moved to Hollywood. For the first time in their ten-year marriage, they had a permanent home. In 1925, Eileen gave birth to Powell's only child, William David Powell.

But for a man with a roving eye, Hollywood was a dangerous home base. The temptations were limitless. Powell liked the glamor of Hollywood and enjoyed making films. He was a social man who won many friends among elite Hollywood 'society'. His wardrobe was impeccable, and he became known as one of the town's best-dressed men.

It was still the day of the silents, and Powell's superb voice was not yet a negotiable asset. Paramount cast him as the heavy in a score of comedy-melodramas, including *Aloma of the South Seas*, *The Great Gatsby*, *Beau Geste*. In *Beau Geste* he excelled, sharing some of the spotlight with his good friend

Ronald Colman, with whom he had worked and lived during the *Romola* shooting in Florence.

Powell made his talkie film debut in 1929, in *Interference*. At a time when the sound track put a sudden end to the careers of many silent-screen stars, Powell's stage-trained voice was a lifesaver. But at the time he was bored and restless, and commented, 'Making pictures isn't fun any more. It's the hardest kind of work. There seems to be such a hurry about making talking pictures. I don't know why. They're like having a Broadway opening every night.'

Even though he'd played villains and bad guys, Powell brought subtle human qualities to the roles, and Paramount decided to try a new image.

The turning point in Powell's career came when the studio cast him as the debonair sleuth Philo Vance in *The Canary Murder Case*. It was a tremendous success, and was followed by further appearances as Vance in *The Greene Murder Case*, *The Benson Murder Case*, and *Paramount on Parade*. Powell actually considered the Philo Vance character 'too much a snob', but the pictures were popular, and he realized that 'Vance made a pile of money for the studio, and for me, too'.

Paramount began using Powell in a variety of roles, among them a number of society dramas. One of these was *Street of Chance*, with Kay Francis (to be his leading lady many more times).

But the inevitable had happened. As his career spiraled, his marriage faltered, and Powell and Eileen drifted further apart, and eventually divorced.

In 1930 the man who admitted to having been 'girl conscious' from the age of fourteen, and who over-tipped waitresses because he 'liked to see their eyes shine', fell hard for a vivacious young blonde on the Paramount lot. And William Powell, who'd eventually be known as the screen's 'perfect husband', was about to woo and win Carole Lombard.

CHAPTER FIVE

'My breasts, my breasts,' moaned the platinum Venus as her nipples enlarged to the size of thimbles. 'Oh, please, please fuck me,' she pleaded with the husky truck driver.

Quotes and scenes similar to this have been attributed post-humously to poor Jean Harlow in the several decades since her death. A veritable mountain of fiction in the guise of fact has been written about lovely, tragic Harlean Carpentier. The truth is straightforward and simple, but events in her private life snowballed to such fantastic proportions that on them the Legend of Platinum Blonde Jean Harlow has been built.

Harlean's unlikely birthplace was decidedly mundane Kansas City, Missouri, on March 3, 1911. It was the year William Powell was graduating from high school in the same city.

Harlean's mother, Jean Harlow Carpentier, was a vapid, plumpish, but pretty blonde. The woman's latent flair for the dramatic was indicated in her chosen name for her little girl. Taking the first part of her last name, and the last part of her first name, she concocted 'Harlean'.

Harlean's father, Montclair Carpentier, was a dentist.

From its inception, the Carpentier marriage was hopelessly dull but, 'for Harlean's sake', they tried to make it work. It was no use. By mutual consent, and 'with no hard feelings', they divorced when Harlean was nine.

Mama Jean took her daughter and moved in with her parents, Sam and Ella Harlow. Harlow was a strait-laced, ultra-conservative, well-to-do real-estate broker who had a penchant for running other people's lives. He was determined to raise his granddaughter strictly, certain that his own daughter 'didn't know what the hell she was doing' when it came to raising a child.

Nor did he. Harlean was enrolled in the respected but some-what stultifying Barstow School for Girls at her grandfather's insistence. Dr Carpentier didn't approve but was overruled.

During the girl's formative years, Grandfather took over completely. He forbade Harlean to play with friends or invite them home because she might 'catch something' – a cold, a virus. Never could 'the baby' enjoy a normal 'play in the sand' existence. Grandpa always insisted Harlean be meticulously groomed and dressed. He lavished gifts on her, and even bought the child an ermine bedspread.

Grandpa was so domineering that Jean Carpentier finally could take it no more. She left Harlean with Grandpa and Grandma and escaped to Chicago – 'to visit cousins', have some *fun*, and maybe find a job. Instead, she found a husband. They met one evening at the College Inn, when Jean, alone, allowed herself to be picked up at dinner by Marino Bello.

Swarthy, sophisticated, well-dressed, and not exactly shy, Bello was a slick character who would haunt Mama Jean's life – and her daughter's – for years. Marino, 'a man's man' who boasted of an endless stream of female conquests, awakened in Jean Carpentier a sexual appetite that only he could satisfy. His awesome influence over the woman – and, through her, her daughter – was a burden neither mother nor daughter would succeed in shaking off. The two major emotional crises Harlean Carpentier had to face as a child were the divorce of her parents and her mother's remarriage.

Sam Harlow became hysterical upon learning of his daughter's new husband. He referred to Bella as 'an Italian gangster' and refused to let them visit the house. But Harlean, very attached to Mama, wanted to be with her. Jean missed her baby too, but Grandpa rigidly enforced his 'stay away' edict. For four years – from 1922 through 1925 – Marino and Jean Harlow Carpentier Bello lived in Chicago, in various second-rate hotels and apartments. The future business manager of his movie-siren-to-be stepdaughter was in turn a waiter, wholesale food salesman, and seller of unlisted five-and-dime stocks.

Mama Jean was permitted by her father to return home to Kansas City only twice during these years, on Christmas Day of 1924 and again in 1925. During this time Harlean continued on at the Barstow School, where she was an average student. She hadn't many friends; her grandfather saw to that. Sam Harlow even offended Harlean's father by accusing him of having intentionally 'plotted' his divorce. After that, Dr Carpentier refused to come to the house, and Harlean had to visit Daddy at his office.

Young Harlean's physical appearance developed spectacularly. At fourteen she was envied by her classmates, and her grandfather became even more protective of her: 'Goddamned if she's going to go out with boys before she's eigh-

31

teen.' And he'd pick the boys.

On that second Christmas visit, in 1925, Mrs Bello developed a bad bronchial cold and, to Grandpa's dismay, had to remain at the Harlow home for several weeks. (Years later, when producers were contemplating scripts on the life of Jean Harlow, Mrs Bello's Christmas cold was transferred to Harlean and amplified into infantile paralysis, spinal meningitis, diphtheria, and/or scarlet fever.) 'But that husband of yours *stays away*,' Grandpa commanded. He was white with fury when Marino flew to join her anyway.

Mrs Bello's bronchial infection did in fact linger for weeks, and by the time she was recovered, she had reestablished her mother–daughter relationship with Harlean.

Sam Harlow detested Marino more than ever. But one trait the 'oily Latin' possessed was a hide as thick as an elephant's. So long as he had his creature comforts, which his new wife saw were provided, and could immerse himself in his mysterious 'business deals' involving undiscovered gold mines, promising stocks, and the like, he was happy, despite Grandpa's outright offensiveness. And so long as Marino satisfied Mama Jean's long dormant sexual passions, she was more than happy.

The moans that ofttimes emanated from the second-floor bedroom occupied by Mama Jean and her husband once prompted her father to ask Bello, 'Are you beating my daughter?' The response made Mr Harlow blush and ask no more questions.

Young Harlean knew better than to ask. Her feminine intuition provided the correct answers.

Bello was a charmer when he wanted to be, and his relations with his stepdaughter were, at this point, cordial. He taught her some of the social graces: how to tango and waltz, even how to apply lipstick 'so as to make a man want to kiss you'.

Even Dr Carpentier was grateful that someone, *anyone*, had arrived on the scene to give Harlean the benefit of some guidance other than that coming from her maniacal grandfather. 'I do what I can,' said Marino. 'A girl that age needs a father, not a grandfather.'

Carpentier felt the best thing that he could do for his daughter would be to 'get her out of that house'. He decided the time had come to act. He confronted Sam Harlow: 'It's about time that Harlean is given an opportunity to grow up.'

This time Grandpa's ravings accomplished nothing. Harlean, now fifteen (and still called 'the baby' by her family), was enrolled at the private boarding school Ferry Hall, in Lake Forest, Illinois.

It was September, 1926. Gable was a struggling actor; Lombard was working in films; William Powell was a star, and the father of a one-year-old son. Teen-aged Harlean was a beauty: tiny – five feet, two inches – with incredible, creamy skin, china-blue eyes, and, most striking, hair that was a shade of white blonde. She resembled a miniature, voluptuous porcelain figurine, complete with kewpie-doll lips.

In later years the Hollywood studios would make much of Harlean's Ferry Hall education. Ferry Hall was a proper finishing school, and the image-makers tried to create the illusion that the girl was one of the school's crowning achievements.

Actually, she was there less than a year. She didn't make many friends, was homesick, and wrote to her mother and grandparents almost daily. Sam and Grandma Ella, who was a quiet, empathetic woman, longed for her to come home. But, 'for the sake of the child', Dr Carpentier, Mama Jean, and Bello insisted that Harlean remain at Ferry Hall.

To further compound the girl's unhappiness at school, she was reprimanded when, now fully developed, she refused to wear a brassiere. After stern lectures by one of her teachers, she still protested: 'I feel I can't breathe when I'm wearing a brassiere.'

Harlean began dating a Chicago lad, Charles McGrew, whose family was in the stock market. He was 'old' – twenty-one – and she wrote her mother that although she liked him very much, she'd give him up if it could be arranged to withdraw her from school and 'take me home'.

Mama was quickly shipped to Chicago to visit Harlean. All were concerned that 'the baby' might not remain 'a good girl'. Harlean tearfully assured Mama that she was still 'a good girl', but, to see that she remained that way, could Mama 'please take me out of school?'

'I'll try, sweetheart,' Mrs Bello reassured her daughter, lying. 'But you know your grandfather ...'

Harlean was furious when, a week later, Mama telephoned that she would take baby out of school but only after the end of the school year.

'No!' cried the girl. 'I want to come home *now. Please.*'

But it had been decided. So Harlean took matters into her own hands. On a Sunday in March, 1927, sixteen-year-old Harlean Carpentier eloped with Charles McGrew. The Ferry Hall School, learning of the union, wired Harlean's grandparents to remove their rebellious granddaughter 'at once'. The school did not permit married women as students. To make matters worse, McGrew was then whisked away from his child bride by his family and sent to 'visit relatives' far away from Chicago.

A miserable, confused Harlean was taken home by her stepfather. And Grandpa Sam had by now thrown up his hands. He wanted 'the whole bunch', including Harlean, out of his house. He gave them enough money to last almost a year.

Mama Jean and Marino packed up their belongings and took an unhappy Harlean to live in Los Angeles in the summer of 1927. They took a small, furnished two-bedroom apartment within easy commuting distance of downtown.

Harlean started smoking, and didn't return to high school. She tried to forget her marital fiasco, and Marino was sympathetic, understanding, and seemed to know the right things to say so she wouldn't cry.

In the California sun, Harlean's hair became even lighter and whiter, although she couldn't sunbathe because her milk-white skin burned easily.

It didn't take a seer to predict the unusually striking young girl would have more than a fair chance in the world of films, though the family hadn't moved to Los Angeles for that purpose. Even at the young age of seventeen, Harlean had the unmistakable appearance of a girl who knew her way around. The assumption that 'no one can look like that and not know the score' was the kind of sentiment she would have to cope with throughout her life.

Soon Grandpa Harlow stopped sending money. Marino wouldn't soil his hands, so Mama Jean tried getting jobs, and went through several: five-and-ten saleslady, restaurant cashier, door-to-door cosmetics saleslady.

One of Harlean's girlfriends suggested that Harlean join her in getting work as an extra. Harlean was a divorced woman now. She changed her name, adopting her mother's maiden name, Jean Harlow, and got a card from the Central Casting Bureau. She made the usual rounds. It was all a lark to her.

When Grandpa learned of Harlean's new hobby, he blew

34

up. But he got over it, as usual, and, according to Mama Jean, 'he's keeping you in his will'. Later Jean said she went for work as a movie extra because 'that was all I was qualified for'. The pay was $7.50 a day plus lunch, and helped pay the family's expenses.

In the summer of 1929, agent Arthur Landau was at Hal Roach Studios, where Laurel and Hardy were filming a comedy. A voluptuous, young, unusually blonde girl in a revealing green gown was called to Landau's attention by Stan Laurel.

Landau was impressed, and inquired about the girl's background. Laurel told him they'd used her a couple of times previously, most recently in a film titled *Double Whoopee*.

"It was the girl's platinum hair that made me look twice,' recalled Landau. He subsequently learned that, in addition to the Laurel and Hardy appearances, she had done bit roles in several Christy comedies and in *Moran of the Marines*, a Richard Dix–Ruth Elder starrer. Recently she had Charlestoned in *The Saturday Night Kid*, in which she got her name on screen for the first time. It was a Clara Bow picture that hadn't yet been released. Jean had also been an extra in the Charlie Chaplin film *City Lights*.

Jean was hopelessly inadequate in the acting department, and knew it. Landau wasn't sure what he could do to advance the girl's career, but her looks had impressed him sufficiently for him to sign her.

A major film of the day had been having endless production problems. Involved was an Arthur Landau client, actress Greta Nissen. Miss Nissen had been signed for the lead in the massively expensive Howard Hughes production of *Hell's Angels*, which had been in various stages of production for over two years. She was an important star, earning $2,500 a week. *Angels* had been shot silent, and now, with talkies suddenly the rage, Hughes wanted to scrap everything and remake the film as 'an all-talking picture'.

Greta Nissen was Norwegian, and was saddled with a heavy homeland accent. In *Hell's Angels* she was playing an all-American girl. She would have to be replaced and Landau saw the opportunity for his neophyte client to try out for the part. Other leading ladies who had marquee value – like Dorothy Mackaill, who was first choice as replacement – were unavailable. In one of those 'gossamer thread of circumstance' occurrences, Landau took an ultra-long shot and suggested that his totally unknown, unskilled client Jean Harlow might be a good choice for the part.

The head cameraman on *Hell's Angels* was Gaetano Gaudio. He recalled that 'we made a test of the girl. The poor thing was sent back to make-up after she first appeared on the set. Her dress was all wrong, too, and that had to be changed.' Despite these setbacks, especially Jean's nervousness, the test didn't turn out too badly, but Hughes, upon seeing it, wasn't impressed.

Harlow didn't have a remotely 'cultured' voice, but, if nothing else, it was 100 percent American, and she was right in type for the role: 'a combination good kid and slut' was how the *Hell's Angels* character was described.

In any case, Howard Hughes felt that the spectacular aerial sequences of the picture, and stars Ben Lyon and James Hall, were the real attractions anyway. Harlow's striking platinum-blonde appearance was at least original, and Hughes gambled that she'd work out. She was paid $1,500 for six weeks' work, and put under contract to Hughes's Caddo Company.

Despite Harold Robbins's insinuations in the fictional *The Carpetbaggers*, Jean Harlow did not have a love affair with Howard Hughes. This was corroborated when Hughes's right-hand man, Noah Dietrich, wrote a tell-all book about his boss, *Howard: The Amazing Mr Hughes*. Dietrich shed further light on what Miss Harlow was like when he described how, sometime later, when Harlow was sent on tour to promote *Hell's Angels*, she offered to sleep with Dietrich if he'd have the Hughes organization pay the bill for an expensive gown she had bought.

Hell's Angels director James Whale, one of several directors who contributed to the film, had to wring a performance from young Jean. Her inexperience stood out like a beacon. She was terribly nervous and insecure, and at one point, playing a seduction scene, none of her attempts at emoting seemed to please Whale.

'Tell me,' she implored, desperate and earnest. 'Tell me exactly how you want me to do it.'

Apparently things worked out. *Hell's Angels* opened in June, 1930, and established Jean Harlow, virtually overnight, as a motion-picture sex symbol. She gained further national celebrity via one particular line of dialogue in the picture. Wearing a sexy, totally revealing negligee-type evening gown, she said: 'Do you mind if I slip into something comfortable?'

Jean Harlow, nineteen years old, was suddenly 'the hottest property in films'. She joined Gable, Lombard, and Powell on the Hollywood scene. And soon their lives would intertwine.

CHAPTER SIX

Hollywood, 1930. Though the stock market had crashed and the Great Depression had begun, Hollywood was still – for a few lucky ones – the land of dreams. The air was heavy with the scent of orange and lemon blossoms. There was no pollution. Mostly palm trees, open spaces. Some newcomers were disappointed. 'It's like Main Street!' exclaimed a very young Bette Davis when she first saw it.

Successful movie people were earning thousands of dollars per week. Parties were still the order of the day. In the right homes, champagne literally flowed like water. Clark Gable and Ria Langham, whose reputation as a superb hostess had preceded her, were welcome new additions to the town.

One of the reasons MGM now signed Gable was because a respected studio executive, Paul Bern, saw potential in the young man's screen test. Gable's first contract was for two years, with six-month renewal options, at a salary of $350 per week.

The first person with whom Clark shared the good news was not Ria but 'old reliable' Frances Doerfler, who was working at a Hollywood dress shop. Gable celebrated by taking Frances to a Christmas dinner at the Brown Derby. But, in true Cable style, he didn't give her a Christmas present. He felt he had to save every penny in case MGM didn't renew his contract.

Because of his early poverty, Gable was driven, throughout his lifetime, to be extremely frugal and penny-pinching, always saving everything 'for a rainy day'. He never gave tips or presents, justifying it to himself as 'not wanting to buy anyone's friendship'.

Clark's first picture for MGM was *The Easiest Way*, with Constance Bennett. She was the Big Star, and Gable was very unhappy. He wrote Frances, 'Constance Bennett doesn't even know I'm alive.' While Clark couldn't further his career by using Miss Bennett, he *was* noticed, and helped, by Metro's fast-rising young star, Joan Crawford.

This intense, young, brunette beauty – Hollywood's 'Hotcha Kid' – was driven by a fantastic passion for living. She fell hard for the Gable charm. 'This magnetic man had more sheer male magic than anyone ... and every woman knew it. He knew it too. It was as much a part of him as his own breathing.'

Joan asked that Clark be cast in her upcoming film, *Dance, Fools, Dance*.

Crawford and Gable had a great deal in common. They had both worked their way up from nothing. And certain columnists sneered that the couple shared a similar reputation – they were both opportunists. Crawford had been accused of marrying Douglas Fairbanks, Jr, to further her career. That marriage was still being publicized by MGM as 'one of the most idyllic in Hollywood.'

Louis B. Mayer was concerned when the romance between Crawford and Gable began getting out of hand. But the attraction between the stars registered on screen, and after *Dance, Fools, Dance* Mayer decided, at Crawford's suggestion, to replace Johnny Mack Brown with Gable in Joan's *Complete Surrender*, renamed *Laughing Sinners*. The studio re-shot practically the entire movie, since Brown had been in most of the scenes.

Joan, her marriage to Douglas Fairbanks, Jr, on the rocks, was afraid to get deeply involved with Clark. 'My misgiving was that he might be one of those men who desire a woman they can't have; once they attain her, they lose interest.' She was fearful it wouldn't last, that she couldn't make it last, 'that every girl who ever worked with Clark would feel the same way I did.'

But she also admitted that in this and other films they did together, 'When the scenes ended, the emotion didn't.' According to Joan, however, they only went to lunch a couple of times, and their love was 'bounded by the flats on the set'.

Clark ostensibly tried to convince her that things between

them could work out. 'We talked of marriage,' said Joan, 'but I dared not ruin the dreams. I'd rather live with them unfulfilled than have them broken.'

Crawford was twenty-six, Gable twenty-nine. While he was not yet officially divorced from Josephine Dillon, he was definitely indebted to Ria. Since Joan was supposed to be happily married to Fairbanks, gossip ran rampant. The studio didn't care yet about Gable's career, but Crawford was too big an investment to be the subject of a scandal.

While continuing his affair with Crawford, Clark Gable met Jean Harlow. It was on the set of MGM's *The Secret Six.* Jean was on loan-out from Howard Hughes. Still, she got billing over Gable – but below Wallace Beery, Lewis Stone, and Johnny Mack Brown, indicating both Gable's and Harlow's low standing at studio front offices at the time.

Jean and Clark hit it off immediately. During the filming, Gable carefully observed the pert twenty-year-old divorcee who slung herself about with a careless abandon which in no way suggested the finishing-school background publicity emphasized. Because Jean could not memorize lines as easily as Clark, they used to arrive early to rehearse. Finally, one day Gable felt compelled to say, 'Honey, why do you act so goddamned phony?' He told her how off screen she was natural and easy-going, but on screen 'phony as hell.' He gave her the advice he had gotten from Lionel Barrymore: 'Be yourself.'

They became pals, and Harlow was especially thankful to have a friend on the set, since she and Wallace Beery had developed an instant animosity toward each other.

'She's a dumb broad,' grunted Beery, always immersed in his characterizations, 'and can't act.' He told one of the assistant directors, 'Keep her out of my way.' The assistant later told a publicist, 'Harlow thinks he's disgusting. She said he invited her into his dressing room and when she refused he became ugly.'

To create further problems for Jean, her stepfather was constantly on the set, always eager to mingle and 'talk business'. Beery disliked Marino as well as Jean, but Gable and Bello, both 'men's men', hit it off. They had a lot in common. Both were experts on women and how to use them. Later on they would even become hunting buddies.

It is a fact Clark Gable was responsive to Jean Harlow's straightforward sexiness. She never wore any underwear, and he never failed to be turned on. There were no complications in their relationship. He was not the father figure she was endlessly searching for, and she certainly wasn't the domineering mother influence he was partial to. Nor was she 'a hot, raw nerve' like Crawford. It was out-and-out cameraderie, an uncomplicated 'friends who could fuck if they wanted to' type of relationship, without the binding strings of an emotional entanglement.

But Jean wasn't under contract to Metro yet, and after *The Secret Six* she moved on to Columbia. Gable's interest returned to Joan Crawford. Louis B. Mayer wanted something done about Gable and Crawford, and Gable's friends at the studio advised him to 'settle things'. In the midst of all this, Clark was still seeing Frances Doerfler, who hoped that somehow Gable would end up with her. But in this moment of decision, Clark Gable sought the advice of a mature woman.

The decision was made. 'I've got to go to New York on business,' he told Frances. What he failed to tell her was that the business was marrying Ria Langham.

There was a technicality. The New York marriage took place a couple of days before the final decree from the Dillon divorce became legally binding. Therefore, Clark and Ria had to be married again, in Santa Ana, California, on June 19, 1931. Justice of the Peace Kenneth E. Morrison officiated. One of the MGM publicity staff, Joe Sherman, was present. From now on, there would always be an MGM representative present at all important events concerning the young actor.

Clark had a ready answer, which had been prepared for him by the publicity department, for the inevitable query about the 'mature' woman he married. 'The older woman has seen more, heard more, and knows more than the demure young girl with a pretty face and shapely figure. I'll take the older woman every time.'

After the marriage, the Gables were 'respectable'. Clark moved into Ria's home on San Ysidro Drive, next door to Mary Pickford (Joan Crawford's stepmother-in-law). When Clark's father joined them, they rented a house at 220 North Bristol Street in Brentwood, where their neighbors were Barbara Stanwyck and Joan Crawford herself.

Ria was a clever woman, and cultivated Joan's friendship. Joan found her to be 'a charming lady, so happy in Clark's success, so anxious not to intrude on his glamour, and you felt like a heel cherishing this emotion for her husband. I wouldn't have hurt her for the world. Neither would Clark.'

Clark's father remained with the Gables for only a few months. Then he married his brother's widow, Edna, 'a quiet, gentle woman'.

For the first time as an adult, Clark could enjoy a sense of somewhat 'normal' family life. Ria's fourteen-year-old daughter, Georgianna, and eight-year-old son, Alfred, were staying with them. Clark had always liked kids. Ria noted, 'He fell in love with them and they with him. The boy was crazy about him, and later Clark took him hunting on many occasions.'

Life fell into a simple pattern for the Gables. Clark, naturally, worked during the day at the studio. Ria entertained only on weekends. She handled the family's fiances, prohibiting Clark from splurging on any personal extravagances until all his debts had been paid. Clark, always frugal with others, was generous toward himself.

It was around this time that Gable first became interested in hunting. He admired the gun collection of a friend, Dr Franklyn Thorpe, the husband of Mary Astor. One day Clark stared at the guns for a while, then said, 'Let's fix up a party, Doc.'

Doc became one of his favorite hunting companions, along with Wallace and Noah Beery. And MGM's publicity department was quick to capitalize on Clark's fantastic accuracy with a gun.

On weekends when indulging in his new pastimes – hunting, fishing, and camping out – Clark frequently took Ria with him. But she was merely an onlooker and never an enthusiast in any of these ventures.

One of Gable's favorite haunts was 'Rainbow' Gibson's fishing lodge on the Rogue River in Oregon. Rainbow was a fisherman and guide who helped Clark locate salmon. The lodge itself, called the We Ask U Inn, was something off a Hollywood set: large living room filled with deep, comfortable chairs and a huge fireplace. The wooded area around the main building held cabins for the guests. Clark was extremely fond of Gibson's three daughters, who ranged in age from fourteen to ten. He felt at home here.

Also close sporting friends of Clark's were Nan and Harry Fleischmann (of the yeast family), who owned a skeet club which Clark frequented, many times with Ria in tow. Nan

Fleischmann, recalling these times, stated: 'Clark's career was just getting started then. He was earning his first important money, and he was cautious about it. He told me that it was his greatest ambition to have twenty thousand dollars in cash.'

After Gable's fan mail began outdrawing Joan Crawford's and Wallace Berry's, Minna Wallis, in an effort to get him a higher salary, decided to use an old ploy. She instructed her client not to show up on the set, in the hopes that the studio, fearful of any delay which would increase production costs, would panic and grant the salary increase.

But the scheme backfired. When Metro called Minna's office, her partner, Ruth Collier, told them, 'Oh yes, we know where Clark is. But he cannot come back until and unless he gets a one-thousand-dollar-a-week raise.'

At this response, Louis B. Mayer took over and roared, 'We've made Gable what he is, and we can break him twice as fast. We won't give in even if he stays away forever.'

Ruth tried to argue, but Mayer interrupted, 'I will not be blackmailed, young lady. You tell that ingrate to be here in the studio by eight sharp tomorrow morning. If he is not here, he'll never work on this lot again – or anywhere else in Hollywood.'

Eight o'clock the next morning found Gable on the set.

Joan Crawford wasn't the only leading lady on the Metro lot who wanted Clark as a co-star. Greta Garbo insisted Gable be cast opposite her in *Susan Lennox, Her Rise and Fall*. It was a Garbo vehicle, but Gable more than held his own, and he was pleased with his performance.

Top director Clarence Brown requested Clark for *A Free Soul,* a major production starring Norma Shearer. Brown had seen Gable around the studio and had been struck by his 'agile, vicious grace'. Brown, who looked like a professor, was small in appearance. He had been an engineer, and approached film in a similar manner, aware of his tools and utilizing them. His request was granted.

But after reading the script, Clark was concerned and tense. There was a scene which called for him to give a hard slap to Miss Shearer. Lionel Barrymore, who co-starred, recalled: "Clark was in agony over playing the scene. He wanted to give it everything and really slap Norma, as Brown directed, but he was plagued by the thought that she was Irving Thalberg's wife and Metro's biggest star. He was afraid that if he really belted her, it might ruin his chances in films. Norma solved his problem for him. When it came to the big slap scene, she told him to follow Brown's orders, slap her and mean it.'

When Thalberg saw the rushes, he changed the script and had Clark throw Norma around even more. He wanted to make Clark more villainous in order to direct sympathy away from him.

Howard Strickling, MGM's brilliant publicity director, had another idea when he saw the rushes. He wanted to feature a new kind of hero in the publicity. Strickling went to Louis B. Mayer, who agreed. They both wisely realized that the era of the poetic matinee idol was over. Violence and mobsters were *in*. The public was ready for a new type of leading man, who wooed his women with his fists and cynicism rather than with suave elegance.

In *A Free Soul* Gable's character took no nonsense from women, and the public loved it. He opened the doors for other Depression heroes like Cagney, Bogart, Garfield, and Raft. Lionel Barrymore may have won an Oscar for his portrayal of the father in *A Free Soul*, but it is Gable's performance that everyone remembers.

Even before release of the film, the studio knew it had a winner. Larry Barbier, an MGM photographer, recalls: 'The secretaries and the girls in the studio stenographic pool are always a good barometer. Something like an electric shock now ran along the studio grapevine. When he walked into the commissary for lunch, all eyes were on him. Suddenly everyone was aware of Clark Gable.'

Men on the lot liked Gable too. His brand of virility was obvious to everyone. A former MGM executive sums it up: 'When Gable walked down the alley, you could almost hear his balls clank.'

When it was released, *A Free Soul* caused a sensation. Instead of booing the gangster who gave Norma Shearer her due, the audience sided with him for putting her in her place. He was giving her her just deserts. And they cried when he was shot by the girl's fiancé.

Norma herself sumed it up: 'It was Clark who made villains popular. Instead of the audience wanting the good guy to get the girl, they wanted the heavy to win her.' Leslie Howard, who played the suitor in *A Free Soul*, was virtually ignored.

In only about a dozen films, and in one year, Gable went from an unknown to a star. This was accomplished in part because Clark happened to be in the right place at the right time. And a good publicity man, recognizing the opportunity, made the most of it.

That man, Howard Strickling, thereafter played an important role in Gable's entire life. The two men became close friends, and Strickling, later Metro's vice-president in charge of advertising and publicity, personally handled all of Clark's private affairs. Although he always remained in the background, Strickling was there. He knew everything there was to know about Clark Gable. Most of it was kept from the press. The rest was released as Strickling saw fit. Every time Gable needed anything, Strickling arranged it.

One instance indicating Strickling's adeptness was the night in 1945 when Clark, drunk and driving home alone on Sunset Boulevard, lost control of his car. The following day newspapers reported that Gable heroically avoided a head-on collision with a drunk. Another, more startling version of the story was that Clark had been a hit-and-run driver. Naturally, this rumor, circulated verbally only, never reached print.

Strickling was confidant to most of Metro's top stars. It is said that he has kept more news out of print than he released.

Under Strickling's guidance, Gable became the most spectacular new Hollywood personality of 1931. Although MGM's roster included Garbo, Crawford, Marie Dressler, Wallace Beery, Norma Shearer, Leslie Howard, Marion Davies, Mary Astor, Helen Hayes, Franchot Tone, Robert Montgomery, the Barrymores, Lupé Velez, and dozens of others, Gable was unique. He had suave brute force. 'There was always the implied threat of violence,' noted a critic. 'He could get away with almost anything.'

A new catch phrase swept the country: 'Who do you think you are? Clark Gable?'

During the year Gable was re-teamed with Joan Crawford, in *Possessed* – an apt title, since their affair resumed with more intensity than ever. During production, Joan was depressed about her still-floundering marriage. Clark was always sensitive to her mood.

'You didn't sleep last night.'

'How did you know?'

44

'Joan, whatever's bothering you isn't worth it.'

He became a sympathetic friend. They'd go for quiet rides by the sea. And, remembered Miss Crawford, 'All day long we'd seek each other's eyes. It was glorious and hopeless. There seemed nothing we could do about it. There was no chance for us.'

Crawford was vital, vibrant, lovely, passionate, much younger than middle-aged Ria, and without the responsibility of children. But this time wasn't it Gable who was 'happily married'? And Crawford was about to be in the process of a divorce.

The attraction between them was so electric that Gable was willing to dump Ria and marry Joan and 'the hell with the consequences'. But Joan wasn't ready to remarry, and nothing could make her do something that might endanger her career. She turned him down, a decision she reportedly would regret for the rest of her life.

Ria Gable had by now become friendly with and hostess to all of Hollywood's top luminaries. She was a woman who knew how to make the most of her money. She was at ease entertaining the most prominent and influential people, and Clark was usually the centerpiece of her social gatherings. Frequent guests included David O. Selznick and his wife, Irene Mayer Selznick (Louis B. Mayer's daughter), the Samuel Goldwyns, Mary Pickford, Irving Thalberg, and Norma Shearer. Other friends were Helen Hayes, Gloria Swanson, Marlene Dietrich, the Countess Dorothy di Frasso, Joseph Schenck, and Richard Barthelmess.

In addition to partying at home, there were jaunts to visit Marion Davies and William Randolph Hearst at San Simeon. Said Ria: 'Clark enjoyed it all for a while, but he was temperamental and for many weekends he'd do nothing but hunt. He always felt more comfortable in sports clothes. Clark had a deep inferiority complex and was highly sensitive. I remember when he bought his first expensive sports car. It was quite flashy, and he was bursting with pride when he drove it to the studio. Then a slighting remark about it, made in jest, infuriated him. He sold the car immediately, at a tremendous loss.

'It was the same way with his clothes. If anything critical was said about them, he never wore them again. I used to urge him to stand up and fight back, to say, "I like this, whether you do or not", but he never would.'

Many years later, George Joelson, who had been a police-man on the MGM lot, remembered: 'The thing that impressed me most about Clark Gable was the fact that he was always dressed to the teeth. He always looked like a million bucks. You knew he was a movie star the minute you laid eyes on him. He wasn't ostentatious or pretentious. But he always looked like the king he was.'

Ria was proud of the role she played in Gable's life. 'Irving Thalberg said I provided the "frame" for showing Clark off. He congratulated me on having seen his potentialities, and said I could surely "pick 'em".' Then, in a revealing statement, Ria also admitted: 'I was always arranging a screen test for some young hopeful.'

Clark and Ria separated for the first time just before he started work on *Strange Interlude*. Ria took her children and went to New York. Upon completion of the picture, Clark telephoned and begged her to return, which she did, and life for them continued as once before. A friend says:

'Actually, Clark was very insecure. His sudden popularity puzzled and confused him, and he didn't quite know how to handle it. He was beginning to find his marriage to Ria restrictive, but he clung to her, for he'd grown to depend on her strength and reassurance.'

On the strength of his appearance in *A Free Soul*, Gable had demanded and received a new contract, starting at a salary of $1,150 per week, with $500 going into a trust fund.

Along with his new contract, Gable literally received a new physical appearance. The make-up people were given instruc-tions that thenceforth Gable was not to be made up in what Hollywood termed the 'Valentino style'. He should be made to look like the rugged he-man that he was. And Howard Strickling was put to work walloping the new Gable image across.

It was now a Hollywood status symbol to have Clark Gable as your leading man. Norma Shearer's rival, Marion Davies, requested him for *Polly of the Circus*. While Norma had Thalberg to push through her requests, Davies had William Randolph Hearst. Marion got Gable for *Polly*, and they had a brief fling off camera as well. Miss Davies was now permitted such harmless liaisons by her mentor, since Mr Hearst was 'past his peak in the boudoir'.

Gable's next film would reteam him with the platinum-blonde girlfriend whose career was making strides as fast as his.

CHAPTER SEVEN

'Mama, I'm tired.'

Jean Harlow had made six films in 1931. Howard Hughes was paying her a couple of hundred dollars a week while collecting a small fortune for her services on loan-out. She had literally worked all over Hollywood: one film at MGM, one at Fox, one at Universal, two at Columbia.

Besides being underpaid, she knew Hughes really had no interest in developing her career. She pleaded with him to be released from her contract. 'Absolutely not' was the reply. When MGM wanted to buy Harlow's contract, Hughes asked for $100,000. He eventually settled for $60,000 and the right to use Jean in two films over the next five years (which he never did).

Jean made the move to MGM in style. She arrived a bona-fide Leading Lady, with a starting salary of $1,250 a week, building to $5,000 a week by the contract's seventh year. Jean also got a secretary, personal maid, hairdresser, car and chauffeur at her disposal, all paid for by the studio.

More important to Jean was the guidance and protection of the giant MGM publicity machine to build her career. Though she was only twenty-one and supporting her family, Jean was not the brightest girl in the world and needed a man who could take some of the burden off her shoulders.

She saw Gable occasionally at the studio, but they were leading separate lives.

At MGM Jean met Paul Bern, known in filmdom's upper circles as Hollywood's 'little father confessor'. Bern was one of those integral men behind the scenes, unknown to the public but whose name and face were known by everyone who was anyone in Hollywood. He had been an intimate confidant of many leading silent-film actresses, including the beautiful but tragic Barbara La Marr and rising young Lucille Le Sueur, renamed Joan Crawford. Bern's best friend was silent-film superstar John Gilbert.

Bern was a protégé of Irving Thalberg's, who had brought Paul into the company as one of his assistants in 1930. Before that Bern had worked at other top studios.

His physical appearance was decidedly unglamorous. He was very short and small-framed, and had wispy hair and a thin moustache. But he was a great listener, and understood the uneducated, insecure actors and actresses who couldn't handle their talent and success.

Bern first saw Harlow on an MGM set. He telephoned her at home later that evening and invited her to lunch. She accepted, and was immediately impressed by Bern's gentlemanly behavior. He was one of the few men at the studio who seemed interested in her brain, not her body.

Even then Harlow was attracting quite a bit of attention because of her ambivalent nature. At one moment she was a delightful waiflike creature, cooking a huge dinner for the crew on a set. The next moment she might be rubbing ice on her nipples to make them erect. Then she'd wear a dress so transparent that the nipples clearly stood out, and there was no question that everything else showed through too.

But Paul obviously brought out the mother instinct in young Jean. She didn't care that Bern was an older man. So what? One of the many things that Harlow had in common with her friend Clark Gable was an attraction for older members of the opposite sex. Gable was ten years older than Jean, but Bern was twice her age. And she was impressed by Bern's loving her for what he described to his pal John Gilbert as her 'spiritual beauty'.

Courting Jean Harlow was consistent with Paul's desire to be known as a man so virile that sex symbols were attracted to him. In his youth, he had been a member of Sarah Bernhardt's troupe, and had waited on her 'as though she were a goddess'. Later he had relationships with silent-film symbols Nita Naldi, Jetta Goudal, Estelle Taylor. When Barbara La Marr married Jack Dougherty, gossip in Hollywood was that Bern tried to drown himself but was saved by John Gilbert and Carey Wilson.

But Paul Bern was no rake, no cad. He was known throughout Hollywood as being sensitive. He came from a long line of sensitive people, and there had been several suicides in Bern's family. It was exactly this sensitivity that attracted Jean.

When Harlow fell in love with Bern, or thought she had, friends called it weird, ridiculous, and perhaps even a little obscene. They speculated that Jean liked Bern for what he could do for her. He had power and influence. But she wasn't exactly a struggling starlet who needed that kind of help. Friends of both maintained knowingly that the relationship was merely platonic, that the couple would never marry, that they were just 'good friends'.

At the time Bern was dating Jean, he was still secretly involved with a woman named Dorothy Milette. The affair had been going on for years. But the world had not yet heard of this mysterious woman whom newspapers would identify as 'Mrs Paul Bern'.

Soon Jean and Paul were seeing a great deal of each other: lunches, cocktails, dinners. He asked her to attend the premiere of the studio's all-star film *Grand Hotel*, at the famed Chinese Theatre on Hollywood Boulevard. It was the couple's first public appearance together.

Not only did Jean like Paul, she liked the company he kept. In addition to John Gilbert, his friends included Thalberg and Norma, David and Irene Selznick.

Jean honestly felt the age difference didn't matter. She had *always* been attracted to older men. She felt comfortable with them. Jean was twenty-one, Paul forty-two. 'Career-wise', Bern was in the chips. He was one of Thalberg's top lieutenants, earning $1,500 a week. He seemed to have dozens of friends and absolutely no enemies.

When he proposed marriage, Jean readily accepted. Since Bern was Jewish, studio chief Louis B. Mayer chided him for marrying a *shiksa* (a non-Jewish girl).

Paul and Jean took out a marriage license on June 21, 1932, and the wedding date was set for July 2, at Jean's home. An elite group would attend the ceremony, to be performed at eight in the evening. Bern chose John Gilbert as best man, and Jean, at the studio's suggestion – 'So you'll avoid insulting anyone' – decided against bridesmaids.

The guest list represented the cream of Hollywood society, including the Thalbergs, Mayers, Selznicks.

These were the days when movie stars made regularly scheduled personal appearances at theaters playing their movies, and Jean Harlow was no exception. On the morning of the day she was to be married, Harlow was on the stage, as advertised, of Loew's State Theatre in Los Angeles, which was playing her latest film, *Red Headed Woman.*

The Saturday-evening wedding was a small, informal affair at Jean's home. The elegant reception would follow the next day, Sunday afternoon, in the garden of Bern's mansion. He had given Jean the heavily mortgaged estate as a much-publicized wedding gift, but in actuality, since California has community-property laws, it really made no difference whose name the house was in.

Most of the men at Jean's wedding, including the groom, wore informal clothes. Paul wore a double breasted blue suit; Gilbert sported a tweed suit with patch pockets. But Marino Bello was, as one would expect, dressed in a tuxedo. All the women were in formal gowns, and Jean's wedding dress was a full-length white silk creation. She wore low heels so she wouldn't be taller than Bern.

The wedding went smoothly, and cameras clicked away, recording the event. At a decent hour the guests made their departure. They would all see each other tomorrow and continue the reveling. The happy newly-weds drove to Bern's house to consummate the marriage.

Later that night Jean's agent received a frantic phone call. 'Come get me!' she cried. 'I'll be waiting outside the house. Come get me, and don't ask questions! He's liable to wake up.'

If ensuing reports are to be believed, the wedding night was Kafkaesque. Mild-mannered Paul Bern turned out to be a sadist, and Jean his victim. The pitiful fact of Bern's under-developed genitalia and impotence had driven him, under the influence of alchol, to beat his young wife. America's reigning Love Goddess was in a state of shock, with welts across her back, shoulders, and buttocks.

She spent the remainder of her wedding night at her agent's house. In strictest secrecy, a doctor was summoned. 'Nothing is broken,' a sobbing Jean was told, 'but there might be internal damage.' It was later assumed that the beating was responsible for severe damage to Jean's kidneys.

Whatever had happened that fateful night, both Jean and Paul had to be present at the elegant wedding reception Sunday afternoon. In the garden of the Bern home, the scent of

50

summer flowers was heavy. The turnout was a veritable 'who's who' of cinema royalty: Clark Gable and Ria, James Cagney, L. B. Mayer, the Thalbergs and Selznicks. None in the glittering group could have guessed the nightmare that had taken place.

Jean had been warned by her concerned agent that if she so much as uttered a peep about the debacle, her career would be over, because no one in the public eye could survive such a scandal – certainly not a sex symbol whose husband turned out to be impotent. The studio would drop her like the proverbial hot potato.

At the reception Louella Parsons cornered Jean and scolded her: 'You have circles under your eyes. You've been working too hard.' She called over Paul and lectured him. 'You're Jean's boss now, Paul. Make her take it easy.'

The cameramen took endless shots. Jean could barely hold up. Finally it was over, and when the last guest had departed, Jean screamed at Paul: 'Don't ever, ever come near me again or I'll kill you.'

That summer of 1932, Harlow and Bern lived together in name only. According to some intimate bystanders, Jean despised him to such an extent that she brought him to tears with insults on the rare occasions they spent time together. According to others, she accepted his weird sexual practices so long as Bern didn't include her.

It was Paul Bern, however, who suggested to Thalberg that Jean be starred in *Red Dust,* a stage play bought by MGM years before. Metro was trying to find a part for John Gilbert, who was costing them $520,000 a year. He needed a role in which he would not appear at great disadvantage because of the poor quality of his voice. They decided to co-star him with Harlow, hoping that her presence would detract from his.

When John Lee Mahin, the former New York reporter hired to write *Red Dust*, saw *Secret Six*, he flew to producer Hunt Stromberg and said, 'You're crazy if you use Gilbert with Harlow. I just saw Harlow with Gable. He would be terrific with Jean again, couldn't miss.' So Jean filmed *Red Dust* with Gable.

The set was sweltering. There was no air conditioning in 1932, and the stage was damp because of the rain machines. Director Victor Fleming ignored complaints about the heat, stating, 'Everybody sweats in the tropics – that's the way it

is!' Jarfuls of live moths were released for each new take –
to insure 'authenticity of jungle location'. It was not an easy
film to make.

The Gable Harlow love scenes had the usual audience of
technicians. Jean was naked for the scenes in which she was
supposed to be bathing in a rain barrel. She and Clark wise-
cracked about the waterline, and occasionally Harlow would
rise a bit too high, giving one and all a 'glimpse of tit'. Gable
loved it, although he blushed every time the nude Jean teased
him.

It was during the filming of *Red Dust* that Paul Bern committed suicide. It was early September, 1932, less than two
months after their wedding. This time scandal could not be
avoided.

There are two versions of the story. According to one, the
body was discovered by the Carmichaels, the couple who
worked for Paul and Jean. They had accompanied Jean to her
mother's house the night before, and in the morning drove
back to the Bern house, where they found Paul dead.

They phoned Jean first, then called MGM.

According to other reports, including that of Hearst's top
reporter, Adela Rogers St John, Jean Harlow was at home the
night Paul Bern shot himself, and it was Jean who called
Howard Strickling. Thalberg and Strickling decided it would
be a good idea to get her out of the house, so Strickling and
Mrs St John took Jean to her mother's house.

In any event, the news of Bern's suicide created panic at
the studio.

Howard Strickling took over. Ralph Wheelwright, a publicity executive, and Whitey Hendry, chief of the MGM
police force, were dispatched to the Bern home. They calmed
the Carmichaels and persuaded them not to call the police.

Jean and Mama Jean were instructed to 'keep away from
the house'. Louis B. Mayer arrived at the house before
Strickling. He found the suicide note Bern had left. The note
read:

Dearest dear,
    Unfortunately this is the only way to make right the
frightful wrong I have done you and to wipe out my
abject humiliation. You understand that last night was
only a comedy.

Mayer hid the note and personally telephoned the police. He waited until the officers arrived and then decided to leave – 'To visit Jean,' he said, 'and make funeral arrangements.'

As he was driving away from the house, Mayer met Strickling, who was driving up. Wheelwright had told Strickling of the suicide note, and Strickling asked Mayer about it. Mayer didn't want to turn it over to the police, but Strickling wisely insisted. They certainly couldn't afford any complications later with the authorities.

But both Mayer and Strickling knew that the mysterious tone of the note would arouse all sorts of questions and speculations on the part of the press and the public. The men had no choice. The studio had to make the best of a bad situation. 'Ride it out' was the thinking.

Strickling and Mayer wanted to control the degree of scandal. They visited Jean at her mother's and insisted she tell them everything. She then revealed Bern's impotence, and the fact that he had made no sexual overtures during the first month of their marriage. To further complicate matters for the MGM brass, on the night of the suicide Clark Gable was off on a fishing trip with Jean's stepfather, Marino Bello. Strickling realized that Gable, because of his intimacy with the Harlow family and his cameraderie with Jean, might somehow be implicated, and that the press might now try to make something distasteful of the Gable–Harlow relationship.

The publicity department dispatched people to keep check on the roads leading to Jean's house so Gable could be told to keep away. Harlow and Gable were valuable properties. The studio had to protect its investments.

Filming on *Red Dust* resumed one week after Bern's suicide. The funeral had been dignified – the studio had seen to that. MGM had done its job well, and had succeeded in keeping Gable's name out of the entire affair. When a distraught Jean returned to the set, the stage was closed to outsiders. She was welcomed by Clark, who gave her a big hug and kiss. She was also hugged by Fleming and kissed by co-stars Mary Astor and Gene Raymond, cameraman Hal Rosson, and other members of the crew.

Jean had been fearful of the reception she might get. Would they all think she was cheap, stupid, unfeeling? She needn't have worried. Though she constantly flubbed lines, everyone understood.

53

The press, however, continued to have a field day with the Harlow–Bern fiasco. They dredged up information about Paul's past. The body of Dorothy Milette, the mysterious woman in Paul's life, was found floating in the river thirty-one miles south of Sacramento. There had been reports that Bern had been married to Miss Milette and was a bigamist. This was not true.

There were reports that Jean and her mother had been in San Francisco two weeks before Bern's suicide and a woman who looked like Dorothy Milette had entered their hotel room. There were even reports that this woman had been in Paul's home the day before his suicide, and neighbors said that on the night of the suicide, after midnight, a car sped away from the Bern estate.

Not since the Fatty Arbuckle–Virginia Rappe scandal of the twenties had a film personality been exposed to this kind of treatment in newspapers. And although the Bern case was closed with an official pronouncement of 'suicide', the case would go down in film history as one of Hollywood's unsolved mysteries.

In later years the mystery would be further clouded. To make the story more dramatic for Harlow biographers and for movies about the legendary sex symbol, it would be hinted that the Bern suicide might possibly have been murder. That blackmail was involved. That Jean Harlow knew about Bern's impotence before she married him. That others in Hollywood knew of Bern's sexual problems.

Adela Rogers St John told Harlow that Bern had once tried suicide by thrusting his head into a toilet.

'He must have looked pretty silly,' Jean remarked.

'I wish they'd let him drown,' responded Adela.

'So do I.'

While the Bern affair would haunt Jean throughout her life, it did not hurt her career. In fact, she became a bigger star than ever.

Red Dust was completed on schedule and rushed into release. Jean was concerned that MGM might drop her, but the studio was planning far ahead, and her option was never in danger. While MGM executives had had their fill of Harlow's messed-up private life and the interference in her career by her stepfather, there was no doubt that Jean Harlow was money in the bank. They'd put up with her so long as her box office held out.

'Here's your next picture,' she was told as she was handed a script of *Hold Your Man*. The man was Clark Gable.

CHAPTER EIGHT

Before *Hold Your Man*, Gable had another commitment, with another blonde.

There was no fanfare; the seas didn't part; the meeting wasn't registered on Los Angeles seismographs. It was 'just another picture' teaming two very popular young actors. The production wasn't anything elaborate, and in fact the leading lady was second choice for the role.

Paramount Pictures was having its problems in 1932. The front office was hoping a low-budget comedy they had planned, *No Man of Her Own*, would bring in some big profits. It was the tale of a fast-talking promoter and a small-town librarian. Miriam Hopkins, one of the industry's most successful young actresses, had agreed to play the librarian, and dependable Wesley Ruggles was the director.

But then Hopkins decided she didn't want to do the film – 'It's not an important enough property' – and contract actress Carole Lombard got the role.

'I suggested Clark for the gambler,' said Ruggles. 'I remembered him from the one-reelers when I'd used him and Janet Gaynor as extras at five dollars a day.' Now Gable was the new rage.

At first the Paramount production office didn't want Gable. As a killer, he was tops. But 'How do you know he can play comedy?' they asked. Ruggles persisted, and MGM agreed to lend Gable for the film.

Contradicting the many stories that Gable and Lombard didn't like each other at first sight, Ruggles stated: 'Clark and Carole clicked right from the start, and made a good comedy team. I was impressed with the progress Clark had made.'

It's interesting that although Gable had had that 'big break', his self-confidence was nil. Ruggles remembered, 'One day I stopped by his dressing room to ask how things were going for him. It was Clark's opinion that he wasn't going to "last long" and he told me he was going to "make hay" while he could.'

By the time of *No Man of Her Own*, Carole Lombard had appeared in a dozen Paramount films and was established as one of the studio's leading ingenues. She had already played opposite top Paramount stars like Gary Cooper, in *I Take This Woman*, and William Powell, in *Man of the World* and *Ladies' Man*.

Powell had met Carole in the fall of 1930. The twenty-two-year-old beauty with the sparkling personality and devastating sense of humor instantly captivated the thirty-eight-year-old movie idol.

At the time Powell was known as 'a private, shy person'. Friends who worked with him recall that many people were bewildered that he found anything in common with a young woman as gregarious as Carole. Some theorized that Lombard was attracted to Powell because he was a father figure, 'of sorts'.

Though Carole was, and would remain, extremely close to her brothers and her mother, she was eager to embark on a new phase of her life. Even Powell said, 'She was ready to spread her wings, and marriage enabled her to do it.'

When they met, Powell was already one of Paramount's top male leads. Though under six feet and only one hundred sixty pounds, he gave the appearance on screen of being a big man. He had presence, on screen and off.

Carole possessed that innate sense of style, in clothing and entertaining, which, in addition to her other attributes, appealed to Powell. These were rare qualities in a girl so young.

Paramount, too, liked the Powell–Lombard teaming. After *Man of the World*, they were re-teamed in *Ladies' Man*. Carole provided no ego problem, as there might have been with other leading ladies. If the stories and titles of their films together spotlighted Powell, Carole couldn't have cared less.

Importantly, the Powell and Lombard families were compatible. They had similar Midwest backgrounds. And Carole easily fit in with Powell's social set, Hollywood's upper-crust Wasp society: Ronald Colman, Richard and Jessica Barthelmess, William Haines, Warner Baxter.

After an eight-month courtship, Carole became a June bride,

a week after Ria Langham had married Clark Gable.

In true Hollywood fashion, before the newlywed Powells set up housekeeping on a luxurious scale, they went on a dream honeymoon: a cruise on the liner *Malola* to Honolulu. And wisecracking Carole sent her friends a telegram after the honeymoon night: 'Nothing new to report.'

Lombard was already known in Hollywood for her salty language. And her reputation for quips regarding the sexual prowess of her partners now began surfacing. Some say that it was Carole's attitude about sex that created the problems in her marriage to Powell.

A long-time Hollywood observer notes that while Powell was known to enjoy sex, Carole was far more interested in other sides of marriage. Her nickname for Powell was 'Pop', and a Hollywood writer claims that the age difference became a problem.

The marriage survived for a little more than two years. During that period Powell became more gregarious, while Carole became more serious. But there were always problems. She had no feeling for maintaining an elaborate illusion regarding life with 'respected, erudite movie star William Powell'. And maintaining that image was very important to him.

Powell was in the forefront of big money earners. After his second film with Carole, Powell left Paramount. Myron Selznick, Hollywood's leading agent (and older brother of David O. Selznick) had negotiated a fantastic deal for three of his clients: Powell, Kay Francis, and Ruth Chatterton. All signed with Warner Brothers. Powell and Miss Francis had been teamed successfully in the society drama *Street of Chance*. Warner Brothers cast them together in another soap opera, *One-Way Passage*. It was a big hit, and Powell was apparently worth the $6,000 weekly salary Warner Brothers was paying him. In addition, Powell's contract gave him story approval – in those days a rare clause in any actor's contract. Powell made nine films for Warner Brothers in only two and a half years.

Meanwhile, Carole's career was steadily climbing. But the studio hadn't yet really taken advantage of her gift for comedy. *No Man of Her Own* gave Lombard her first opportunity to combine comedy and drama.

There was no unusual chemistry between Clark Gable and Carole Lombard off screen. Each was concerned with his own private life and career at the time. They were talented pros and worked beautifully together. While Carole was pleasant toward Clark, she in no way pursued him, and throughout Gable's life he had relationships only with women who went after him.

But Gable and Lombard certainly liked each other. Gable found her sense of humor refreshing. He admired her antics. She was, after all, fascinating. Not only was she a man's conception of 'the perfect woman' but she could 'cuss and swear' with the best of them. Gable didn't approve of the language, and said so. 'What a stuffed shit – I mean shirt' was her retort.

Carole's candor was appealing. While Gable had enjoyed working with Jean Harlow because she could enjoy a joke and 'be one of the boys', here was a woman who had these abilities plus wit and intelligence. What a change from the slew of serious women in Gable's life: Dillon, Langham – even Crawford.

It was during the filming of *No Man of Her Own* that Carole and Clark nicknamed each other 'Ma' and 'Pa'. Clark had a penchant for nicknames. He liked calling Jean Harlow 'Sis', while almost everyone else at MGM called Jean 'Baby'. A psychological inference of these nicknames might be that Clark and Carole viewed each other as possible mates, while Clark saw his relationship with Harlow as brotherly.

No Man of Her Own was completed on schedule. When the picture 'wrapped', Carole, a devout practical joker whose barbs always hit home, gave Clark an oversized ham (a stunt she would repeat with other leading men). She felt it was an adequate expression of how she viewed him. Clark presented her with a pair of ballet slippers that would have fit an elephant – a suitable gift for a sailor-tongued girl he felt possessed an oversized ego.

And back to their separate lives they went.

Carole's marriage to Bill was in its last days. She wasn't, as he'd hoped, becoming more 'dignified' with the passage of time. He'd had it with her practical jokes, some of which embarrassed him. There was the hilarious story about Lombard teaching Frederic March an object lesson. March considered himself a great lover and felt it was his duty to put the make on each of his leading ladies.

When March was filming *The Eagle and the Hawk*, Lombard, as a favor to director Mitchell Leisen (who had taken over from director Stuart Walker), agreed to do a small part. March, of course, tried to use his charm on Carole. She played along and asked him to her dressing room, 'for a drink'. She led March on and, as his hand started up her dress, he felt a strange object. He was horrified. His hand was grasping a rubber dildo which Lombard had strapped on to discourage further advances.

Antics like this, and Carole's fondness for epithets at what Powell sometimes considered the wrong time, may have made Bill and Carole finally realize that they were 'basically incompatible', although he still loved her. Mitchell Leisen (whom Carole called 'Junior') was a good friend of both Bill's and Carole's. 'As well as I knew her,' Leisen remarked, 'I never knew why they divorced.'

In the summer of 1933, Carole went off to Reno and filed for divorce. Carole's mother said, 'They just decided all of a sudden that they could not agree.' It was a very amicable affair. Carole did not want any alimony, and she and Bill were determined to remain good friends.

Warner Brothers had asked Powell to take a salary cut to $4,000 a week. All the studios were trying to economize during the Depression. While some at Warners had to take the cut, Powell was still in demand. His agent was able to negotiate a deal with MGM, and Powell made what would ultimately be the smartest move of his career. With the new contract, Powell bought an expensive new house in Beverly Hills.

His first film for Metro was *Manhattan Melodrama*, which teamed him with Clark Gable and Myrna Loy.

This was the only film Powell and Gable would make together. While they worked well and were cordial, there was hardly any basis for an away-from-the-studio relationship. Their friendship existed through the years because of the women in their lives: Lombard and Harlow.

W. S. Van Dyke, the director of *Manhattan Melodrama*, liked Powell and Loy's performance so much that he asked L. B. Mayer if he could use them in a small-budget detective comedy: Dashiell Hammett's *The Thin Man*.

Mayer told Van Dyke, 'You're crazy. Powell and Loy are both best as heavies.' Myrna Loy had up to then successfully portrayed 'shady ladies'. The director, however, convinced Mayer to allow him to have the two players. 'I'll get it done in two weeks,' he promised, and the studio would be able to use Powell and Loy in other projects.

The Thin Man brought Powell back to the role of a debonair detective. And now Bill Powell, who in real life had resumed the role of bachelor, on screen became 'the perfect husband'.

The moral of *The Thin Man*, and the sequels that followed, seemed to be: 'Marriage can be merry.'

The Thin Man was produced on the lowest of budgets, and William Powell and Myrna Loy became, for millions of fans, Nick and Nora Charles. They were sophisticated, wisecracking, martini-drinking people who, with their wire-haired terrier, Asta, solved murders. *The Thin Man* was a totally unexpected block-buster, grossing over two million dollars and earning an Oscar nomination for 'Best Picture of the Year'.

In addition, the witty comedy provided Powell the first of his Academy Award 'Best Actor' nominations. Ironically, he lost the award that year to Clark Gable.

CHAPTER NINE

When Clark returned to his home lot after *No Man of Her Own*, he was disillusioned with Metro's plans for his future. After *White Sister*, with Helen Hayes, *Hold Your Man*, with Harlow, and *Night Flight,* the studio re-teamed him with Joan Crawford in *Dancing Lady*.

Crawford's career was in trouble. She had had two major flops, *Rain* and *Today We Live*, and MGM poured all its considerable resources – top talent on the lot all the way down the line – into *Dancing Lady*, so Crawford would regain her box-office standing. It worked. The movie, produced by David O. Selznick, was considered so commercially successful that for years it was the yardstick by which MGM measured the success of its other products.

During a break in the filming, Clark – who was fed up with both the studio and his home life with Ria – went on a hunting trip with his friend Doc Thorpe, to Jackson Hole, Wyoming.

They camped there overnight and the next day headed for Turpin Meadows, twenty-five miles away.

On this trip Gable told Thorpe, 'I have a pain, Doc,' motioning to his abdomen. 'Can you give me a cathartic?'

'I didn't have to do much examining,' remembered Dr Thorpe. 'The first time I touched the sore spot, I knew he had a red-hot appendix. It had flared up on him some months before. That time it had subsided under ice-pack treatment.'

It was more serious now. 'We'll have to turn right around and go home,' said Dr Thorpe.

Gable groaned. 'And miss the hunting, after we've come all of this way?'

Dr Thorpe tried to reason with him. 'But it soon became obvious that I wasn't going to get anywhere just with pure logic. So I said, "If you won't do it for yourself, do it for me." He asked, "What do you mean, do it for you?" "Suppose you conk off out here in the wilds? Where will that leave me? I will have to get out of Hollywood. I'll lose all of my patients. I will have to start out all over again some place where Clark Gable was never heard of. That's if I can find any such place."

' "Okay", he said.'

It took two days to drive back, with Gable in constant pain. 'He winced once in a while,' recalled Dr Thorpe, 'but he did not complain.'

The doctor brought Clark to Cedars of Lebanon and scheduled the operation for the next day. Gable told him, 'You're the surgeon, but I insist on being boss about one thing. You're not going to put an old crow of a nurse in here with me. I want a pretty one.'

They got him Jean Hoffman, described by Dr Thorpe as 'the prettiest nurse at the hospital'. And, according to Dr Thorpe, 'the operation came none too soon. His appendix when it came out looked like a dirty piece of pork.'

Dr Thorpe wouldn't accept a fee for the operation, so Gable gave him a magnificent watch, inscribed: 'To my pal – Dr Thorpe.'

Gable often confided in Thorpe. He complained about Ria and her social activities. Ria was constantly inviting people to dinner, and Clark, who was fast developing a penchant for quiet evenings at home, repeatedly told Thorpe, 'I never sit down to eat in my home without hearing at least nine sets of jawbones crunching food.'

Clark also griped about Ria's extravagances. But in a few moments of reckless spending himself, Gable ordered a car which he specified had to be a foot longer than Gary Cooper's. He also purchased custom-tailored suits.

When he returned to finish *Dancing Lady*, Gable was disgruntled. He hated what he called 'these gigolo roles'. He said, 'People are bored to death when I rough up disagreeable women. And I'm getting pretty sick of it myself.'

Dancing Lady was the final straw. According to a friend, 'Clark felt this was a step down for him, that he hadn't done anything really worthwhile since *Susan Lennox*, and that he'd fallen into the category of "just a good leading man".' He went to the front office and complained to his friends Howard Strickling and Eddie Mannix.

Mannix, a cigar-chomping former bouncer for the Schenck brothers, was a 'man of iron'. He was known for his direct, salty language. 'You always knew where you stood with Mannix,' recalls a former MGM executive. 'He was not the knife-in-the-back type so common in Hollywood.' Like Gable, two of Mannix's hobbies were women and drinking. (Later in his life, Mannix suffered several heart attacks and was told to cut out 'booze and broads'. He wouldn't heed the advice. 'When I go,' he said, 'I want a cigar in one hand, a drink on the table, and a hot broad underneath me.') Mannix remained one of Gable's closest friends and advisers.

Both Mannix and Strickling warned Gable not to incur Mayer's wrath, but he didn't heed their advice. L. B. was annoyed that 'this ingrate' dare question the studio's (that meant his) judgement. He thought he'd teach Clark a lesson.

At Columbia, then a small studio on what used to be poverty row, director Frank Capra was having problems with a script he had written with Robert Riskin called *Overland Bus*. After several revisions he took the script to his boss, studio chief Harry Cohn.

Cohn imediately liked the new version, and Capra said, 'Now, Harry, if we can cast a good man first, it'll be easier to get a girl. MGM has a great light comedian, Robert Montgomery.'

The script was sent over to MGM. Montgomery turned it down, and Cohn was distraught. Louis B. Mayer told Cohn, 'Harry, Montgomery says there are too many bus pictures,

And, Herschel, no offense, stars don't like changing their address from MGM to Gower Street, But, Herschel, you caught me in a good mood. I got an actor here who's being a bad boy. And I'd like to spank him. You can have Clark Gable.'

'Louis,' interjected Cohn, 'suppose *he* don't like the script?'

'Herschel, this is Louis Mayer talking. I'm *telling* you to take Gable.'

Clark, learning that *Overland Bus* was an MGM reject and one in which Robert Montgomery had refused to participate, stormed into the office of Eddie Mannix yelling, 'What a pal you turned out to be, selling me down the river like this.'

Mannix replied, 'I'm not selling you down the river, Clark.'

'What do you call it, then?'

Over at Columbia, director Capra wasn't exactly thrilled either. 'Clark Gable! I've only seen him in *The Last Mile*. He played a tough killer.'

'It's Gable or nothing,' said Cohn. 'Understand? He's on his way over to see you.'

Capra realized that he had no choice. Cohn would do whatever Mayer wanted, and if Mayer wanted to punish Gable, Cohn would have to make *Overland Bus* with Clark Gable.

Gable arrived at Capra's office in quite a state. Capra assumed that he had hit every bar along the way.

'Is thish *Mishter* Frank Capra's office?'

'Yes, Mr Gable. I'm Frank Capra. Come in, please, come in.'

'Gla-ad to meet cha.'

Trying to get his eyes to focus, then belching, Gable finally said to Capra, 'Well-l, what's the poop, shkipper – besides me?'

'Well, Mr Gable, I –'

'That son of a bitch Mayer. I always *wanted* to see Siberia but damn me – I never thought it would *smell* like this. Blech-h-h!'

Capra knew that the people at MGM considered working for Columbia equivalent to being banished to Siberia. Furious, he said, 'Mr Gable, you and I are supposed to make a picture out of this. Shall I tell you the story or would you rather read the script yourself?'

'Buddy, I don't give a fuck *what* you do with it.'

Capra had no quick reply to Gable's statement, and merely gave him the script, muttering that his own Siberia was

MGM.

Gable laughed. 'Hee hee-e-e! Sez you.'

He went off, stumbling, smacking into the door, and singing, 'They call her frivolous Sa-a-al, a peculiar kind of a – hey, you guys!' He had spotted some Columbia people in the courtyard, and said to them, 'Why ain't you wearing *parkas* in Siberia?'

Capra was sure that he would never see Gable again, and that Gable would not show up on the set. But Cohn assured him that if Mayer wanted Gable to make the picture, the actor would, and that they should not worry about Gable; instead, he suggested, they should turn their attention to finding a leading lady.

All the important leading ladies of the day had already turned down the script. But Capra persuaded Claudette Colbert, who was about to go on a vacation from Paramount, to say yes. She wasn't anxious to do it, but $50,000 – exactly twice her going price – convinced her.

Joe Walker, Capra's cameraman, recalls that the film was tightly budgeted at $350,000. 'Many nights we worked all night. The bus scenes were very difficult, because we didn't have breakaways in those days. We had to shoot in the actual cramped quarters inside a bus. We shot the night-in-a-haystack scene under a circus tent on the RKO ranch. Capra devised the dubbing in of the sound of frogs and crickets, which was an innovation at the time.'

To take the onus off the picture's being a 'bus film', the title was changed to *It Happened One Night*.

It was completed right on schedule, in one month. Clark thought no more about the film, certain it was a dud. Back at MGM, he was growing more and more discontented. Although *Manhattan Melodrama* had been a top production, Gable was still playing a gangster, and he considered his career to be 'petering out'. Apparently his agent, Ruth Collier, agreed. She sold his contract to two rising young talent entrepreneurs, Phil Berg and Bob Coryell.

That Clark Gable had been, in Hollywood parlance, 'unloaded' by an agent was not a promising sign for a supposedly successful star. In addition, his marriage to Ria was floundering, and he was, understandably, depressed and discouraged. He drank heavily.

But Berg and Coryell saw a big future for Gable. 'We paid

twenty-five thousand dollars for his contract,' Bob says, 'and we soon had reason to congratulate ourselves on a profitable buy.'

It Happened One Night turned out to be a landmark film. Although it started out a poor grosser when it opened at New York's Radio City Music Hall – 'Well that's what we thought would happen' – when it hit the hinterlands the results were astounding. It outgrossed every other film released by all the studios that year. The film, Capra, Colbert, and the screenplay were all nominated for Academy Awards.

Gable did not want to go to the Academy Award ceremonies, which were being held at the Biltmore Hotel on February 27, 1935. But Ria and her daughter, Georgianna, persuaded him to attend. However, he looked 'damned uncomfortable in a stiff collar and dinner jacket'.

The scene at the Awards was tense. A thousand people were in the dining room, and six thousand more were jammed into the lobby and foyer. Vote counting went on until just before 8 P.M., the time of the dinner, because in those days the voting polls closed at 5 P.M. on the day of the ceremony.

William Powell, who had been in films since 1920 and had many friends in Hollywood, was the heavy favorite to win 'Best Actor' for *The Thin Man* – MGM and other major studios usually 'block voted' – and it was a surprise to all when the little film from the Poverty Row studio swept the Awards.

It Happened One Night was named 'Best Picture'. It won for 'Best Screenplay'. Capra was named 'Best Director', Colbert 'Best Actress'. And Clark Gable was 'Best Actor of the Year'.

Gable was shocked. Ria and Georgianna were thrilled. Clark was in a fog on his way up to accept the statuette, and was led from the stage by two publicity men, John Leroy Johnston and Vance King. King later recalled, 'Gable was absolutely stunned that night. As Johnson and I grabbed him by the arms and led him off the stage, he clutched the Oscar. He kept mumbling over and over: "I am still going to wear the same size hat! I'm still going to wear the same size hat!"'

MGM had, by accident, been responsible for making their bad boy into the biggest star in the country.

Once Gable had won his Oscar for *It Happened One Night* (in later years he used it as a doorstop), he was granted star privileges, including choosing of the crew. His choices were Sug Keller as head lighting man, Ted Tedrick for wardrobe, Larry Barbier for publicity pictures, and Lew Smith as his stand-in. And for his cameraman: Hal Rosson, who had married Jean Harlow.

CHAPTER TEN

Even before his Oscar-winning performance in *It Happened One Night*, Clark Gable was David O. Selznick's first choice for a lead part in the all-star *Dinner at Eight*. Selznick also wanted Jean Harlow, Joan Crawford, John Barrymore, and Alice Brady, among others.

The idea of Gable, Crawford, and Harlow together in one film was mind-boggling, and only a showman like Selznick would have had the guts to try to set it up. *Dinner at Eight* would place the stars in a spectacularly prestigious property.

Ultimately Selznick had to settle for Edmund Lowe instead of Gable and Madge Evans instead of Joan Crawford. But he got Harlow for the role of the dumb but shrewd blonde wife of promoter–political aspirant Wallace Beery. The film also starred Marie Dressler, who became one of Harlow's best friends, John Barrymore, Lionel Barrymore, Lee Tracy, and Billie Burke.

Mama Jean was thrilled that 'the baby's' career was moving forward so wonderfully. Even Marino treated his stepdaughter with a bit more 'reverence'. 'You're a star, sweetheart,' he told her one day on the set. 'You must always behave like one.'

Jean had the assistant director ask Marino to leave.

Filming went amazingly fast, and the picture was wrapped in a month. A classic line in *Dinner at Eight* closes the picture. As the group is preparing to go in to dinner, Harlow announces to Dressler: 'You know, I read a book today.' Dressler does a hilarious double take as satin-gowned Harlow continues: 'It says that machinery is going to replace human beings.'

'My dear,' answers Dressler, looking her up and down,

'*you* have absolutely nothing to worry about.'

Director George Cukor recalls, 'It was my first encounter with Jean Harlow. I'd seen her in *Public Enemy* and *Hell's Angels*, where she was so bad and selfconscious it was comic. She got big laughs when she didn't want them. Then I saw *Red Dust* – and there she was, suddenly marvelous in comedy. A tough girl and yet very feminine, like Mae West. They both wisecrack, but they have something vulnerable, and it makes them attractive. Harlow was very soft about her toughness. I liked that scene [in *Dinner at Eight*] when she told off Wallace Beery. She's lying in bed wearing a new hat ... Beery comes in, she sits up and pushes back her hat, as if she's sitting on the toilet. And she says, "You big windbag!" and so on, and doesn't pull her punches – she has such charm!'

Cukor also notes, 'And I'll never forget – when Wally Beery, who's a big businessman and kind of in with the government, says he has to go to Washington – I'll never forget the way she looks at him and says, "Yeah, you better go and fix things." Like a waitress! Totally vague, no idea what it's really about!'

Even before *Dinner at Eight* was completed, Jean was assigned to the film *Bombshell*.

Hal Rosson was one of two cameramen whom Victor Fleming used on *Bombshell*. Lee Tracy and Franchot Tone were the leads opposite Harlow, in what Tone referred to as 'a garbage script filled with stupid dialogue'. Franchot was saddled with such memorable lines as: 'Your hair is like a field of silver daisies. I'd like to run barefoot through your hair.'

Jean, however, felt comfortable with the story. 'It's *me*,' she laughed to intimates.

It was very similar to her own life, a tale about a sexy movie queen with a parasitic family. As shooting progressed, Jean found companionship with Rosson. He was an excellent cameraman, and, unlike others, not only attended to every detail but came up with new ideas that would improve Jean's appearance on screen.

Rosson had known Jean since *Red Dust*. (Ironically, she had been introduced to him by Paul Bern.) Rosson was also director of photography on Jean's next two films, *Hold Your Man* and *Dinner at Eight*.

But it wasn't until *Bombshell* that the relationship developed. Jean and Rosson began seeking each other's company off the set as well. He was sixteen years older than she, and again Harlow was attracted to someone who gave her advice, listened when she spoke, and treated her a a person, not a movie star.

Gradually Hal began to assume the place Bern had initially filled. He talked with Jean, was gentle, understanding, tactful. Some of her loneliness began to fade.

Rosson was a Hollywood veteran. He came from a family immersed in moviemaking. Before going to MGM Rosson had been a top cameraman at Paramount, where Queen-of-the-Lot Gloria Swanson insisted that Hal photograph all her movies. Rosson's brothers Arthur and Richard were film directors; their sister, Gladys, had been Cecil B. De Mille's secretary.

By the time *Bombshell* was nearing completion, Hal and Jean were inseparable.

During the course of shooting films, people's emotional feelings are often intensified within a short period of time. Actors, especially, usually absorb the emotional climate of a film they're making. This was a classic case.

Jean and Hal eloped on September 18, 1933, with the help of Allan Russell, the famous 'honeymoon pilot' who flew Hollywood stars to Yuma, Arizona, for quickie weddings. Jean was twenty-two, Hal thirty-eight.

When Louis B. Mayer learned that Harlow and Rosson had tied the knot, he exploded. He had specifically ordered her not to get married again without checking with him. According to one report, Mayer ranted: 'Aren't there enough gentile men around for that one? Why does she keep picking on nice Jewish boys?' It was meekly pointed out to Mayer that 'Hal Rosson isn't Jewish.'

Hal had no fear of Mayer's ire. Rosson was one of Hollywood's top cameramen, and knew he could work at any studio. Hal also knew that if his marriage with Jean was to have any chance for survival, she would have to escape from the clutches of Mama Jean and Marino. At Hal's insistence, the newlyweds moved into an apartment instead of Jean's family-filled mansion.

In Los Angeles, the couple took a $250-a-month suite at the Chateau Marmont. MGM announced Hal would go to Mexico to photograph Selznick's production *Viva Villa!* Then Mayer had a change of heart and said Rosson could postpone the Mexican trip and take Jean on a honeymoon.

At first Jean loved fixing up the new apartment and planning for the Hawaiian honeymoon. But four weeks after her marriage, she fell ill. Rosson wanted her to call a doctor, but Jean's mother insisted 'the baby' follow the dictates of Christian Science.

Arthur Landau was called, and the agent immediately contacted Mayer. The mogul phoned the Rossons' new apartment and learned that Jean was unconscious. L. B. ordered Rosson to call a doctor immediately.

Rosson and Marino agreed with the doctor that Jean should be rushed to the hospital for an emergency appendectomy. But Mama Jean still held out for Christian Science.

The doctor phoned Mayer personally. The studio chief overrode Mama Jean's protestation and ordered Harlow to the hospital to have the operation. Jean remained at Good Samaritan for two weeks. She needed a long rest. Mama Jean insisted that after this ordeal Jean should move back into the Bello home, rather than the apartment. The Hawaiian honeymoon was shelved.

After convalescing, Jean was supposed to go to the studio for wardrobe fittings on *Living in a Big Way*. But she was holding out for a salary increase and refused to report. When Mayer suspended her salary, Jean was unmoved. 'He can go to hell,' she screamed. After all, Rosson was still drawing *his* salary.

Instead of Hawaii, Jean and Hal settled for a trip to San Francisco. Then they returned to their apartment. Mayer was angry that Jean's supension was not causing her financial pain. The bills were piling up, but Jean didn't care. When she wasn't working, Jean could let herself go. She seemed content staying home and fussing in the kitchen. She didn't worry about her hair or weight and allowed herself to get chubby. This often happened between films, and she'd have to diet drastically to get back into shape.

An old friend of Paul Bern's, Carey Wilson, was now a neighbor, and Jean and Hal enjoyed spending time with him. Wilson was an important writer-producer and associate of Thalberg's. He would eventually work on the Andy Hardy and Dr Kildare series of films, although he never took producer credit. One of his famous films from the forties was

The Postman Always Rings Twice, in which a platinum blonde named Lana Turner played a role that surely would have gone to Jean Harlow had the film been made in the thirties.

It was during Jean's marriage to Hal Rosson, and the six-month suspension, that Harlow turned author. Through the years there has been much speculation whether the novel *Today Is Tonight*, actually was written by Jean Harlow. But there's no doubt that the story idea was hers.

According to Jean's good friend Ruth Hamp, Carey Wilson 'helped edit it' but Jean 'actually wrote it. She told me that she had a dream and wanted to put it on paper and it might make a good story.'

According to Carmelita Wilson, Carey's widow, 'My husband helped her with the construction, characters, and character development. They wrote it together. Jean dictated a great deal of the dialogue.' Mrs Wilson also remembers, 'The book was her idea. It was purely fictional. She wrote it with the idea that she would play it and MGM would produce.'

There is no doubt that Jean did want to sell MGM the idea of doing the story. She felt they had been typecasting her, and was eager to do something 'meaningful'. 'I don't want to play hard-boiled girls,' she complained. 'It's so different from the real me. I hate the type. Why can't I be something else?'

There is also no doubt that she thought of herself as having more talent to offer than merely the attributes of a blonde sex goddess.

But MGM was not interested in *Today Is Tonight*. They wanted Jean Harlow as the public *liked* Jean Harlow: the dumb blonde with a heart of gold. The studio did, however, publicize that Jean had 'taken the time off to write'.

During her suspension Harlow daydreamed, 'I don't care if I never go back to work.' But Mama Jean and Marino needed the money, and Mayer wanted her back. Before her suspension Harlow had been earning $1,500 a week. Now Metro relented and granted her a $500-a-week raise. When Jean returned, *The Girl from Missouri* was the property selected as her new vehicle.

Mama, Marino, and studio influence were too strong for the Harlow–Rosson marriage to withstand. Jean and Hal separated after eight months, and Rosson moved into the Hollywood

Athletic Club. Though less than a year in duration, it was Jean's longest marriage. But the couple parted 'amicably' with 'no hard feelings' – not unlike Mama Jean and Dr Carpentier so many years earlier. Harlow wittily joked that her three marriages had been 'marriages of *in*convenience'.

The long tentacles of Metro-Goldwyn-Mayer would back around its commercial sex symbol and once again pulled her into the fold. 'Don't give out any statements,' she was advised, 'unless the studio okays them. Don't meet with the press unless we set up the interviews.'

Howard Strickling assigned vivacious young Kay Mulvey, a new girl in the publicity department, to handle Jean's publicity. Jean and Kay soon became the best of friends. Miss Mulvey has very strong feelings today about all that has been written about Jean Harlow. Over the years, many stories have been told about Harlow's obsession with sex. That she was an exhibitionist. That she liked to touch her body and wanted others to see her doing it. According to Kay, 'Jean liked sex as much as the next person, but she wasn't the kind of girl to go around unzipping men's flies. She was no nymphomaniac.'

Kay helped Jean through the difficult period of the Rosson divorce. When the Rossons separated, Hal's life took a dramatic turn for the worse. Shortly after breaking with Jean, disaster struck. Rosson contracted polio. For a time this reconciled the estranged couple. Jean visited him at his sister Gladys's home, where he was under treatment. But divorce proceedings went through as planned.

Rosson was lucky. After a short stay at Orthopaedic Hospital, he recovered. He left for New York en route to London, where he worked briefly for Alexander Korda. But Rosson soon returned and resumed his position as top cameraman at MGM. The Metro lot was, for better or worse, one big family. Even though Clark Gable had chosen Rosson at his personal cameraman, out of deference to Jean it was not Rosson who photographed the three more films Gable and Harlow would make together.

Jean shot only one film in 1934. But the studio had big plans for her. They announced she would star in her first musical (a vehicle which Joan Crawford had turned down). It would be produced by David O. Selznick and directed by Victor Fleming. Harlow's co-star: William Powell.

CHAPTER ELEVEN

In 1934 Gable had *It Happened One Night*. Powell scored with *The Thin Man*. Harlow had clicked with *Dinner at Eight*. And Lombard, too, made her landmark film that year.

Carole had made six pictures in 1934. One, Howard Hawks's *20th Century*, has become a classic. And there are classic stories concerning Carole Lombard during these peak years. She was the most popular girl at Paramount. 'If we held a contest,' said studio czar Adolph Zukor, 'Lombard would be queen of the lot.'

On the social scene, Carole, legally free of Powell, fell in love with the leading 'crooner' in the country, Russ Columbo. Handsome, dark-haired Italian Columbo reminded many of Valentino. He was currently more popular than Rudy Vallee had been, and even briefly eclipsed the exciting new sensation, Bing Crosby.

For almost a year Columbo and Lombard were inseparable. To fan-magazine readers, it was a wonderful match: beautiful, blonde Carole and darkly handsome Russ. 'These two have found each other, and it's a glorious beginning for them both,' gushed *Modern Screen*.

But those in the know were aware of certain major problems that would crop up should marriage be the ultimate goal. The couple's simpatico relationship was based on many things. 'But not sex,' noted flinty, frank Hedda Hopper many years later.

Carole did love Russ, and tried to help him launch a movie career. She often invited him down to her sets to watch the shooting. And she asked him to coach her for songs she had to sing in *White Woman*.

Unlike her more masculine suitors, Russ was not offended by Carole's sometimes outrageous behavior. He was more like her brothers, Frederick and Stuart. And he sympathized with her when she was unhappy making *Bolero* with George Raft.

Carole felt Paramount was wasting her 'in a stinker like this'. She got along with Raft, though, and they dated quite often. He has shed a great deal of light on her uninhibited attitudes.

One day George discovered that Carole wasn't a natural blonde. 'We're sitting and chatting in her dressing room, and as we're talking she starts undressing. She had one of the sexiest, most sensational figures I've seen in my life.' George was, however, aware of the unlocked dressing-room door and the fact that the call to return to the set might come at any minute.

'I didn't know what the hell to do after she undressed. She's talking away and mixing peroxide and some other liquid in a bowl. Still talking casually, with a piece of cotton she begins to apply the liquid to dye the hair around her honey-pot.

'She glanced up, saw my amazed look, and smiled. "Relax, Georgie, I'm just making my collar and cuffs match."' (Harlow, too, was known to bleach her pubic hair.)

Raft and Carole became close. He said, 'We talked about everything, and I could express exactly how I felt because she liked the sort of words you were used to only using with guys.'

He also notes, 'Carole was wholly generous, always seeing to it that people she knew or felt sorry for worked as extras. If they didn't work, she wouldn't go on the set.'

And Raft noted, 'She was always playing jokes. One day she put little tin stars all over my dressing room, even in my toilet.' And she wasn't adverse to repeating a previously successful joke. 'Another time she sent me a big package from Bullock's, tied with a big floral ribbon bow. I opened it. There's another box, then another. Finally I get to the last box, and there's a ham!'

Apparently Raft was really in love with Lombard, although to this day he has never revealed the full story of their romance, and all indications are that Carole never intended carrying their flirtation any further. Raft explains his not marrying Lombard by saying, 'What was the sense of it? I had nothing to offer her. By then I had signed over ten percent of my earnings to my wife, and she refused to divorce me. I was trapped.'

Meanwhile, Carole's relationship with Russ Columbo was apparently not at all hindered by her brief fling with Raft.

When *Bolero* was finished, the studio wasn't satisfied with it. At Carole's suggestion, Mitchell Leisen was brought in to shoot over her big dance scene with Raft. Asked if Lombard was a good dancer, Leisen reminisced: 'She certainly was. Everything she did was exquisite.'

Next Carole was cast opposite Columbo's crooning rival, Bing Crosby, in *We're Not Dressing*. Columbo stayed away from the set of this one.

Then came Carole's big break. Paramount lent her to Columbia (where Clark had recently made *It Happened One Night*) for Ben Hecht's and Charles MacArthur's film version of their Broadway play *20th Century*, starring John Barrymore.

Howard Hawks, the director, specifically wanted Carole for the film. But on the first day of rehearsal he was aghast: 'She acted like a schoolgirl. And she was stiff; she would try to imagine a character and then act according to her imaginings instead of being herself.' Hawks recalled that 'Barrymore began to hold his nose. I made him promise that he wouldn't say anything until three o'clock in the afternoon, but I could see him getting very worried over her stiffness, and obviously nothing was happening with this girl.'

Hawks took Lombard for a walk around the stage.

'You've been working hard on the script,' he said.

'I'm glad it shows.' Carole beamed.

'Yes, you know every word of it,' said Hawks. 'How much do you get paid for the picture?'

She told him.

He said, 'That's pretty good. What do you get paid for?'

She paused. 'Well, acting.'

Hawks replied, 'Well, what if I would tell you that you had earned all your money and you don't owe a nickel, and you don't have to act any more?'

Carole just stared at him. Hawks said, 'What would you do if a man said such a thing to you?'

'I'd kick anyone who said that,' Carole said through clenched teeth.

Hawks told her Barrymore had said it.

Carole smiled, with, as Hawks remembers it, 'one of those Lombard gestures'.

Hawks told Carole, 'Barrymore will say that to you in the script. Now, we're going back in and make this scene and you kick him, and you do any damn thing that comes into your mind that's natural, and quit acting. If you don't quit, I'm going to fire you this afternoon. You just be natural.'

'Are you serious?'

'I'm very serious,' replied Hawks.

'All right.'

They went back in. 'We're going to make this scene,' said Hawks.

Barrymore groaned. 'We're not ready.'

'Who's running this?' said Hawks.

'You are.'

'Okay.'

They shot an eight-page scene, and Carole kicked Barrymore. He jumped back. He started reacting, and they both went through the scene. Barrymore exited on cue, and Hawks shouted, 'Cut and print it.'

Barrymore came back in and said to Lombard, 'That was marvelous. What've you been doing, kidding me?'

Carole started to cry and ran off the stage. 'What happened?' asked Barrymore.

Hawks replied, 'You've just seen a girl that's probably going to be a big star, and if we can just keep her from acting, we'll have a hell of a picture.'

20th Century, about an egotistical Broadway director who transforms a salesgirl into a successful stage and movie star, was a sensation. John Barrymore later gave Lombard an autographed portrait, on which he wrote: 'The finest actress I have ever worked with, bar none.'

Carole was ecstatic. With *20th Century* she achieved recognition on a level she had never known before. But, as often happened, instead of maintaining the quality of *20th Century*, Paramount cashed in by lending her out for potboilers – Columbia's *Lady by Choice* and MGM's *The Gay Bride*.

On the home lot she was starred opposite Gary Cooper in *Now and Forever*. But the real star of the picture was a child, Shirley Temple.

Lombard's romance with Russ Columbo had reached the stage at which talk of marriage was inevitable. Carole's friends still didn't take the affair seriously.

Then: 'He's dead,' the voice said over the phone. Carole, vacationing at Lake Arrowhead, rushed back to Hollywood. 'An accidental death' was how the police report finally read. The facts were clouded then, as now.

Russ had been visiting his best friend, portrait photographer Lansing Brown, Jr. A servant at Brown's house later reported that he had heard the two men argue violently. Brown was a collector of antique guns. The story he told police was that he was 'playing with the gun' and didn't know it was loaded. It accidentally went off, and Russ fell to the floor. Dead.

Subsequent investigations reported that the bullet had ricocheted several times and hit Columbo in the forehead. Death was instantaneous.

Lombard was in shock. She attended the funeral, at which her brother Stuart was a pallbearer. She went into mourning. Carole was deeply, emotionally affected by the sudden tragedy. 'His love for me was the kind that rarely comes to any woman,' she said.

However, Carole had been aware of the close relationship between Russ and Lansing Brown. She knew that the kindest gesture would be to console Brown. 'I know you loved Russ,' she told him. 'I don't blame you. It was an accident. Russ would want us to go on being friendly, and of course we will.'

After Russ Columbo, the only other serious suitor in Carole's life was screenwriter Robert Riskin, co-author of *It Happened One Night*. Again she was attracted to a man for his wit and intelligence, rather than his blatant sex appeal. Her friends knew it was not a serious attachment.

But Riskin was the perfect secort for Carole's new social role. She had decided life was short, and wanted to make the most of it. Carole had been taking herself too seriously. She liked the character she had played in *20th Century*, and decided to use it as a model for her new off-screen image. A serious believer in numerology, the actress somehow felt – and expressed the feeling – that she didn't think she would live to be old.

It was easy for Lombard to turn into 'America's Madcap Number One Playgirl'. 'She was already halfway home,' noted a columnist. She began giving wacky parties. William Haines, the former silent-film star, and a friend from her marriage to Powell, had become a top interior decorator. Haines had decorated Powell's house, and now he decorated Carole's. She announced she was throwing a party to launch her new showplace. Then she had the house stripped completely before the guests arrived. It made all the columns.

Another famous party was a formal affair for which she had her living room covered with hay.

76

She invited all her Paramount friends, stagehands as well as stars, to a bash she threw at the Venice Amusement Pier in honor of A. C. Blumenthal and William Rhinelander Stewart. That too made all the papers.

Carole's career got another lift when Ernst Lubitsch took over as head of Paramount production. Lombard's friend Mitchell Leisen rescued her from thankless roles and starred her in the first of her really good films for Paramount, *Hands Across the Table*.

The cameraman was Ted Tetzlaff. Lombard had loved the way he had photographed her years before in *Brief Moment*, and induced him to move over from Columbia to Paramount.

Leisen originally asked Ray Milland, his next-door neighbor in Beverly Hills, to play the lead opposite Lombard in *Hands Across the Table*.

'Oh no,' said Milland, 'find someone else.' Milland had worked with Carole in *We're Not Dressing*, and had found her to be so high-strung that she made him nervous. His official excuse: 'Please don't ask me to do it because I know I can't play comedy.'

Leisen felt that an actor had to have a flair for comedy; it was something that couldn't be directed. He took a chance with newcomer Fred MacMurray. MacMurray possessed the flair for comedy, but was very shy in those days. Leisen and Lombard had to draw it out of him. One day Leisen found Carole sitting on top of Fred, pounding his chest with her fists and saying, 'Now, Uncle Fred, you be funny or I'll pluck your eyebrows out.'

Leisen's and Carole's attempts to make MacMurray funny paid off. One scene, in which Lombard impersonates a long-distance telephone operator calling from Bermuda, was so funny that when it finished, Lombard and MacMurray collapsed in laughter on the floor of the set. Leisen was smart enough to keep the cameras rolling, and the additional footage was added to the film.

MacMurray, reminiscing about his association with Lombard, said: 'I owe so much of that performance and my subsequent career to her. She worked with me on every scene. The first scene we shot had me playing hopscotch on the linoleum of the hotel as Carole walks by. Now, that's something I would never do myself in a million years, but Carole coached me and somehow I got through it.'

Hollywood often tailored films to suit the talents of an individual star. Such was the case with *Hands Across the Table*, written to show off Carole Lombard. It was the standard boy-meets-girl plot, but with some excellent dialogue, and with the combination of Lombard and MacMurray, it became a better-than-average movie.

Leisen used a reversal of the woman and man roles as the theme of the movie, a play that was to become his stock in trade. The woman became the aggressor, a successful personality in the man's world. The man was merely a sex object, valued for his looks and charm.

Lombard and MacMurray would appear in four more films together, and he became a close friend. Fred recalls that the first day he worked with Lombard, they were doing still photography – publicity shots. When he got home his wife, Lily, asked, 'Well, how did it go with Carole Lombard?'

He replied, 'I have never heard such profanity from anybody, man or woman.'

Lily persisted, 'Other than that, what's she like?'

Fred answered, 'She's wonderful.'

Surprisingly, Carole's wonderful performance in *20th Century* didn't receive an Oscar nomination. At the Awards, she had rooted for Bill Powell, and was disappointed when he lost to Clark Gable.

CHAPTER TWELVE

As it does today, the Oscar in 1935 meant a higher asking price for the recipient. Gable now got a new seven-year contract, which gave him four thousand a week for the first three years, forty-five hundred for the next two years, and five thousand for the last two years.

Clark had an Oscar and a fantastic new contract, and life should have been rosy. It wasn't. He and Ria were having their troubles again. Ria was frank:

'Clark was restless and unhappy. He was like a child who has been surfeited with candy. His success was too sudden, too overwhelming. He couldn't adjust to it. We would separate, and then he couldn't rest until we were together again.'

One of the separations occurred when Clark went to the State of Washington for almost three months to film *Call of the Wild*. His co-star was Loretta Young, and soon the Hollywood grapevine was buzzing with reliable news that Clark and Loretta were in the midst of a torrid affair.

The year before the actress had had an intimate relationship with Spencer Tracy, but because they were both Catholics and Tracy was married, they agreed to part. (Years later, when Loretta was on the MGM lot, a cheeky photographer had the bad taste to ask her to pose with both Gable and Tracy.)

Ria took the news about Gable and Loretta in stride. At the end of filming *Call of the Wild* it was announced Miss Young was 'ill' and would take a year off from work. Many in Hollywood supposed that the very Catholic Loretta was pregnant by Gable and refused to have an abortion.

MGM got Gable back on the lot, 'where they could keep an eye on him', and his work schedule was truly prodigious. First came a re-teaming with Harlow, in *China Seas*. Then Irving Thalberg wanted Gable for the studio's biggest production of the year, *Mutiny on the Bounty*.

'I won't do it,' Clark told Eddie Mannix. He was reluctant to do *Mutiny* because he felt that he would seem sissyish in breeches and pigtails, with a British accent.

Mannix finally convinced Gable that should play the part of Fletcher Christian. 'You've got the personality for Christian. And, besides, you're the only guy in the picture who has anything to do with a dame.'

Gable gave in.

When the movie was finished, Gable said, 'I was wrong. It *was* something you could get your teeth into. It wasn't the usual load of movie horseshit.'

Before the release of *Mutiny*, Clark, with Ria again at his side, went on a personal-appearance tour. Everywhere the scene was the same. Women rioted in all the cities he visited. In Kansas City nearly three thousand hysterical ladies mobbed the train station, some of them even climbing over coal cars to get to him. In one hotel a chambermaid managed to sneak into his room, and he awoke to find her stroking his chest. In another city, a smitten teen-ager trapped him in an elevator and covered him with kisses. In New York he had to have constant police protection and be smuggled in and out of every place he went to because the fans blocked traffic everywhere. Admirers even tried to break down the door of his dressing room. Women gave him anything to autograph, even their bras.

On the tour, Gable sacrificed dozens of handkerchiefs, ties, and cuff links to his souvenir-hungry fans. Mystified by the adulation, Gable somewhat modestly stated, 'This power over women that I'm supposed to have was never noticed when I was on Broadway. I don't know when I got it. And, by God, I can't explain it.'

For the women of the thirties he was The Beatles, Elvis, Sinatra, Paul Newman, and Robert Redford all in one irresistible package.

After the publicity tour, Clark took off for South America – alone – to think things over regarding his marriage. His flight over the Andes was rough. At one point the plane lost altitude and barely missed some of the mountain peaks. A friend recalled, 'Clark said he wouldn't have missed it for anything, but wouldn't do it again. He was not too keen about flying after that.'

In South America he was again mobbed by fans, and was glad to get back home. He then told Ria of his decision that they should officially separate.

Ria understood what was happening. 'He was under tremendous pressure. It was a combination of too much work, too sudden success, and the fact that women fairly threw themselves at him all the time. Basically he had good sound Dutch principles, and no one could be sweeter at times, but he could also be stubborn and perverse. I tried to make him see that his happiness would have to come from within himself.'

Clark made the separation complete. He moved out of their house and into the Beverly Wilshire Hotel in December, 1935. He refused to give any information to reporters, saying only, as he had when he had separated from Josephine, 'Let the lady tell it.'

Perhaps some of the problems with Clark's and Ria's marriage were best summed up by agent Corney Jackson, who remarked: 'She had quite a motherly quality. Clark was always rather suppressed when he was with her, like a small boy on his good behavior.'

80

However, Ria's motherly quality was balanced by an IBM-type mind when it came to assessing the 'practicality' of a divorce. This particular Mrs Gable was no Josephine Dillon. If Clark wanted his freedom, fine. He would pay accordingly. She had invested a lot of time and money in him.

When Clark and Ria finally separated, Ria soft-pedaled it and gave out the statement:

'Clark has been working very hard in recent months and has been quite temperamental. Little differences, ordinarily of minor consequence, arose between us, which under stress assumed grave proportions.'

Although Clark was having a difficult time in his personal life, he was happy that things were looking up for 'Sis'. Jean Harlow was a different girl now. She had finally met an older man who might possibly provide the happiness that had eluded her for so long.

On the set of *Reckless*, Jean and William Powell had discovered each other. The girl's pressure-cooker home life with Marino and Mama was becoming increasingly difficult to cope with, and Jean began spending more and more time with Powell and Kay Mulvey.

Powell's older, refined, and knowledgeable manner, his suave, cultured, sexy male baritone, and his distinguished position as a film star of long standing appealed to Jean. He had 'real class'. And of course Powell couldn't help but be attracted to the sexy, famous young woman who respected him and sought his advice.

Gradually it was more than fun for Jean to be with him: It was necessary. She could tell him everything; she could get advice, even on such mundane matters as whether or not she should change the color of her hair. She didn't like fussing with her hair. In fact, in most of her films she wore wigs.

Jean's life was in its usual emotional turmoil, and Powell was a steadying new force. With Bill's encouragement, Harlow had even decided to sell her gorgeous white elephant of an estate, despite Mama's and Marino's loud protestations.

After *Reckless*, which was lambasted by critics but did big business (it was Jean's first and last musical), Metro rushed her into *China Seas*, with Gable. Her popularity had steadily climbed, and the studio was arranging the publicity coup of the year: a cover of *Time* magazine.

81

The *Time* cover made Jean Harlow the envy of every star in town. Even L. B. Mayer was impressed. And surprised, since MGM's Garbo and Crawford were surely more deserving and had achieved greater prestige. But so far as *Time* was concerned, it was Jean who they thought would sell the most magazines.

Strickling and his crew fed the *Time* reporters what the studio felt would be flattering material. The article turned out well, calling Jean 'the foremost U.S. embodiment of sex appeal'. The text smoothly handled the details of the Bern marriage.

Jean was unhappy with the news magazine's slant, but everyone, including William Powell, congratulated her. Powell was impressed and pleased with her rising success. But the person most impressed with Jean's August 19, 1935, *Time* cover was Mama Jean. The article somewhat inaccurately attributed a great deal of credit for Harlow's career to Mama. Mama kept a leatherbound copy of the magazine with her at all times from that point on.

Through the years there has been much discussion concerning Mama Jean's influence on Harlow. People like Adela Rogers St John feel that while many female stars had mothers who stood behind them or beside them, the most obsessed mother, one who stood *in front* of her daughter, was Jean Harlow's. Some contend that Mama Jean was an aggressive, domineering, cunning woman who let nothing stand in the way of her daughter's success. Others, however, including Kay Mulvey, say Jean's relationship with her mother was extremely close. Jean did not hate her mother. Kay says that Jean was as close and warm with her mother as Carole Lombard was with hers.

Jean could deal with Mama, but not with Marino. Something had to be done, but there was little time. Metro had rushed Harlow into *Riff Raff*. The thinking was that it would help establish Spencer Tracy as a sexy leading man.

During production, Jean finally convinced her mother to divorce Marino Bello. But it was, to say the least, a trying time. Harlow had even hired private detectives to gather information needed to persuade Mama of Bello's infidelities.

When the divorce went through, Jean thought she was at last rid of Marino, and felt that she had really helped her mother gain physical as well as emotional freedom. Nothing could have been further from the truth. The divorce unsettled Mrs Bello to such an extent that she became more of a problem than ever.

However, Jean Harlow was in high spirits that November of 1935. *Riff Raff* was finished, she was earning $4,000 a week, she had sold her house and gotten rid of Marino, and her affair with William Powell was in high gear. She even liked her next part, with Gable and Myrna Loy in *Wife vs. Secretary*. It was always fun to work with Clark, and she admired Myrna. How Jean longed to play those well-bred ladies Loy portrayed so charmingly opposite Clark and Bill.

Often Powell would visit the set to cheer Jean on. Bill and Jean were an accepted duet on the lot, and the MGM 'family' hoped that 'the baby' – as everyone now called her – found some happiness.

Wife vs. Secretary wrapped in January, 1936, the same month Clark Gable began his affair with Carole Lombard.

CHAPTER THIRTEEN

When it came to pretentiousness, Hollywood could not be out-done. The inhabitants of cinema town were unrivaled in their attempts to maintain an extravagant off-screen lifestyle to keep pace with their on-screen activities.

Full-dress balls were popular in Hollywood in the thirties. It was appropriate that Billy Gable and Janie Peters, the reigning King and Queen of the town, should 'find each other' at the Hollywood social event kicking off the 1936 season: the White Mayfair Ball.

This was a lavish affair sponsored by the Mayfair Club of Hollywood as a benefit for the Motion Picture Relief Fund. The club was led by David O. Selznick. It consisted of what some might describe as a snooty bunch of Hollywood's elite trying to emulate British royalty.

The White Mayfair Ball was strictly white-tie-and-tails, and that year the women were asked to wear white *and only white*. The entire motif was white: the flowers (roses and gardenias), the decorations – even footmen were dressed in white.

Carole had persuaded Selznick to let her be hostess. Lombard was, of course, already famous for her own charmingly bizarre parties, and thought it would be a nice change of pace to host a formal 'do'.

Hollywood's top echelon turned out in force: Darryl F. Zanuck, Claudette Colbert, Spencer Tracy, Merle Oberon, Adolph Zukor, William Randolph Hearst and Marion Davies, Basil and Ouida Rathbone. Irving Berlin was slated to perform, debuting his new score for the upcoming Fred Astaire–Ginger Rogers film, *Follow the Fleet*. For dancing, Cab Calloway and his orchestra alternated with the Eduardo Durantes Latin band.

Carole had thrown herself wholeheartedly into preparations for the event, and was determined it would be a smashing success. It was – for an hour. Then Norma Shearer arrived. Heads turned. Eyes popped. 'Why, that fucking bitch!' muttered Carole, astonished and furious. Shearer was wearing a bright crimson gown.

'Daaaarling!' exclaimed Norma, floating over to her. Her entrance had been as dramatic as would be Bette Davies's to the New Orleans ball in the film *Jezebel*.

Carole restrained herself for the moment. Only Shearer would have dared disregard Hollywood's rigid social rules.

'Thanks *so* much, Norma darling,' growled Carole, eyes flashing.

Norma laughed and made her glittering way among the crowd. The jealous eyes of the many top actresses present followed Shearer around the room.

Carole had been escorted to the White Mayfair Ball by Cesar Romero. But now another tall, dark, and handsome man strode over to her.

'Wanna dance?' It was Clark Gable, smiling his famous half smile. He was amused at Carole's anger.

'Did you ever see a bitch with so much nerve?' She motioned to giggling, flittering Norma.

'She's a good kid,' answered Gable. 'Want to dance?'

He led Carole onto the dance floor. Lombard, like Harlow, often wore no underwear, and Gable held her tightly as they danced.

'I go for you, Ma,' he smiled.

She was quick. She remembered the nicknames from *No Man of Her Own.*

'I go for you too, Pa.'

While they were dancing, it became more than apparent that Carole was turning Clark on. They both knew it. Carole laughed good-naturedly at his obvious embarrassment. Clark Gable, the all-time Hollywood he-man, began blushing like a young boy. He regained his composure, and Carole said, 'Let's sit down until you cool off.'

'I've got a better idea,' he said. 'Let's get out of here.'

In true Hollywood fashion, he whisked Lombard away from the party, 'for a ride in my new Duesenberg convertible.' The story goes that they drove around and around Beverly Wilshire Hotel, where Clark was living, and that Carole, on his obvious invitation – 'Want to stop up for a minute?' – kidded him: 'Who do you think you are? Clark Gable?'

Whatever they did in or out of the Duesenberg, they returned to the ball shortly afterward and Carole, glowing, resumed her duties as hostess. People, of course, had noticed that Clark and Carole were missing. When they returned, tongues wagged as Gable and Lombard danced cheek to cheek. Among those to take particular notice was Ria Langham Gable.

Lombard was in top form that night. Her bitchy streak had been aroused when Shearer stole the spotlight, and now, as Lombard and Gable danced past Ria, Carole said snidely, 'Isn't that old bag yours?'

Another to notice Clark's infatuation with Miss Lombard was Loretta Young, whose recuperative period from her undisclosed illness was over. Louella Parsons and Marion Davies, considered Hollywood's two top matchmakers, were eager – and this time justified – in predicting 'a budding romance' between Clark and Carole.

While Lombard flitted around, Gable wandered over to the bar for a drink. He became furious at actor Lyle Talbot. Talbot was the first to say what everyone at the ball was thinking, namely that Clark and Carole had slipped away for 'a quickie'.

Clark was about to punch Talbot when Lombard rushed over and pulled him away. She was in a belligerent mood herself, and soon turned Clark's attention to her own continuing anger at Norma Shearer. Clark was always amused

85

at battles between women.

The other women at the ball were complaining to Carole about Shearer's gall at wearing red. After all, they all could have pulled a stunt like that! And they longed to tell Shearer off, but Norma and Thalberg wielded such influence in the industry that none could afford to scale the Hollywood heights without MGM's help.

All eyes were focused on Carole confronting Shearer. Their argument was the high point of the evening.

Shortly after midnight, Carole went over to Clark. 'Let's go.' She told Cesar Romero, 'I'll see you later, Butch.'

'Butch' Romero, as his intimates had dubbed him, was one of a select group invited to a pre-dawn breakfast party at Carole's home. Gable knew that there were at least two or three hours before guests would arrive, and he thought that would leave plenty of time to score. But when they arrived at Carole's, it was clear she wasn't to be had that easily.

Like a scene from one of her frothy comedies, almost like a scene from the film they'd done together, Carole skillfully avoided Clark's advances without turning him off completely.

Clark, not a social butterfly, wasn't anxious to stay on for the breakfast party. 'I've got a date,' he told Carole, 'I've got to go.'

'With who? Loretta Young?'

Gable, not amused by Carole's comment, left in a huff. But now that Carole knew he was interested, she wasn't about to let him slip away.

The morning after the White Mayfair, a pair of doves in a gilded cage were delivered to Clark's hotel room – a gift from Carole. Clark telephoned, and they made a date. He was encouraged because of the note she had sent with the doves: 'How about it?'

When he picked her up in his Duesenberg it was raining, and the canvas roof of the incredibly expensive car was 'leaking like a sheet of toilet paper'. Carole was in hysterics, especially at Clark's embarrassment.

Clark told Carole he loved the doves, but it was impractical to keep them in his hotel apartment. She said, 'I'll keep them for you', and subsequently sent her butler over to the Beverly Wilshire to retrieve the birds.

Clark invited Carole to a party he and his friends Donald Ogden Stewart, the screenwriter, and John Hay Whitney, multimillionaire entrepreneur, were planning. Bea Stewart, Donald's wife, hadn't been able to attend the White Mayfair Ball. She was recovering from a nervous breakdown.

Stewart and Gable had become friends on the MGM lot, and Gable, on rare occasions, could be as zany as the other stars of his day. 'What about a party for Bea?' he suggested.

Since her doctors said that Bea couldn't go out at night, the party was scheduled for high noon. In true thirties screwball fashion, the affair was dubbed 'Bea Stewart's Annual Nervous Breakdown Party', and the guests were requested to wear their dressiest evening clothes.

Robert Taylor, Kay Francis, Ronald Colman, Wallace Beery, and other top stars were mingling that afternoon in Whitney's fabulous mansion when a screaming ambulance screeched to a halt in front of the house. Two attendants jumped out, rushed into the back of the ambulance, and scurried into the party carrying a stretcher. On it was Carole Lombard, apparently unconcious, a white sheet draped over her lifeless body.

After a crowd had gathered, wondering what the hell was going on, Carole jumped up and began her famous laugh. But most of the guests thought the joke in bad taste.

'What the fuck's the matter with you shitheads?' she asked. 'Can't you take a joke?'

The prank was typical of Lombard. Gable was incensed. His sense of propriety had been offended. She, in turn, was 'pissed off' at him.

When he called her a crazy neurotic, she countered, 'You old fogey. You've lived too long with that old battleaxe.' Each stormed away. After an hour, though, they were back together. Along with some of the others, they wandered out to the tennis courts. Carole beat Clark in every set – but consoled him with a kiss.

Her subtle pursuit continued. To show Clark there were no hard feelings, Lombard decided to send him a Valentine's Day gift the following week.

Because the sixteen-thousand-dollar Duesenberg had a faulty roof, Carole felt that Clark needed a new car. She bought a beat-up old heap for sixty dollars and then spent over two hundred dollars to have the Model T put in running order and painted white with big red hearts. She scrawled, 'You're driving me crazy', and attached the note to the steering wheel.

She sent the car over to MGM, and now it was Clark's turn to laugh.

Gable abandoned his Duesenberg and rode around in the old heap – for a few days. 'Carole bought it for me,' he told his cronies, wanting them to know 'Carole's my girl'.

Then Clark had the last laugh. First he phoned Carole and asked her out for Valentine's eve. She accepted.

For the occasion Carole dressed for optimum effect. They were going to the Trocadero, the *in* spot, where stars went to see and be seen. Her blonde hair was pulled back to accentuate her cheekbones. Her sparkling gown had been designed by Irene, and a sprinkling of Lombard's famous diamond jewelry glittered in the evening light. Carole topped the outfit with a chinchilla jacket.

She was surprised at what awaited her, and delighted to discover that Clark had a sense of humor after all. He had picked her up in the Model T. Some people still talk about the sight of Hollywood's two biggest stars clunking down Hollywood Boulevard in an old Ford.

Gable was thirty-five, Carole twenty-seven. He'd been married twice, she'd been to the altar once. Still, they were acting like a couple of schoolkids who had just discovered each other, love and sex at the same time.

Perhaps they had.

CHAPTER FOURTEEN

Clark Gable was long accustomed to being pursued by women. When Clark and Carole had first met, back in 1932, she was married. But now she was free. And she made it clear to Clark that she was available.

But, unlike her scores of predecessors, Carole wasn't about to 'just jump into bed'. She required more than that from a man. She was looking for qualities that would make for a long-term relationship. She wasn't a girl who settled for second best in anything. Marrying a top star held no allure for her. She had already done that.

Throughout 1936 the Gable–Lombard romance proceeded as Carole wanted it to – slowly. Most upset was MGM. This wasn't a time when married people, even legally separated, flaunted their extracurricular affairs. And Gable and Ria were still married.

Paramount, less concerned with its stars' personal lives, didn't even scold Carole. She was a top professional and didn't give the studio any problems. *Hands Across the Table* had been a good grosser, and Paramount put her into *The Princess Comes Across*. Her co-star: George Raft. But Raft balked, complaining that cameraman Ted Tetzlaff 'gave Carole all the good shots'.

Carole wouldn't do the film with a different cameraman, so Paramount replaced Raft with Fred MacMurray – but not before Lombard was, in her usual fashion, instrumental in helping MacMurray solve a major problem he was having with the studio.

Although MacMurray was getting star billing, right after Carole, he was receiving his stock contract salary. Carole advised him: 'Go on strike.'

He did. But each day, as threatening notes arrived from Paramount, he would panic that the studio really meant to let him go. Carole made him stick to his guns. She said: 'Listen, I know how to handle them. Don't go back until they offer you a lot more money. You're worth it, they know it, and sooner or later they'll have to give it to you. Besides, I'll tell them I won't make *The Princess Comes Across* with anybody else.'

MacMurray recalls, 'So I went down to Palm Springs and the threats kept coming. Finally the studio told me it was willing to renegotiate the contract. The money was a lot better, and I think they respected me a little more. I owe all of that to Carole.'

If there had been any doubts voiced by cynical observers that Lombard's divorce from William Powell had been anything but amicable, they were dispelled once and for all when Bill insisted on Carole as his leading lady in Universal's *My Man Godfrey*. Powell was on loan-out, having completed what many consider his best film, *The Great Ziegfeld*, for MGM.

My Man Godfrey would turn out to be another classic sophisticated film comedy.

A touch of irony was that old Gable flame Alice Brady was cast as Lombard's mother. Nothing fazed Carole. She knew of Brady's involvement with Gable years ago on Broadway, and the two very frank ladies had a discussion. Carole wanted to know if Alice had any words of advice concerning Clark. To Carole's amusement, Miss Brady couldn't remember anything at all special about Clark Gable, in or out of bed.

But to the women of America, Clark was Number One. Agent Charles Feldman remarked many years later, 'Even in the mid-thirties Gable was an unbelievable draw. He should have been paid a million a picture *then*.'

Over at MGM, Jeanette MacDonald, dubbed 'The Iron Butterfly' by her co-workers, had found a script and wanted Gable as her co-star. Gable had just completed two pictures back to back with Joan Crawford: *Chained* and *Forsaking All Others*. Jeanette was at her peak, and a Louis B. Mayer favorite. Fresh on the heels of her success in *Naughty Marietta* and *Rose Marie*, she had been approached by Robert Hopkins, who told her he had a story that would be perfect for her and Gable.

It was the tale of a Midwest girl who made good by singing in a San Francisco cabaret, graduating to the local opera house, where she became the favorite of society people. She would be pursued by the cabaret owner, a love-'em-and-leave-'em type, with the climax of the story occurring during the devastating earthquake of 1906, when the hero would risk all to reach his love.

Gable wasn't available for the picture. Jeanette, certain that he was right for the part, decided to wait for him rather than go into production on *Maytime*, thereby making a huge sacrifice, since she was on a per-picture contract.

Gable wanted no part of *San Francisco*, saying: 'She's a prima donna. I just sit there while she sings. None of that stuff for me.'

However, with the usual persuasion from Eddie Mannix, and impressed by the knowledge that Jeanette was willing to go off salary to wait for him, Gable finally relented. *San Francisco* was Gable's first film with Spencer Tracy. Clark and 'Spence' developed a friendship, but, contrary to popular opinion, they seldom met off the lot.

When the film was released, some critics said that Tracy stole the show, and Gable agreed. Clark never had any pretensions about his ability as an actor. He knew he was good, but he also knew that 'there are better actors around'. However, Gable's fears about Jeanette MacDonald overshadowing him were unfounded.

Over the years *San Francisco* has become something of a classic. Even today, audiences still marvel at the special effects. Clark, however, did not have altogether fond memories of the film. In the earthquake scene, which called for him to be buried beneath a falling brick wall, he injured his shoulder, even though the bricks were made of papier mâché. Clark suffered periodically from the injury for several years.

Clark and Carole were both so active professionally that there was little time for socializing. Today few realize that in the thirties movie people usually worked ten-hour days, six days a week. The time Gable and Lombard did spend together, they were alone at her house. Occasionally the couple enjoyed a rare night out on the town.

Lombard now hit a turning point in her career. *My Man Godfrey* was released in the fall of 1936. It was her most successful picture to date, and she received her first – and only – Academy Award nomination for 'Best Actress'. She was again playing a 'zany debutante' type, while William Powell was a Harvard graduate-turned-bum-turned-butler. *My Man Godfrey* is often referred to as one of the most outstanding screwball comedies of the thirties.

The picture was so well received that Lombard, who had been having difficulty with Paramount regarding a raise in salary – the studio had been insisting that her pictures didn't do all *that* well and that at $3,000 a week she was overpaid – now slapped them with a salary demand that would make her the highest-paid female star in Hollywood.

Carole demanded – and got – $15,000 per picture. More important, she got certain concessions, like the right to make a picture a year for an outside studio, the right to choose her own cameraman, director approval, supporting-cast approval, and other lesser concessions, like the right to drive her car onto the studio grounds instead of using the parking lot. In addition she could select her own make-up man, hairdresser, and crew.

But the biggest coup of all was having the studio agree to knock out the infamous morals clause in her contract. This was a clause in all actors' contracts that gave the studio the right to fire them if scandal erupted in their private lives. The deletion of this clause meant that Carole could literally flaunt her affair with Gable and not worry about job security.

Clark Gable wasn't as successful in his contract negotiations. But then again, Gable wasn't willing to take the financial risk of not being under the protection of a big studio and receiving a steady salary. For that protection, he was tied to MGM.

Through the years, Clark's frugality has been the topic of many discussions. Most defend him by explaining that he was stingy because of the hardships of his youth. Greta Garbo and Wallace Beery were other stars who didn't give gifts to crew and cast members after a film. Gable was known on the lot as 'a cheap-skate'.

Larry Barbier tends to contradict some of the statements made about Clark's stinginess. He recalled that Clark sank about $1,500 into the gag car which Carole had given him.

'He got a belt out of passing Cadillacs and Lincoln Continentals in that old rattle-box,' remembered Barbier, 'but after eight months or so he became bored with it. Ford dealers offered him a couple of thousand dollars for it. I suppose they planned to paint it white with red hearts and put it in their show window on Valentine's Day.

'Clark turned down the offers. When I went out to his house, I would see it standing in the yard. One day I told him, "I have a kid of sixteen going to high school. I have to buy him a car. What about that Ford of yours? Will you sell it to me?"'

Clark said 'No', but Carole nagged him about it: 'Pa, you stingy old bastard, haven't you given that car to Larry's kid yet?'

The next day, over lunch, Clark said to Barbier, 'Have you got a buck on you, Larry?'

Barbier said, 'Yes', and Clark said, 'Well, hand it over.'

When Barbier gave him the dollar, Clark handed him the owner's registration for the car.

Barbier says, 'That was just like Gable. He didn't mind giving away the car, but he wasn't also going to pay the buck he'd put out for the owner's registration.'

The crew was amazed when Barbier told them what Clark had done, saying, 'You must have hypnotized him. That's the first thing he ever gave away.'

After *San Francisco* Gable was put into one of the worst

pictures of his career, *Cain and Mabel.* William Randolph Hearst had had a disagreement with L. B. Mayer and moved his film company, Cosmopolitan, and its star, Marion Davies, over to Warner Brothers. Marion's career was failing alarmingly, and Hearst asked Mayer for Gable to be lent for her leading man. The thinking was that anything with Gable would gross well, and Marion would again be in a money-making picture. Mayer didn't want to anger Hearst any further, and lent Gable.

Although Marion had successfully pursued Clark when they made *Polly of the Circus*, he was 'off limits' now. Carole was a good friend of Marion's, and Marion liked her and didn't want to offend her.

After *Cain and Mabel* came another clinker, *Love on the Run.* It re-teamed Gable and Crawford (she still got top billing), who was married to Franchot Tone now, and was trying hard to lead a more 'society lady' type of existence. Clark was too big at this point to put up with any temperamental outbursts from leading ladies. Columnist Whitney Bolton tells a funny story. On the set one day, when Joan found out they had to film through the weekend, she complained to Clark: 'I bought wonderful new clothes so I could go to the opera in San Francisco on Saturday night with friends.' She then elaborately described her new gowns.

Gable, suffering that day 'from a bit of a hangover', was obviously bored with Joan. He turned to Bolton and did a mocking imitation of his co-star: 'Whitney. I have brand-new dancing pumps, a Sulka white tie, a gorgeous dress shirt, blue plush suit, a pea-green opera cloak, and where am I? At the opera, no. Down here in this very, very unsocial Pismo Beach. Yes.'

Bolton was shocked. 'The reason I was shocked is that it was Clark Gable talking. Any other star talking like that would not have surprised me. But I spent a lot of time with him and Carole, and that was the only time I heard him say or do anything that was even ungracious.'

By now, Gable was becoming suspicious of everyone's motives. He felt the studio was 'using him', and he was definitely being underpaid. When Irving Thalberg made a deal with Mayer to have his own special unit at MGM, it was agreed that he could take a small, select group of stars to use in his productions: Shearer, Harlow, Robert Montgomery, Franchot

Tone, the Marx Brothers, and 'one half of Greta Garbo'. He could have Tracy or anyone else on the lot, 'except Clark Gable'. Gable was not unaware of his value. And he was fed up with being used as 'chattel – an object of bargaining.'

It was while Gable and Crawford were making *Love on the Run* that Thalberg died. Clark was asked to serve as an usher at the funeral. At first he refused. Gable and Thalberg had never been close. Clark always thought Thalberg was responsible for the slow progress he had made in his early MGM days. And even when Thalberg had used Clark so successfully in *Mutiny on the Bounty*, it was only after Thalberg had been made aware of the star's box-office value. So Clark felt he owed Thalberg nothing. But the persuasive studio executives convinced Gable that it would offend the entire industry, which had loved and respected Irving Thalberg, if Gable refused to be an usher. He relented.

Life with Gable and Lombard now assumed a somewhat melodramatic flavor. They were lovers and living together, but even though the world knew it, they had to live their lives 'so the world wouldn't know'. He kept his suite of rooms at the Beverly Wilshire. But Carole moved to a more isolated house in Bel-Air so that she and Clark would have more privacy.

'Ria has detectives following you,' Gable was told. 'Fuck the old bag' was Carole's reply. But the lovers remained cautious. Gable was wary that his wife's financial demands would increase if she felt publicly humiliated.

There could be absolutely no doubt now that Gable was in love with Lombard. With the settlement that Ria was asking, Clark would have dumped *any* woman he was carrying on with, regardless of how he felt about her, unless he literally couldn't get along without her.

Carole's first picture under her new Paramount contract was *Swing High, Swing Low*, directed by Mitchell Leisen. It was rewritten expressly for her by Virginia Van Upp and Oscar Hammerstein II from the famous play *Burlesque*. *Swing High, Swing Low*, today a forgotten film, was Paramount's highest-grossing picture for 1937.

For the movie, Leisen insisted that Carole do her own singing, which she did. And, as usual, Carole had a lot to say about the production. Two newcomers on the Paramount lot still remember how she helped them.

"This poor girl's eyebrows are too thin. Get Wally West-more.' It was Carole talking, and the girl was Dorothy Lamour. Lombard refused to continue the scene until Westmore had arrived and fixed Miss Lamour's eye make-up.

Also in *Swing High, Swing Low* was Anthony Quinn. He boldly asked Carole for a date. Lombard liked to be seen publicly with men other than Gable, to confuse and annoy Ria. And Carole knew the publicity certainly would be good for Quinn. She acquiesced.

Quinn, however, stood Carole up. When she saw him a few days later, she stormed over to him: 'You shithead. You bas-tard. You son of a bitch. I've never been stood up in my life, you little prick.'

Quinn meekly explained that he hadn't shown up because he didn't have any money. Carole's mood changed instantly. She believed him, and went so far as to direct him to agents who would be able to advance his career.

As Christmas time, Carole persuaded Clark to join her in Sun Valley, away from Hollywood and the watchful eyes of Ria's detectives. Carole and Clark ended that first rather busy year of their affair cozily reminiscing in front of the fire. It had been one of the happiest years of their lives.

CHAPTER FIFTEEN

Nineteen thirty-six was easily the best year in Jean Harlow's life, too. The studio had promised, while she was making *Suzy*, with Franchot Tone and Cary Grant, that they would cast her in another picture with Bill Powell.

'Why not?' she asked Eddie Mannix. 'We'd be box office, and that's all Mayer cares about anyway.'

Finishing *Suzy*, Jean took a six-week vacation. She played golf and loved spending time at Kay Mulvey's house by the beach, playing with Kay's little son, Dick, teaching him how to make mudpies.

'Jean was happiest in slacks and sneakers,' remembers Kay fondly. 'She loved children. She loved cooking. She was nothing like the Jean Harlow on screen. She was not clothes-conscious at all. The gowns she wore in films were, to her, just props. She was basically a casual person.'

Arthur Landau confirmed this when he revealed, 'In her private life Jean was an introvert given to introspection, music, and reading. At the studios and on the stages Jean was an extrovert, for that was the role she had to play.'

During the vacation Jean spent her nights with Bill Powell, and they often were with the Carey Wilsons. Jean had adored Powell's recent movie with Carole Lombard, *My Man Godfrey*, and dreamed of doing a similar film with Bill.

'Write me one,' Jean asked Carey.

But time was running out. Jean Harlow had less than one year to live.

Though the studio did cast her with Powell, it wasn't what Jean had in mind. The film was *Libeled Lady*, and in it the romantic duo was Powell and Myrna Loy. Bill and Myrna were solidly established as a box-office draw together, and the studio refused to tamper with the combination. Jean's love interest in the story was Spencer Tracy. 'What has Mayer got against me?' complained Jean to her secretary.

There were several reports that Jean and Powell were secretly married, but all were false. Myrna Loy confided in a friend that during this period she often 'helped out' Bill and Jean. Studios rigidly enforced the morals clauses in stars' contracts in those days, and the celebrity set couldn't travel together openly as they can today. So Miss Loy, Powell, and Jean would often go away together for weekends, with Myrna and Jean ostensibly sharing a room and Bill taking a single. Naturally, Myrna, not Bill, was the one who wound up sleeping alone.

But if things were peachy in Jean's love life, Mama Jean minus Marino was totally distraught. The woman became more and more neurotic. She wanted Marino back. The fact that Jean was planning to marry Powell made Mama even more frantic at the thought of being alone.

'You have someone and you don't care about me,' cried Mama one evening while she and Jean were dining out.

Heads turned.

'Mama, please,' Jean begged, as ears perked up and others swiveled around discreetly to eavesdrop on the scene.

Gable in his early film
days. (*Ronald Grant*)

Two of Hollywood's
timeless superstars, Gable
and Garbo, in *Susan Lenox*
(1931). (*Ronald Grant*)

Gable and Harlow filming
together for the sixth time in
Saratoga (1937).
(*Ronald Grant*)

A more mature Gable.
(*Ronald Grant*)

Above: Carole Lombard with 'Edmund', her rooster. (*Ronald Grant*)

Right: Carole Lombard when her name was Jane Peters. (*Ronald Grant*)

Above: Carole with her leading man George Raft in *Bolero* (1934).
(*Ronald Grant*)
Below: Two very different attitudes of the very glamorous Lombard.
(*Ronald Grant*)

Jean Harlow – 'the hottest property in films'. (*Ronald Grant*)

Powell and Harlow in *Reckless* (1935), Jean's first and last musical.
(*Ronald Grant*)

Above left: The debonair William Powell. (*Ronald Grant*) *Above right:*
Powell with Luise Rainer in *The Great Ziegfeld* (1936). (*Ronald Grant*)
Below: Powell with Myrna Loy in *Another Thin Man* (1934). The most
popular screen team of their day, they were also best friends. (*Ronald Grant*)

'You don't care,' whispered Mama.

'You know I care,' said Jean, trying to look unconcerned. But she was very concerned ...

At the wrap party for *Libeled Lady*, Jean and Powell announced their engagement. The crew applauded, champagne corks popped, and 'the baby' beamed as everyone wished her well.

The film was finished in early September, 1936, shortly before Irving Thalberg died. After his death, Mayer assumed total control of the studio. Thalberg had been Jean's friend at court, and now her career would be at the total mercy of a man who disliked her. Exhausted, she made no more films for the remainder of the year, but was forced to spend much of her free time with Mama.

For Christmas, Powell surprised Jean with a massive 150-carat star sapphire ring. It was an 'unofficial engagement ring', and had cost Powell $20,000. Although this sum seems modest by today's standards, in 1936 the average man earned about $1,000 a year. The $20,000 ring would cost about $160,000 today.

The publicity about the engagement kept Harlow front and center in newspapers throughout the land. The girl's popularity was sustaining, and now 'Put 'er with Taylor' was the executive order. Robert Taylor was the new MGM heart-throb, and Harlow was assigned as his next leading lady for the frothy *Personal Property*. It would be Jean Harlow's last completed picture.

Harlow and Taylor shocked the movie community when they defied Louis B. Mayer by accepting an invitation, in January of 1937, to go to Washington, D.C., for President Roosevelt's Birthday Ball. 'I'm going. L. B. can shove it,' Jean told Eddie Mannix.

Mayer was a staunch Republican. Naturally, it would appear unpatriotic if he refused to let Jean and Bob attend, so he made it as difficult as possible without actually forbidding them.

He told them, 'There can be *no delay* in the start of this movie or in its shooting schedule.' The cast and crew and director Woody Van Dyke all cooperated with Jean and Taylor 'beyond the call of duty', enabling the film to be completed in an unbelievable seventeen days.

It was a great strain on Jean. During production she began

97

drinking to calm down and taking sleeping pills to sleep at night. She had to be roused with other pills in the morning. But Jean was determined to 'beat Mayer at his own game'. She maintained a cheerful attitude on the set, kidding with all the technicians and with Taylor.

It was a weary Jean Harlow who finally boarded the *Santa Fe Chief* for the trip east. She was completely exhausted, and seldom got out of bed. The effects of the long journey were still evident when she arrived in Washington and was greeted by March of Dimes representatives and MGM publicity people. 'Is she all right?' asked a Dimes executive.

'I'm fine,' cut in Jean. 'Let's get started.'

Though it had been her idea to attend the festivities, the studio didn't waste the opportunity to milk maximum publicity for *Personal Property*.

She made, in all, twenty-two personal appearances, including a trip to nearby Annapolis to visit the Naval Academy. The Birthday Ball was held at seven different hotels, and Jean and Taylor appeared at all of them. The trip took its toll, and on the return train journey both Jean and Taylor came down with bad colds.

Throughout the ensuing months of February and March, Jean stayed home, 'a wreck'. Finally, she and Powell decided that a visit to Palm Springs was in order. She began thinking seriously of retiring after she married Powell. She was tired. Why not retire from the screen before the screen tired of her? She was, after all, 'an old lady of twenty-six!'

But MGM had an iron-clad contract and was determined to hold her to it. While *Personal Property* was no more than an adequate film, it would make a lot of money, and so would another picture with Clark Gable.

Saratoga would team Gable and Harlow for the sixth time. It was another instance in which Joan Crawford had originally been slated for a project but turned it down. 'They never write anything for me,' groused Jean. 'Always hand-me-downs, damn it.'

Mayer was still furious with Harlow for having gone to Washington. As a slight, and to show her that *Saratoga* was just another picture, albeit an 'A' film, Mayer assigned Bernard Hyman to produce. This indicated the extent to which Jean was out of favor. Hyman had been a Thalberg favorite, and Mayer was assigning less important pictures to the executives who had been close to the late studio chief.

Gable had no complaints, because Jack Conway was one of his favorite directors, and Clark always enjoyed working with Jean. Some movie buffs think that the love scenes between Jean Harlow and Clark Gable are sexier than love scenes played between other screen couples because he was particularly responsive to her brand of sex appeal. They both got a kick out of using their bodies to arouse each other. It was a game they had played beginning with their first film together.

Though she was jealous of other women Clark worked with, Lombard was not jealous of Jean. For one thing, she knew that Jean was madly in love with Bill Powell. For another, Jean and Clark now had a 'buddy-buddy' relationship that was beyond the earlier, sexier days.

'I like her because you can talk to her like a man,' Gable said of Harlow.

'I like her because Pa thinks of her as a man,' joked Lombard.

Carole and Jean often joined Gable and his pals for hamburgers at lunchtime, at a little 'greasy spoon' just outside the studio gates.

Prior to the start of *Saratoga*, Jean was seriously ill. Her Washington cold had developed into a severe case of the flu. Then her teeth began bothering her and at one point the pain was so great that she defied her Christian Scientist mother and implored Landau, 'Pops, please, get me a dentist!'

Landau secretly took her to one, who discovered that several of Jean's molars were impacted and her gums were infected, and the infection had spread through her entire body. Oral surgery was quickly arranged, and she was sent to a private hospital to recuperate. The entire episode was kept from Mama Jean until surgery was completed.

Jean took an additional week of rest at home before reporting for *Saratoga*. But the girl obviously hadn't fully recovered. She was still tired, lethargic, and was snappy even with Powell and Kay Mulvey.

Few people are aware that, at this point, a new man had entered Harlow's life. He was Donald Friede, a handsome publisher from New York, supposedly interested in publishing Jean's novel. Gossips rumored that there was trouble between Jean and Powell. It was printed that Powell had resented Jean characterizing her new 150-carat ring as 'vulgar'. One Holly-

99

wood savant claims that Powell walked out on Jean and this rejection caused her to lose interest in everything.

Saratoga was soon running behind schedule, a jinxed film from the start. Mayer had issued an edict to producer Hyman and director Conway: 'Finish that picture by June 5th.' He refused to talk to either one until the film was completed.

Eddie Mannix was dispatched to the set several times a day to check that production was not lagging. On Saturday morning, May 29, they were shooting a key bedroom scene with Clark and Jean. Conway was annoyed because Jean was moping and unresponsive. 'Come on, kids, speed it up,' ordered Conway. The Gable–Harlow chemistry was intrinsic to the scene's success.

Clark lifted Jean. He was supposed to drop her onto a chaise longue for a comic response. But when Clark picked her up, he was horrified to see the girl had broken into a cold sweat. Instead of dropping her, he gently lowered her onto the chaise and waved his arm to Conway as a signal to 'cut'.

'She's sick, Jack,' he said.

Jean struggled to get up from the chaise. 'No, no, I'm fine,' she said. 'Let's go on ...'

Then she collapsed.

Someone rushed for smelling salts, and the assistant director, Tom Andre, helped her to her bungalow. She was weak, but kept muttering apologies: 'I'm sorry, I'm all right, let's do the scene ...'

A few minutes later, both Conway and the studio nurse, who had been summoned quickly, told Jean she had to go home and 'rest for the weekend'.

On her way, Jean's car stopped at the set where Powell was working. Harlow canceled her lunch date with Bill. 'I'll be all right by tonight, call me,' she told him.

But Jean wasn't all right. When Powell phoned that evening, he spoke with Mama Jean and was told 'Jean is resting quietly.'

All weekend the phone kept jangling. Clark and Carole. Powell. Myrna. Kay Mulvey. Bernie Hyman. Conway. Finally, by noon on Sunday, Mama Jean was delighted when Jean suggested she take the receiver off the hook. Later that day Jean became violently ill. She vomited, and complained of pains in her stomach and back. Mama Jean attended to her, and, foolishly believing she could cure whatever illness Jean had, she gave no thought to calling a doctor.

On Monday, Conway and Hyman were frantic. Jean hadn't shown up and they couldn't reach her on the phone. A messenger was sent to her house. Mrs Bello refused to admit the boy but told him, 'Tell Mr Conway I'll call later.'

'Jean's feeling wonderfully well, she'll certainly be at work tomorrow. Right after lunch,' Mama Jean later assured Conway. 'Just another night of rest and she'll be fine.'

The director, relieved but still anxious to finish the picture on schedule, used the day shooting closeups of Gable and doing other scenes that didn't require Jean.

But Harlow wasn't there Tuesday afternoon either. Clark was worried. He hopped in his car and drove to her house. Mama Jean answered the door. She was cheerful but refused to let Clark in. 'Jean's sleeping' was all she would say.

Gable arrived back at the studio around three and held a caucus with co-star Frank Morgan and Conway.

'If she's still sleeping, it must mean that she's weak and should have a doctor,' said Gable.

Conway called Hyman. It was obvious now the picture could never be finished by Saturday. The producer, frantic, phoned Landau. He was afraid to call either Mayer or Mannix.

'The mother said she was thrilled I had come to the house,' Gable told the others. 'But why wouldn't she let me in?'

'Did you ask to see Jean?' inquired Landau.

'Of course I did,' snapped an irritated Gable. 'I even asked if a doctor had been there. She just laughed and told me that pretty soon she'd have to introduce me to Science.'

Landau knew that Mama Jean was referring to Christian Science, and that they were going to have major trouble convincing the woman to allow a doctor to see Jean.

At this point no one quite realized the gravity of the situation. The producer and director were still hesitant about calling studio chiefs. They hoped that if they drove out to Jean's house with Landau they could get in to see her. Gable and Morgan went along. Landau went up to the door of the Harlow house; the others stayed in the car.

Mama Jean answered, but the safety chain was on, and she opened the door only about six inches. After some nonsensical small talk, Landau insisted Mama Jean open the door. She relented, and Landau signaled to the men in the car. They all rushed up to Jean's room.

'Doesn't she look better now than last Saturday?' Mama asked.

The men were aghast. On the bed lay a pathetic, pale young woman. She was only half conscious, moaning in pain—in her stomach, her chest, her back, her shoulders. She had recently vomited. She was wracked with fever, and she was calling for Bill Powell, for Kay Mulvey, for 'Pops'.

Frank Morgan took her pulse. His voice trembled. 'Get a doctor,' he said.

'Bernie, you've gotta call Mannix!' screamed Landau.

But Mama Jean steadfastly insisted that Jean couldn't be moved. Now the top MGM brass descended. Metro was in a bind. They had to help the star but couldn't press Mama too hard. She might call in members of her Church, and news of Jean's illness would leak to the press. People would discover that Mama Jean had endangered her daughter's life by playing faith healer.

The finest internist in Los Angeles, Dr E. C. Fishbaugh, was called to the house, and Jean's ailment was diagnosed as inflammation of the gall bladder. 'This girl's got to be hospitalized and operated on immediately.'

But Jean was unconscious and couldn't give her consent, and Mrs Bello was adamant: 'No. She is not leaving this house.'

Gable, Morgan, and the group pleaded with the woman. She finally agreed to allow nurses to come to the house. Time was running out.

Blood and urine samples were rushed to a lab. Jean was being fed intravenously, and had been given a hypodermic to relieve some of the pain. The vigil lasted through the night, and reporters had gotten wind of the news: 'Jean Harlow is very ill.'

The studio told newspapers that Jean's illness was exaggerated. 'Just a stomach ache. A small cold,' stated the press releases.

Mama Jean covered her ears, closed her eyes, stamped her feet, refusing to listen to everyone's pleas that Jean be transferred immediately to a hospital if her life were to be saved.

It was a nightmare. Conway and Hyman telephoned Mannix and begged him to have Mayer intervene. 'Only L. B. can order Jean into a hospital, overriding her mother.'

The story is that Mannix went to Mayer but at this point

the mogul refused to do anything. Rumors later circulated that Mayer turned a deaf ear because he wouldn't forgive the girl for insulting him by rebuffing his sexual advances.

Gable was aghast as Jean's condition worsened. An acute infection from the gall bladder spread throughout her body. Her kidneys were badly damaged. Uremic poisoning was setting in.

Hyman called William Powell. 'Jean's seriously ill. She may be dying,' he moaned. 'Her mother won't let us take her to a hopital.'

Powell was shocked. Hyman told him, 'I'm going to Mayer direct. He's the only one who can do anything.'

Hyman burst into Mayer's house. 'Harlow's dying,' he screamed. 'Her crazy mother won't let us get her to a hospital or operate. You're the only one who can save her.' To prove his point, Hyman dialed Jean's home. 'She's unconscious,' he told Mayer, holding the phone out to him. 'Don't you believe me?' he implored. 'She's dying ...'

'Give me the phone,' Mayer snapped. 'Why didn't you come to me right away?'

With Mayer's go-ahead, the group at Jean Harlow's bedside defied Mama and rushed the girl to Good Samaritan Hospital.

It was too late for surgery. She was now too weak. Through the night Jean was given two blood transfusions. Then her breathing began to falter. In a last-ditch attempt to save her, the hospital sent for the L.A. fire department's rescue team. She needed oxygen, quickly.

Captain Warren H. Blake vividly recounts the scene: 'We knew Jean Harlow, and we did everything that years of training, experience in hundreds of cases, and daily life-saving drills had taught us. We made the trip to the hospital in record time. From the first it appeared a hopeless task to resuscitate her. We went into the hospital on the run. Miss Harlow was semiconscious. We set up four oxygen tanks and connected them with a mask over her face and began to pump oxygen into her lungs. Her mother was talking and shaking her lightly, trying to rouse her. Miss Harlow was talking, incoherently. William Powell stepped up to say something to her, but couldn't. He broke down and stepped back. We've faced a lot of tragic scenes in our work, but nothing so tragic as that. Miss Harlow was pronounced dead at eleven thirty-seven A.M. We kept pumping oxygen until eleven forty.'

With Jean at her death were her wailing mother, a solemn and weeping William Powell, and the internist, Dr Fishbaugh. When the doctor confirmed that Jean was dead, Bill sobbed and rushed out of the room. Mama Jean became so hysterical that she had to be taken away and put under heavy sedation.

It had all happened so fast. For those not directly involved, the news of Jean Harlow's death would be a terrible shock. Why had a beautiful young girl who had everything died so suddenly and seemingly without cause? The MGM switchboards were jammed with calls. The operators were in tears.

Rumors flared rampantly. No one believed MGM's statement regarding the cause of death. Some thought Harlow's kidneys had been ruined by heavy drinking. Others circulated the lurid story of the Bern beating. Still others said that Jean had been the victim of a clumsy abortionist. Were rigid dieting and hair bleaching the cause of death? Many hollered 'scandal', accusing MGM of covering up yet another blunder because 'Harlow had actually died of syphilis'.

The MGM commissary was famous in the thirties as a bustling meeting place where hundreds of studio employees, including the stars, gathered for lunch. Harry Ruskin, an MGM writer for many years, recalls: 'The day "the baby" died there wasn't *one sound* in the commissary for three hours. Not one *goddamn* sound.'

The studio shut down the following day in memory of Harlow. At other studios, a minute of silence was observed. MGM brass released statements. From New York, Nicholas Schenck said: 'She was a marvelous girl and a great actress. I feel terribly sorry and sympathize with all of her friends, of which there are many.'

In Hollywood, Ed Mannix was quoted: 'A sweet child has passed from us. It will seem strange not to see that lovely face and bright smile in the doorway of my office. It was a rare delight to work with her always. She was not only a great artist, she was a wonderfully sincere, honest human being.'

While such sentiments gushed forth for public consumption, the real issue at MGM was what to do with *Saratoga*. There was a fortune to be made, but would release of the film generate so much ill will – 'trying to cash in on a tragedy' – that the studio would be better off shelving it?

Meanwhile, Jean was buried. Thousands of people began assembling at dawn on the morning of June 9, 1937, at Forest

104

Lawn. But only two hundred fifty famous guests had admission cards to the Wee Kirk O' The Heather, the little church where the funeral would be held.

It had been a 'hard ticket'. Those not invited were 'out'. Reputations would rise or fall depending on whether they had wangled their way into the proceedings. Over fifteen thousand dollars' worth of flowers filled the church. L. B. Mayer sent a giant heart made of red roses, pierced with a golden arrow. But the most notable flower was one white gardenia which was clasped in Jean's tiny pink hand. Attached was a note: 'Good Night, My Dearest Darling.' No one has ever found out whether the flower was placed in Jean's hand by William Powell or Jean's mother. Or was it sent by one of Jean's other lovers? wondered Walter Winchell.

Harlow's mother was in a state of shock. She was accompanied by Beverly Hills police chief Charles Blair and Carey Wilson. A haggard-looking William Powell and his mother, Mrs Nettie Powell, were next to enter the chapel. Then Jean's stepfather, Bello, and her real father, Dr Carpentier.

A warm breeze floated through the crowd. The church's bronze doors were closed, and the casket was opened for a few moments so that Jean's family and closest friends could see her for the last time. In Jean's death, as in her life, MGM had the final word. The studio's make-up people and hairdressers saw to it that for the star's final appearance she looked radiant. Her hair – actually a wig – was a shade of soft honey blonde. There was a faint smile on her lips. 'She looked as though she were asleep ... she looked so natural it was frightening,' one of her friends remembers.

The lid on the coffin was then closed, and Jean's family and close friends were seated before the rest of the invited were allowed in.

Clark Gable was one of the pallbearers and ushers. After escorting a visibly upset Carole Lombard to a seat in the back of the chapel, Clark executed his duties as usher. Among the people he seated were his pal Hal Rosson, Jean's third husband, and Charles McGrew, Jean's first husband.

As Gable was about to join Lombard and the services were about to begin, Barbara Brown, one of Harlow's stand-ins, became hysterical. Gable jumped up and helped escort her from the church.

A blanket of fifteen hundred lilies of the valley was placed on Jean's casket. And the services began. The organ played 'None But the Lonely Heart'. And then Jeanette MacDonald stood and sang 'The Indian Love Call' – a rather unusual song to be sung at a funeral, but it had been one of Jean's favorites.

Mrs Genevieve Smith, a Christian Science Reader, officiated. She read from the Bible and from *Science and Health*. Later it would be reported, erroneously, that Mrs Smith was the Reader who had officiated at services for Paul Bern. This, of course, was ridiculous. Bern had been Jewish, and a rabbi presided at his funeral.

Jean's services ended with Nelson Eddy singing 'Ah, Sweet Mystery of Life', the song that closes with the haunting lyric: 'It is love and love alone that rules the world.'

What ruled MGM's world was money. The New York offices of Metro, where the ultimate power resided, were upset when Mayer gave out the statement: 'Production on *Saratoga* will be indefinitely delayed until we can rewrite the story to fit some other feminine personality. All that has been photographed to date, and we were within one week of the picture's completion, will be discarded.' He also noted that MGM had been about to lend Jean to Fox for *In Old Chicago*, with Tyrone Power and Don Ameche (the role went to Alice Faye). Mayer stated that other properties Metro had scheduled for Jean Harlow would be rewritten.

Those in the know, however, realized that the pap about shelving the picture was a prelude to the announcement that overwhelming public demand insisted that *Saratoga* be released. Even as it was announced that the picture 'will be discarded', after a discussion with New York executives the script was frantically reworked so that the scenes Harlow hadn't filmed could be faked. They would require no dialogue. Through clever photography Jean's double, Mary Dees, could be used in long shots, and often with her back to the camera.

Gable had no taste for having to film those final *Saratoga* scenes. However, it was during this time that Clark met a vivacious actress with whom he would enjoy a long-term on-again-off-again relationship.

When the studio tested young contract players as possible replacements for Harlow in *Saratoga*, one was Virginia Grey, a delicately beautiful blonde. Clark made the test with her personally, and they became more than close friends. Though she didn't get the part in *Saratoga*, Clark saw to it that Virginia was cast in several of his succeeding films.

Almost everyone at the studio was personally affected by Harlow's death. Kay Mulvey was shattered. Jean had willed Kay some jewelry, including a charm bracelet supposedly presented to Harlow by a Chicago gangster. One of the charms was a diamond-and-platinum pig, an obvious reference to Jean's tendency to gain weight. Jean's admirer had affectionately referred to her as 'Piggy'.

Kay remembers that Dr Carpentier, when he came to the Coast for the funeral, asked to see Jean's dressing room. 'May I take these?' he asked. They were a pair of Jean's tiny shoes, size three, and a rabbit's foot she had considered a good-luck charm.

After Harlow's funeral, her body was removed to a mausoleum, where it would remain until a decision was made: Should Jean be cremated or placed in a permanent crypt?

William Powell, as a gesture of his love, purchased a twenty-five-thousand-dollar crypt, in which Jean was eventually placed. On her casket was a silver nameplate which gave the years of her birth and death and a replica of her own signature. The Jean Harlow room had space for three bodies: Jean's, her mother's, and a third. Some believe Powell is reserving the space for himself.

While it was assumed that Harlow left her mother a sizable fortune, the facts reveal the opposite. She left only about ten thousand dollars, no annuities, no insurance policies. There were various jewels, cars, furs. After all claims on the estate were settled, Mama Jean was left with about twenty-eight thousand dollars in cash – a respectable sum for 1937, but it wouldn't last very long in Mrs Bello's extravagant hands.

When Mama Jean eventually ran out of money, a mysterious contract was negotiated with MGM. Arthur Landau says: 'Harlow's mother was hard up for money and then through Bill Powell and Eddie Mannix the novel [Today Is Tonight] was sold to the studio for five thousand dollars.' It has been reported that not only did Mama Jean receive this sum, but in addition she received a pension of five hundred dollars a month for the rest of her life. MGM bought only film rights to the novel, and Mama Jean retained publishing rights.

When Saratoga was rushed into release in early July, only a month after Harlow's death, it received better reviews than it would have had Jean been alive. It was, of course, a box-office blockbuster, and, in addition, it gave Gable's career, in momentary lull because of the poor reception of *Parnell*, a lift. In *Saratoga* Gable was playing Gable, and that's what the public liked to see.

The critics had never really praised Jean Harlow's work, except for *Dinner at Eight*. In *Saratoga* she was suddenly discovered to be 'a bright, budding master comedienne'.

CHAPTER SIXTEEN

At the time of Jean Harlow's death, in 1937, Carole Lombard was twenty-nine years old and had less than five years to live. But they would be five glorious years.

Lombard's affair with Clark was now taken seriously by all. Ria's private detectives continued to follow Gable and watch Carole's house. Constant surveillance was the order of the day.

This placed Clark under quite a strain, further compounded when he had to endure making one of his rare clinkers, *Parnell*. It was a ponderous historical drama of the Irish rebellion, directed by John Stahl. Gable didn't like the script, felt uncomfortable in the period costumes, and disliked 'endless retake' Stahl.

Leading lady Myrna Loy was Clark's only pleasant association on the whole project. Joan Crawford had refused to do the film, and Clark was peeved that she had been able to get out of it and he hadn't. But the commitment had been made, and production moved forward.

An actor, unlike an accountant or a plumber, cannot leave a day's problems at the office. Emotions cannot be turned off like a faucet, especially if things aren't going well. It is during stressful times like these when home life can make all the difference. 'Carole,' stated Mitchell Leisen, 'knew how to make life at home fun for Clark. As an actress she knew exactly the pressures he was under and knew just how to relieve them.'

Publicity for Gable was at a peak. He was invited to put his hand- and footprints in the cement in front of Grauman's Chinese Theatre. Lombard teased him. 'Why don't you give

108

'em a prick print as well?' She also warned him, 'I'm inviting Lee Francis and some of her girls. They'll be cheerleaders.' Miss Francis was the town's leading madam, and Lombard knew that Clark had been one of her best customers.

Throughout his life, Gable often preferred a call girl or waitress 'for a quick roll in the hay'. He told a pal, 'With one of those floozies, I don't have to pretend I'm Clark Gable.'

Whenever Clark boasted of his sexual prowess, Carole blew up. She wasn't temperamental, but her temper could suddenly flare up when she was provoked. On one occasion, she soared to the boiling point when Clark bragged of the unusual circumstances and sites for some of his lovemaking. He talked of it happening in a canoe, in a telephone booth, on a fire escape, and then finally boasted, 'I once did it in a swiming pool. You know, it's hard to do under water.'

Controlling herself superbly, Carole merely smiled and said: 'Yes, I know.'

Gable was irate. 'What the hell kind of girl are you? Doing a thing like that! And then having the nerve to tell me about it!'

Both before and after her marriage to Gable, Lombard was not averse to revealing to friends that Clark was 'a lousy lay'. She told her mutual friend, Doc Thorpe, that Gable's poor performance in the bedroom was probably because he was 'sex-starved for years', having been married to and involved mainly with older women who never put any demands on him. If the many Hollywood people who knew Carole are to be believed, it would appear that she relayed this 'lousy lay' information to all of them, from Anita Loos to, of all people, Groucho Marx.

Was Carole putting everyone on because *everyone* in the world wanted to know what Clark Gable was like in bed? Not according to Groucho, who is basically a very serious man. 'Carole was a wonderful woman,' states Groucho. 'If she felt you were her friend, she'd be very frank with you. She meant it, what she said about Gable. Just because a guy has a great build doesn't mean he's a great lover, you know.'

During the thirties Gable kept himself in good physical shape by working out several times a week at the Terry Hunt Health Club, where he would box and take steam baths and massages. Hunt reminisced about his one-time client: 'Unlike some of my other celebrated customers, I never heard Clark

109

gripe about anything. A health club and gymnasium is a good place to let off steam about terrible scripts, unfair reviews, stupidity in the front office, all of that stuff. You even have a captive audience. But there was never even a mild beef out of Gable.

'I've heard people say he drank quite a bit. But if he was ever drinking or suffering from a hangover when he came to my place, I never knew it.

'Clark had a physique that compared favorably with that of Johnny Weismuller and other athletes who worked out here. What was unusual for a man with so muscular a figure was that Clark always looked so good in any sort of clothes.'

The actor was obviously very fond of Hunt. 'While Gable was one of my customers, I started a mail-order course in physical training. He was one of the stars whom I asked for a signed endorsement. He gave it, but MGM ordered me to stop using his name for commercial purposes. They said that, according to their contract, his name could not be used without their consent. I told Clark that, and he said, "The hell with them. Keep using it, Terry!" That's the sort of man he was.'

Gable was so universally known that merely his name provided a youngster on the MGM lot with a stepping stone to stardom. Roger Edens, one of MGM's top creative musical writers, was excited about a pudgy thirteen-year-old singer and wrote a specialty number for her to sing at Clark Gable's thirty-sixth birthday party on the set of *Parnell*. The song, 'You Made Me Love You', was an old standard. But the new introduction, 'Dear Mr Gable, I am writing this to you ...', was an inspired touch. Judy Garland made the most of it, and Gable was duly impressed. In the midst of the song he strode over so she could direct the song to him. Afterward, he helped her off the stage. 'Thanks, honey. That was a real thrill,' he said, kissing her on the cheek.

Judy recorded the song and sang it in *Broadway Melody of 1938*. Soon the world was singing the lyrics, and Carole Lombard played the record at home constantly. 'Too constantly,' laughs a publicist. 'He found it irritating, but Carole loved to chide him so he'd keep his ego in proper perspective.'

Clark was more famous than ever, but fame had disadvantages as well as blessings. In 1937 Gable suffered the same fate that stars like Charles Chaplin and Marlon Brando were to experience in later years. He was named in a paternity suit.

110

The news hit like an explosion. Violet Norton, an English-woman, charged that Gable was the father of her daughter Gwendolyn, who had been born on July 23, 1923. Violet had even written a number of letters to Gable from England and then from Winnipeg, Canada, demanding child support. She alleged that at the time of conception Gable had been living in England under the name of Frank Billings. Since this was the same time Gable had been working with the stock company in Oregon, wouldn't Frances Doerfler be the ideal witness?

Gables lawyers were skeptical about Frances testifying. They asked Gable it he thought she would do it.

'Of course she will. So will any member of her family.'

'What happened to the engagement?' the lawyers asked.

'Well, Frances and I drifted apart.'

'What makes you so sure that in view of that the Doerflers would testify to help you clear your name?'

'They're good people. They would not lie for me. But they would tell the truth for me – or anyone else.'

'Are you sure this girl you were engaged to would testify?'

'Of course.'

'After you threw her over?'

'What makes you think I threw her over?'

'You must have. No one ever heard of a girl walking out on Clark Gable.'

They asked him when he had last seen Frances, and he told them it had been on the MGM lot three years before, when she had been looking for a job. 'Did you help her get a job?'

'No, it didn't occur to me.'

'And you *still* think that if we can find her she'll help *you* by testifying?'

Gable, puzzled, responded: 'Why not?'

Finding Frances was not easy. The Depression had wiped out her father's farm, and the old man had died soon afterward. Frances had been forced to take a job in a dress shop, and then as a cook.

MGM finally tracked her down. Would she testify? 'Of course. I know he was not in England during the fall of 1922.' Deciding that it would look better for her to be an employed actress, the studio put her under contract.

Before the trial Mrs Norton received overwhelming press coverage. And she was quite willing to talk. She told fanciful tales of how she and Clark had been next-door neighbors. And of why she was so positive he was the right one: 'I can tell by the way he mykes love to that Joan Crawford – just the same as 'e did to me.'

And on and on.

On the witness stand Mrs Norton identified Gable as 'Frank Billings – 'im that clymes now 'is nyme's Clark Gyble! Hit's 'im all right. Hit's the syme big ears.'

As absurd as the charges were, MGM and Clark had to take them seriously. Testifying for Gable at the trial were his father, who swore to Clark's never having been in England in his life, and several persons who had worked with Gable in Oregon during 1922.

When it was Frances's turn, Gable led her to the witness stand. He kissed her and said, 'It's good to see you again.'

She produced playbills that she had nostalgically saved from the 1922 stock productions.

The suit was, of course, thrown out of court, and later Violet Norton was indicted by the United States Post Office for using the mails to defraud.

The ordeal was over, and Gable invited Frances to a celebration party. They reminisced about old times. But after that evening, whenever their paths crossed at the studio, he pretended not to see her. Subsequently, MGM dropped Miss Doerfler. Too proud to ask Gable to intervene, Frances left Metro quietly, and never saw Gable again.

MGM had seen to it that during the trial Clark took advantage of his personality by becoming chummy with reporters covering the proceedings. Clark was impressed by Los Angeles *Examiner* reporter Otto Winkler. They became friendly, and Gable told Howard Strickling, 'Let's get Otto. I'd like to have him working for me.'

When the trial was over Winkler went to work for MGM, and Strickling assigned him specifically to Gable.

Since the trial was held at the Federal Building, Clark decided to use the opportunity to check personally his income-tax returns. Ever watchful of his money, and always suspicious of the studio, he wanted to compare his earnings report with that submitted by the studio.

'Hah! That's Gable for you. Always an eye on those payroll figures,' quipped Carole when she heard about it.

Naturally, Lombard hadn't attended the trial, and in fact MGM had ordered Gable not to be seen publicly with her until it was concluded. But Carole followed the proceedings with her usual eagle eye. She was appalled at Gable's treatment of 'that poor Doerfler dame. Christ, Pa, what a way to treat a woman!'

Lombard also never approved of the way Gable treated his father. She could understand the situation intellectually, but not emotionally, and often was responsible for Gable's being kinder to the old man.

Gable and Lombard made their first public appearance together after the Norton trial in an appropriately safe and glamorous harbor: William Randolph Hearst's seventy-fourth birthday party. Each year on Hearst's birthday, Marion Davies would be hostess at a fabulous costume party.

This year's bash was held at Marion's Santa Monica 'beach-house', actually an enormous, magnificent chateau. The theme of the party was 'The Circus.' Cary Grant and Randolph Scott, who were rooming together, came as a pair of clowns. Dolores Del Rio dressed as an aerialist. Marion was a bareback rider, and Hedda and Louella both came as lion tamers. Gable and Lombard had gone riding that day, and wore their western outfits.

At the party Lombard and Marion adjourned to one of the ladies' rooms for a cozy chat and a few drinks. (Hearst didn't approve of Marion's fondness for alcohol, so she hid bottles of Moet et Chandon in the many powder rooms – often in the toilet tanks – of her various vast establishments.) Meanwhile, Gable had gravitated toward a bubbling, beautiful young blonde actress, Anita Louise. While Anita's career never really gained any kind of important momentum, she enjoyed great success on the Hollywood social circuit. She had wit, charm, personality. When Carole returned and spotted Anita and Clark together – 'Why, that son of a bitch!' – she reclaimed Gable immediately.

Lombard was always annoyed when Clark displayed interest in another woman publicly. Carole had changed her life considerably to accommodate Clark. She had given up the night-club circuit because Clark didn't like nightclubs. She learned about things he did like: fishing, hunting, guns. She even took up duck hunting.

As her feelings for him had grown stronger, she had been faced with a dilemma. She knew he needed to escape every so often from the Hollywood rat race and go back to nature,

113

where he could come alive again. She wanted to share in his rigorous pursuit of outdoor sports. But she sometimes suffered from extreme exhaustion. Few people knew that the screwball comedienne who seemed so full of life went straight home from the set, had dinner in bed, and was asleep by eight thirty.

Carole was basically an indoor person, but she wasn't going to make Ria's mistakes. Lombard would be involved in everything Clark wanted to do, not be merely a good-looking broad 'in tow'. She succeeded in this, yet never sacrificed her individuality. And her career hardly suffered; it was rolling along beautifully. Although she didn't win the Oscar for *My Man Godfrey* (it was won by Luise Rainer for *The Great Ziegfeld*), Carole's nomination was 'better than money in the bank' Under her new deal with Paramount she could do outside pictures. Agent Myron Selznick brought her to his brother, David.

Selznick owned a story which he thought would be a great screwball-comedy followup for Carole's *Godfrey* hit. Ben Hecht had written the screenplay, and Russell Birdwell came up with the title: *Nothing Sacred*. It was one of the first films to be photographed in Technicolor. The director would be William Wellman.

The Selznick–International Studios, fronted by the beautiful replica of Mount Vernon which was later used as Tara in *Gone with the Wind*, became the setting for some of Carole's more outrageous antics, many of which she pulled off with the aid of Russell Birdwell, the former Hearst reporter whom Selznick had hired as chief publicist.

Carole could usually be found at the center of any unusual activity. Her racing between her dressing room and the sound stage on a little motor scooter had raised a number of eyebrows. Then she began traveling around the lot in a red fire engine she had discovered. Often she'd have the fire bell and siren going full blast. The studio manager, having heard a rumor that Carole and so-star Frederic March intended to set fire to a small yacht being used in *Nothing Sacred* in order to test the fire engine's equipment, placed a twenty-four-hour guard around the pool where the yacht was moored.

Russell Birdwell was and remains the epitome of the Hollywood press agent. He adored working with Carole Lombard. Birdwell says that Lombard could easily have been a top press agent. She had an incredible talent for knowing not only what was newsworthy but how to present it so it would *make* news. One day at Selznick–International, she stormed into Birdwell's office, shouting: 'That fucking son of a bitch! Complaining about the taxes he has to pay!'

She was talking about one of the foreign-born directors working on the Paramount lot. 'He should be grateful he's in this country, the shithead. Christ, I paid over three hundred thousand dollars in taxes last year, and I was glad to do it.'

Birdwell recognized a great story when he heard one. It was the middle of the Depression, and a tale like this would show the world that though movie stars seemed to live glamorous, charmed lives of wealth, most of their cash actually went to the government. Birdwell set up a press conference, and Carole revealed that out of $465,000 she'd earned in 1937, she'd kept only about $50,000 – $339,000 had gone to federal and state taxes, and the rest to her agent and other business expenses. Carole, the screwball-comedy queen, got plenty of press coverage with headlines to the effect: LOMBARD HAPPY THE U.S. TAKES MOST OF HER PAY. Even President Roosevelt was impressed by her patriotism, and sent her a note thanking her.

Birdwell and Carole had fun as well as garnering plenty of coverage on her pictures for Selznick. Birdwell's wit and sense of humor matched hers, and one day he arranged to have her made Mayor of Culver City and the day declared 'Carole Lombard Day'. Her only official act was declaring a studio holiday. Selznick was not amused when he drove onto the empty lot.

'What the hell's going on?'

'David,' explained Carole, 'everybody on the lot looked so tired, I thought an extra day's rest would do them good.'

Selznick had laughed when Carole managed to get her director, 'Wild Bill' Wellman, put into a straitjacket for several hours, but this was too much. He told her that in future she should limit her antics to activities which would not cost him thousands of dollars.

After *Nothing Sacred*, Paramount re-teamed Carole with Fred MacMurray in the comedy *True Confession*. She was so busy during this period that she and 'Pa' saw relatively little of each other, and he was annoyed. So when the film went on location to Lake Arrowhead, Carole asked Clark to join her for the weekend. She enjoyed the fact that Ria's detectives would have their hands full keeping tabs on them up there. It is

115

amusing that Hollywood was such tightly knit group – Lombard and Ria actually shared the same manicurist. The girl kept Carole informed on all the latest gossip.

Although Ria and her detectives were making it difficult for the couple, Lombard was preoccupied with a more important problem after Harlow's death. Both Carole and Clark were concerned about their friend William Powell.

The Bill Powell who returned to the set of *The Emperor's Candlesticks* was not the same man everyone had known. He could not hide the sorrow, and only his work kept him going. When the film was completed, he escaped for a month aboard Ronald Colman's yacht. Then he left in August for a three-month European trip.

In New York a very tired and depressed Powell registered at the Waldorf. His friends at the studio had told him, 'See people, Bill. Don't be a recluse. Jean wouldn't have wanted that.' Reporters were told by an MGM press agent, 'You can ask him anything else, but *please* don't ask him *anything* about Harlow.'

It was obvious, however, that Harlow was very much on his mind. 'I'm really awfully tired,' he told a reporter. 'This is my first real vacation in seven years. You know, I had quite a nervous shock two months ago.' He couldn't say any more, and newsmen felt uneasy and tried to look away as Powell covered his eyes with his hands. It was obvious that Harlow's death had already began to have an effect on Powell's outlook. 'From now on I will make fewer movies ...' Of Europe, he said, 'We, Al Kaufman and I, have no definite plans. We'll be more or less a couple of feathers in the wind.'

The next day Powell sailed for England aboard the S.S. *Statendam*, attempting to board incognito by wearing sunglasses. He was, of course, recognized. Arriving in Plymouth, England, en route to Holland, he refused comment when asked what he thought about Twentieth Century–Fox's having chosen *Jean* as the title of the film he was scheduled to do when he returned to Hollywood.

By Christmas Powell was back in Hollywood for *Jean*, now retitled *The Baroness and the Butler*. It was an imitation *My Man Godfrey*, for which he received a salary of $40,000 per week for six weeks. Powell drove a hard bargain. In addition to his salary, Fox agreed to place Eileen Wilson under contract. She was Powell's ex-wife, and the mother of his teen-age son.

Right after *Baroness*, Powell was faced with the most grueling personal ordeal of his life: 'I began bleeding from the rectum.' It was the most dreaded diagnosis of all. 'The doctor found a cancer, smaller than the nail of your little finger, between three and four inches up inside my rectum.... I'd have had to have a colostomy and evacuate into a pouch through an artificial opening for the rest of my life. I didn't feel I could go for this. But the doctor said that for my particular case they could offer an alternative – a temporary colostomy and radiation treatment. I took it.'

The cancer was removed. Radiologist Orville Meland of the Los Angeles Tumor Institute implanted platinum needles containing tiny radium pellets. And then, for the next six months, Powell 'simply waited'.

MGM gave out press releases that Powell was taking a hiatus from films because of 'eye trouble'. Later his operations were reported as 'abdominal operations'. Through these dark days, it was Carole Lombard and Fieldsie who stood by him.

Circumstances now dictated a change in Powell's lifestyle. It would have to be a simpler, slower-paced existence. He shunned most Hollywood social gatherings and spent much time with his son, often attending local sports events. 'I had a lot of examinations but led a reasonably normal life,' recalled Powell. 'I did quite a few radio shows, though I couldn't make movies. The worst thing about it was the esthetics of it.'

The cancer didn't recur, and after six months Powell's colon was restored as it had been before. Powell knew full well: 'I was one of the lucky ones.'

CHAPTER SEVENTEEN

Gable and Lombard were in the prime of their lives. With Carole, success in all her endeavors was vitally important. Her determination to make their relationship work was paying off.

It was now that Gable began to be referred to as 'The King'. Few remember how he got the title. One day in 1938 Spencer Tracy, arriving at MGM, found himself unable to get onto the lot because a throng of autograph hounds had surrounded Gable's car. No one noticed Tracy. Annoyed, yet amused, Tracy stood up in his convertible and shouted:

'Long live the King! And now, for Christ's sake, let's get inside and go to work.'

When word of the incident spread around the studio, someone got a brass crown from the prop department and covered it with white rabbit fur. Tracy, appointed to officiate, that afternoon crowned Gable King in the MGM commissary. Within a short time the whole incident was forgotten.

But Ed Sullivan, then a syndicated Hollywood columnist, had heard about the joke and had a brainstorm. He suggested that entertainment editors around the country poll their readers to find out who really were King and Queen of Hollywood. The editors were skeptical, what with the host of Hollywood stars around, but the idea caught the imagination of the public and the contest went on. When the results were finally in, Gable was indeed King, and Myrna Loy Queen. An official coronation ceremony was held, with Sullivan crowning the couple.

Gable, probably pleased by the whole thing at the time, grew to hate the title. 'You know, this "King" stuff is pure bullshit,' he said in retrospect. 'I eat and sleep and go to the bathroom like everybody else. There's no special light that shines inside me and makes me a star. I'm just a lucky slob from Ohio. I happened to be in the right place at the right time, and I had a lot of smart guys helping me – that's all.'

At the time of the 'King' contest, Tracy and Myrna Loy were starring opposite Gable in *Test Pilot*. It was the most ambitious film about aviation since the production that had catapulted Jean Harlow to stardom, *Hell's Angels*. It's interesting that Tracy, in real life, hated flying and was afraid of it.

'Spence' and Gable were friends – 'but only professional friends', recalls an ex-MGM publicist. While Gable admired Tracy's skill as an actor, Tracy was always a bit jealous of Clark – not of Gable's success, but of his personality and ability to get along with people, and of the relative ease with which he handled his private life. Furthermore, everyone knew Gable gulped he-man drinks with no apparent effect. But with Tracy, it was 'he's on the wagon' or 'he's off the wagon'. There was no in-between, and Tracy envied Gable's talent to drink *and* work. During *Test Pilot*, a great deal of which was shot at March Feld, about sixty miles from Hollywood, MGM had

118

a difficult time keeping Tracy off the sauce.

Gable was proud of his own work on *Test Pilot,* and every night he'd regale Carole with news of how well he was doing. She'd simply mention *Parnell* and that would shut him up. Carole even went so far as to have leaflets printed: IF YOU THINK GABLE IS THE WORLD'S GREATEST ACTOR, SEE HIM IN 'PARNELL', YOU'LL NEVER FORGET IT. IF 'PARNELL' WAS AS GABLE PORTRAYED HIM IN THAT PICTURE, IRELAND STILL WOULDN'T BE FREE. When Carole couldn't arrange to have the leaflets dropped over the MGM lot, she had them handed out at the studio gate.

Clark had given and taken a lot of ribbing in his time, but he was no match for Carole. However, her kidding didn't bother him, because he was secure in her love for him. And Lombard knew what she could kid Gable about and what she couldn't. In today's parlance, she 'kept Clark's head together'.

Three important new friendships developed for Clark when he was on location for *Test Pilot.* One man who soon became a close buddy was Al Menasco, founder of Menasco Motors. He was a former World War I test pilot, close friend of Jimmy Doolittle, and inventor of the first inverted inline engine. It was Menasco who managed to obtain the Sikorsky test plane which Gable used in the picture. Another who became a friend was Paul Mantz, a famous flier of the day (he'd be known as 'The Honeymoon Pilot'). Mantz directed the film's aerial sequences. The third pal was Ray Moore, Clark's stunt man in this film.

Clark liked having friends who were not involved with movies or show business. He didn't have to be wary of their motives. Gable was always suspicious of people in the industry. At one point he was even suspicious of Carole. This occurred when she signed a two-picture deal with David O. Selznick following the success of *Nothing Sacred.*

Selznick was casting for the most important film of the century. Every leading star in Hollywood, including Carole, wanted the female lead. The film would be a project fraught with dissension, haggling, and bitterness.

CHAPTER EIGHTEEN

The making of *Gone With the Wind* has been the subject of many books. Stories about Gable's reluctance to make the film and his unhappiness during production are legion. Even more popular are tales of the grudge Gable held against both MGM and David O. Selznick because the actor felt he'd been grossly underpaid, considering the film's ultimate success.

As soon as it was announced that Selznick had bought the rights to the best-seller, thousands of people began writing to suggest that Clark Gable play Rhett Butler. When Selznick spoke to Clark, Gable was adamant. He couldn't see himself in the role, and suggested Ronald Colman.

Selznick, now independent of MGM and his father-in-law, Louis B. Mayer, wanted to produce *Gone With the Wind* through his own company, Selznick–International Pictures. He already had a distribution deal with United Artists. But L. B. Mayer sought the project for MGM, and knew that if Selznick wanted Gable, 'the bastard will come round'.

When Lombard signed with Selznick, Clark was upset. He thought Selznick was using Carole to get him to agree to play Rhett. This, of course, may have been a very small consideration on Selznick's part, but in reality Gable's willingness or unwillingness to do the role was not the issue. MGM controlled Gable, and he'd have to do what *they* decided.

Selznick had signed Carole, even though she got a whopping $150,000 a picture, because she was 'hot', a top box-office draw. Of course, Lombard *was* eager to play Scarlett O'Hara, and *did* try to persuade Gable to change his feeling about portraying Rhett.

Back in March of 1937, Selznick had told his New York representative, Kay Brown, 'Chances of getting Gable are practically nil, if not in fact actually non-existent.' Initially Ronald Colman was a top contender for the role of Rhett Butler. In fact, as early as May, 1936, Selznick had discussed the role with Colman. But by 1937, when Selznick had purchased the property and signed George Cukor to direct, their choices were Gable, Gary Cooper, and Errol Flynn.

In early 1938, Gary Cooper was front runner for the part.

Selznick was negotiating with Sam Goldwyn for Cooper's services. In late May, L. B. Mayer phoned his son-in-law to suggest that Selznick produce the project as a package for MGM.

Selznick considered this. One plus factor was that Metro had all the money necessary to finance the project. Selznick informed his Selznick–International backer, Jock Whitney, that the casting problem 'would of course be much simpler there [at MGM] ... which would make the picture less of a risk for them than it would for us, since Gable would give them an insurance we would not have. From my personal standpoint, I could probably make the picture with less trouble and, indeed, probably make a better picture with their resources than with our own'.

But Selznick wanted to retain complete control, so Whitney arranged for the additional necessary financing, but ultimately Selznick still had to deal for Gable. The producer didn't want to negotiate directly with his father-in-law, so Al Lichtman, an MGM vice-president, negotiated with Selznick. The terms were stiff. Selznick would get Gable and financing for half of the production ($1,250,000) from MGM. In return, MGM would release the film and share equally with Selznick's company in the profits – only *after*, however, paying off the production costs and taking 15 percent of the gross profits for distributing. Selznick pondered.

Meanwhile, Warner Brothers offered a deal in which they would pay for the production in full, provide Bette Davis for Scarlett, Errol Flynn for Rhett, and Olivia de Havilland for Melanie, and take only 25 percent of the profits.

But only one actor was the right choice for Rhett, so Selznick had to accept Metro's terms. Although agreement on the deal to have Gable was reached in early 1938, the announcement and contract-signing ceremony were delayed until August because of Selznick–International's distribution deal with United Artists.

Carole was shooting *Made for Each Other* at Selznick–International for United Artists. Her two-picture deal had stipulated that her first film be dramatic. She wanted to prove – especially to Selznick – that she was a good dramatic actress. Every actress in Hollywood was out to show Selznick she'd be the perfect Scarlett O'Hara. Lombard was no exception. Though she didn't express her interest as vocally as the others, she was

121

'plenty interested'.

The reviews of *Made for Each Other* were encouraging. *Newsweek* said Carole gave 'the best performance of her career'. However, the picture was disappointing at the box office, and Selznick never seriously considered Lombard for Scarlett.

While Carole was filming at Selznick, Gable was across the street on the Metro lot. He'd finished *Test Pilot*, and *Too Hot to Handle* (again with Myrna Loy), and now MGM rushed him into *Idiot's Delight*, with Norma Shearer. The studio wanted him to complete *Delight* before the year was out, since Gable would be tied up with *Gone With the Wind* for months.

Norma Shearer had dropped out of the race to play Scarlett because polls indicated the public did not want her in the role. But although Shearer's days as a top box-office draw were almost over, her power at Metro was undisputed, and she demanded and got Gable as her leading man for *Idiot's Delight*. The picture reteamed them for the first time in seven years, and Norma received top billing.

Lombard hadn't liked Shearer since the Mayfair Ball episode, and wasn't happy that Gable would be working with her. Miss Shearer had become known as Hollywood's Merry Widow since the death of her husband. She was dating George Raft – an unlikely suitor, since Shearer was the screen's epitome of The Lady, while Raft was The Gangster. She was dating others as well, but talk at parties was that Norma was really out to get Gable.

In connection with this gossip, there is the naughty 'no underpants' story, which relates how Norma ostensibly tried seducing Clark during a photography session at which she wore no underwear. This is often confused with another 'no underpants' story, in which Clark was approached by a famous Hollywood beauty at a party. She came over to where he was sitting and straightaway lifted her dress. She was wearing no underwear, and proceeded to straddle Gable's knee. Clark, a quick thinker when it came to repelling unwanted advances in public, simply tilted the cushioned chair backward till both he and the lady fell over, exposing her 'virgin island' to the congregated crowd.

In any case, if Carole was annoyed at tales of Norma's advances, she retained her sense of humor. Besides, she knew that Clark had other concerns about the film.

Idiot's Delight required Gable to perform a tap dance, and

122

MGM hired Joe Yule, Mickey Rooney's father, and an old burlesque comedian, to coach Clark. Carole was also helping him with the routine. She hadn't hoofed since her old Mack Sennett days, but she delighted in teaching Clark the time step.

'No, no,' she'd shout. 'Remember, it's one, two, three, kick! One, two, three, kick!' Then the two would collapse on the sofa laughing.

Carole asked Jean Garceau, a friend from the Myron Selznick Agency, over to the house. Ostensibly it was to bring some papers from the office. It was the first time Mrs Garceau had met Gable.

'Are you excited about playing Rhett?' she asked. It was a question he had heard many times.

'Frankly, I'm scared to death,' he replied.

Mrs Garceau's meeting with Clark Gable was not sheer coincidence. The following day Carole asked Jean to be her exclusive personal secretary and business manager. (Fieldsie had recently retired to marry director Walter Lang.)

At first Jean hesitated. She had been married for eight years, and liked the idea of a strictly nine-to-six job. She felt, and rightly so, that to replace Fieldsie she'd have to be secretary, friend, companion, alter ego. Carole promised Jean they'd keep things on a strictly business basis. And she confided, 'Clark and I are going to be married as soon as he is free.'

As soon as Lombard completed *Made for Each Other*, she asked Jean to help her house-hunt. Their first choice was a home on the 'B' circuit: Beverly Hills, Bel-Air, or Brentwood. But it turned out that Raoul Walsh, the director, had a twenty-acre ranch in Encino which he had decided to sell. Both Clark and Carole had visited Walsh and knew the ranch. It consisted of a main house, hay barn, workshop, garage, and stables for nine horses. In addition to the twenty acres, there were five acres of adjoining land that could be purchased.

The main building was designed to resemble a Connecticut farmhouse, with tall brick chimneys. The two-story structure had been designed and built thirteen years previously by Malcolm Brown of MGM. Walsh had never really lived there, utilizing the ranch as a weekend retreat where he kept his horses and sulky. There was even a small track for the horses to work out.

Though it seemed to good buy, a lot of work had to be done on the house. New furnishings would have to be installed, servants' quarters added, the kitchen enlarged. But Clark was delighted the minute he saw it.

'I've always wanted a place like this,' he told Carole. 'It will be the first home that I've had since I was a boy that I can really call my own. Ma,' he said, putting his arm around her, 'I think we're going to be very happy here.'

Since all of Clark's money was tied up, Carole paid for the ranch. Walsh wanted cash, and Carole came up with fifty thousand dollars. At the time, no one outside the immediate family was aware that it was all Carole's money. Since money never meant much to her anyway, Lombard was happy to spend it on Gable.

'Clark isn't the happy-go-lucky, carefree man the public sees,' Carole confided to a friend. 'He hasn't had a very happy life, and is inclined to be depressed and worried. I want to make it up to him if I can.'

Carole wanted Clark to relax and be happy, and she was a constant gagster for his benefit. She sent him a full ballet outfit with gigantic dancing slippers while he was rehearsing the *Idiot's Delight* dance scene. Corney Jackson, the agent who later married actress Gail Patrick, was on the set of *Idiot's Delight*, and remembered that Carole had a huge bouquet delivered to Clark after the dance was filmed. 'Just as if he were a prima donna,' said Corney. 'Clark thought everything Carole did was terrific.'

Even with Carole in the background subtly urging him on, Gable still didn't want to play Rhett Butler.

'I never asked for the part. I was one of the last to read Margaret Mitchell's novel, and did so only because everyone insisted that Rhett was so obviously written for me. I replied that when the book was being written I was a four-dollar-a-day laborer in Oklahoma and was not in anybody's mind for anything, much less the hero in a Civil War novel.'

Clark discussed his qualms. 'Rhett was *too* popular. Miss Mitchell had etched him into the minds of millions, each of whom knew exactly how Rhett would look and act. It would be impossible to satisy them all, or even a majority. I knew that. So when Dave Selznick offered me the part, I told him with some pleasure that I was sewed up by my MGM contract. And added that I didn't want the part for money, marbles, or chalk. He said that he'd try to make a deal with the studio.

And since my contract states that I have no choice in roles, I said nothing. I could see myself being sold down the river.'

Throughout the entire project and for years afterward, Clark kept the feeling of being 'sold down the river'. Even the hundred-thousand-dollar bonus MGM gave him didn't change his attitude.

When the news was finally released in August, 1938, that Clark was officially set to play Rhett, the public went wild. Corney Jackson remembered: 'Clark's publicity was simply fantastic. The studio was giving him the "A" treatment, of course, but he made a lot on his own by just *being* Clark Gable. Everywhere he and Carole went, they were mobbed. They almost stole the show from Norma Shearer at the world premiere of *Marie Antoinette*.'

Clark and Carole became the leading subjects in all the fan magazines. *Photoplay* magazine created a sensation with an article stating, 'To the ouside world Clark Gable and Carole Lombard might as well be married. So might Bob Taylor and Barbara Stanwyck. Or George Raft and a minor actress, Charlie Chaplin and Paulette Goddard. Unwed couples, they might be termed.'

Now, in 1975, with divorce, illegitimate children, lesbianism, homosexuality, and other intimate details of stars' private lives accepted as casually as weather reports, it's hard to realize that an article in 1938 about a few couples living together could create such a stir. This piece also mentioned Constance Bennett and Gilbert Roland. A blatant but understandable omission was Marion Davies and William Randolph Hearst.

The article was tame, really, never specifically stating the couples lived together. But newspapers of the day picked up on it, and suddenly the nation's moralists were incensed. *Photoplay* reporters and editors were instantly barred from the major studios, even though the magazine ran a public apology in the next month's issue. But the damage had been done, and the Will Hays office brought pressure to bear on studio heads to 'get those bums married'. With the exception of George Raft and Virginia Pine, all the couples eventually complied.

The situation forced Louis B. Mayer to take action regarding Gable. Mayer, who had a habit of controlling people's lives through money he lent or advanced them, was hoisted by his own petard. For years the mogul had been sympathetic to Ria Gable's desire not to divorce Clark. Mayer had even encouraged Ria, via her attorney, a close Mayer friend, to make things as financially difficult as possible for Gable. This kept the actor in line. He couldn't afford a suspension, with its loss of salary. But now Mayer realized that Lombard was no passing fancy, and he wanted Clark to divorce Ria and marry Carole as quickly as possible. But Ria was holding out for 'at least three hundred thousand dollars' as a settlement.

Gable was still fuming that he'd been 'sold' for *Gone With the Wind*. Mayer now offered Clark a new contract, which upped his salary from $5,000 to $7,500 a week. In addition, Mayer offered Clark an advance which would enable him to pay off Ria.

Meanwhile, Selznick still had the Gargantuan task of coping with Gable and all the incredible problems inherent in making *Gone With the Wind*. The producer took a great deal of interest in the development of the character of Rhett, and he was still searching for a woman to play Scarlett. Tallulah Bankhead, Miriam Hopkins, Paulette Goddard, Jean Arthur, Loretta Young, Lana Turner, and a dozen others were tested.

Selznick wanted Lionel Barrymore for the part of Dr Meade, but the role was eventually given to Harry Davenport. Judy Garland was considered for Careen, but that role went to Ann Rutherford. Olivia de Havilland and Leslie Howard were cast as Melanie and Ashley. The producer was also trying to line up the best crew possible. MGM promised him Hal Rosson as cameraman, and any of their other people.

The film was originally budgeted at $2,250,000 but Selznick was confident he could bring the cost down to two million.

Gable was a problem from the start. He was wary of having to perform with an accent. Metro finally informed Selznick that Gable refused 'under any circumstances to have any kind of Southern accent'.

As a symbol of peace and love, and a subtle hint to Gable that he should make an effort to get along with Selznick, Carole sent Clark a string of stuffed white doves on the first day's shooting. She also sent him a single red rose, which Clark kept in a bud vase on his dressing table, along with his favorite photograph of 'Ma'. From that day on, every day that Clark worked on the MGM lot, he received a single red rose from Carole.

Filming on *Gone With the Wind* began on December 10,

1938. Scarlett still hadn't been cast. The burning of Atlanta was the first sequence shot, on the back lot of Selznick studios in Culver City. They were the old Pathé Studios, at which both Gable and Lombard had worked early in their careers.

Troubles plagued production from the beginning. Most stemmed from the attempt to condense the long novel (1,037 pages) into slightly less than four hours of film. The script, although credited solely to Pulitzer Prize-winner Sidney Howard, was molded by many, including Ben Hecht, F. Scott Fitzgerald, a half dozen others, and, of course, Selznick himself. Rewriting continued right up to the last day of shooting.

Selznick finally hired a relatively unknown British actress, Vivien Leigh, to portray Scarlett O'Hara. Her screen tests had been superb. Vivien and director Cukor adored each other. Gable was displeased with both Cukor and Leigh.

There has been much discussion concerning Gable's being responsible for Cukor being replaced. This has been exaggerated. Throughout the project, Selznick and Cukor 'hadn't seen eye to eye'. Selznick had considered other directors as early as September, 1938: Victor Fleming, Frank Capra, and Jack Conway. Selznick later said, 'I felt that while Cukor was simply unbeatable in directing intimate scenes of the Scarlett O'Hara story, he lacked the big feel, the scope, the breadth of the production.'

The industry gossip was that MGM had pressured Selznick to remove Cukor because the director did not film quickly enough to stay on schedule. Metro and Gable also felt that Cukor, 'a woman's director', was highlighting Scarlett and Melanie and not Rhett. Cukor later remarked, 'It is nonsense to say that I was giving too much attention to Vivien and Olivia. It is the text that dictates where the emphasis should go, and the director does not do it. Clark Gable did not have a great deal of confidence in himself as an actor, although he was a great screen personality; maybe he thought that I did not understand that. My own theory after all these years is that for David Selznick *Gone With the Wind* was the supreme effort of his career; he was enormously nervous about the whole thing ... it was a great trial, but also his undoing, and he did things he had never done before. For the first time he wanted to come down on the set and watch me direct something that we had worked out together. It was very nerve-wracking.'

Selznick decided to replace Cukor. The new directors considered, all under contract to Metro, were Jack Conway, King Vidor, Robert Z. Leonard, and Victor Fleming. The producer showed the list to Gable, and Clark chose Fleming. The day after Cukor left, Gable's buddy Vic left *The Wizard of Oz* (completed by Mervyn LeRoy) to take over direction of *Gone With the Wind*. There was a two-week hiatus while the script was revised. Then Fleming announced, 'I'm going to make this a melodrama.'

Though Gable was happy with the new director, Leigh and de Havilland felt betrayed. Both actresses continued secretly to consult Cukor, without Fleming's or Selznick's knowledge.

Neither Fleming nor Gable got along with Vivien Leigh. Even Selznick later admitted, '. . . during the hundred twenty-two days she was on the set she groused plenty: before a scene she would be muttering deprecations under her breath and making small moans. According to Vivien, the situation was stupid, the dialogue was silly, nobody could possibly believe the whole scene. And then, at a word from Victor Fleming, who was not merely a very fine director but a man who had the ability to conceal the iron hand in the velvet glove, she would walk into the scene and do such a magnificent job that everybody on the set would be cheering'.

The ordeal was taking its toll on the director and on Gable. One day, when they were filming a climactic scene involving Rhett and Scarlett, Vivien cried, 'I can't do it. I simply can't do this scene. This woman is a terrible bitch.'

'While we're at it,' interjected a distressed Gable somberly, 'I might as well tell you, Vic. I can't do that "don't give a damn" scene tomorrow.'

This was too much. Fleming roared, 'Miss Leigh, you can insert this script up your royal British ass.' He stormed off the set and wouldn't return. Three days later Selznick, along with Gable and Leigh, went to Fleming's Malibu home and induced him to resume working.

Gable hated Leigh's temperament, but, unsure of himself for the first time in years, he too was temperamental. 'I can't do it,' he raged to Olivia de Havilland about the key scene, involving his crying over the death of his daughter, Bonnie. 'I won't do it! I'm going to quit acting and go off to my tractor in Encino. I'll quit pictures. Starting with this one.'

Clark was annoyed over many things, not the least of which was his wardrobe. Few of his fans knew it, but Gable was always very careful about supervising his clothes in all his films. Gable had had the same tailor for years – a man named Schmidt. For some unknown reason, when Clark moved over to Selznick–International for *GWTW* he was told he could have any tailor *but* Schmidt. This reinforced Gable's 'what the hell' attitude concerning the picture. When Selznick learned of this stupid error, it was immediately rectified, but Clark wasn't easily mollified.

Except for Miss Leigh, Gable liked the other cast members. One of his favorites was the youngster Cammie King, who played his child, Bonnie. Even Carole went out to watch the day Cammie filmed the scene in which she is thrown from her horse.

But most days the mood remained tense. The cast and crew worked hard and often to relieve the tension. They sometimes played gags on each other. Clark was the target of one the day they filmed the scene in which Rhett carries Scarlett up the long, winding staircase. Vivien Leigh, in on the joke, managed to convince Gable that she had done something wrong which required the scene to be re-shot, and so they did it twelve times. Clark was exhausted but didn't utter a word of complaint. Finally Fleming said, 'The first take was perfect, Clark. The others were just for laughs.' Clark wasn't amused.

There was little time for humor now. Right in the midst of his most traumatic acting chore, Clark had to resolve a pressing personal problem. The *Photoplay* story necessitated a speedup of his divorce. For years financial negotiations with Ria had dragged on. Clark hadn't cared. 'Let her ask for the moon' was his attitude, since he had no intention of marrying again. But now things had to be settled so he could marry Carole.

Russell Birdwell suggested to Gable and Lombard that they retain the famous lawyer W. I. Gilbert, Sr. Gilbert took the case, and a divorce settlement was finally reached. Ria would get approximately $286,000 after taxes. She went off to Reno to get the divorce, which was granted on March 6, 1939.

Ria stated, 'Clark knew he could have a divorce any time, since we ironed out our little differences some time ago. But he never seemed to want one.' Ria couldn't help but add, 'I think a marriage between a cinema star and a society woman has a better chance of succeeding than one between two stars.'

But the two stars were determined to make a go of it.

Clark was finally free. He turned to Otto Winkler to handle

arrangements for the wedding. 'Get it all set up,' he told Winkler, 'so we can do it the minute I get some free time.' Both Gable and Lombard wanted a quiet, simple wedding, with no fanfare. Louella Parsons had suspected as much, and confided to Fieldsie, 'They won't tell me when they marry. I know it.' She was right.

Two incidents made it possible for the lovers to elope. One was that Clark had two days off from shooting: March 29 and 30. The other was that Twentieth Century–Fox was sponsoring a glittering premiere for *The Story of Alexander Graham Bell* up in San Franciso on the evening of the 28th. Important members of Hollywood's press corps would be at the premiere, and the coast would be clear.

Plans proceeded secretly and according to schedule. At four in the morning Clark drove to pick up Carole. They gathered Otto, and the trio drove to Kingman, Arizona, in Otto's unpretentious car. Kingman, around four hundred miles from Los Angeles, was the inconspicuous town Winkler had chosen for the momentous event. They went to the courthouse for the license. Viola Olsen, the clerk at the marriage bureau, almost collapsed when she recognized Gable and Lombard. She could scarcely fill out the forms.

'Take it easy, honey,' Gable smiled, and she fumbled even more. Winkler then whisked the couple to the house of the Reverend and Mrs Kenneth Engel, of the First Methodist Episcopal Church. Clark and Carole changed clothes and then exchanged vows in a quiet and dignified ceremony, with Mrs Engel and a dumbstruck neighbor as witnesses.

Back in Carole's home on St Cloud Road (which reporters were watching, lest the couple try eloping), Jean Garceau was spending the day with Carole's mother and brother Stuart. They knew when the phone rang that it was the newlyweds. Clark told Bessie, 'You've got a son-in-law, Mom.'

While Clark and Carole were relaying the good news to Bessie, Winkler was on the telephone calling the wire services and leading columnists. It was a tricky public-relations task, because Winkler was dealing with one of the biggest Hollywood news stories of the decade. It was of utmost importance to Gable and Lombard that no influential columnist feel snubbed at having missed an exclusive on the hottest item since the ex-king of England had married Wallis Warfield Simpson, three years previously.

130

When Louella Parsons, Willian Randolph Hearst, and Marion Davies received telegrams – MARRIED THIS AFTERNOON. CAROLE AND CLARK – Louella's first reaction was 'That's impossible. They wouldn't dare.'

They had dared, but to be sure that Louella wouldn't hold a grudge, they later gave *her* a wedding surprise, and had one of her bathrooms completely redone in mirrors, onyx, and fourteen-carat-gold fixtures.

There was no honeymoon for the Gables. The couple had to rush back from Kingman. The only stop, at a Harvey House for their wedding-night supper, created pandemonium.

By the time Clark and Carole arrived home, it was three A.M. and, exhausted, they fell asleep immediately. They had to be up in a couple of hours for a press conference. Strickling had convinced them, 'You can't offend the press. This is too big a story.' He had sympathized with their desire to have a private wedding that wouldn't turn into 'a fucking circus'. But now the Gables had to pay their dues.

The MGM police stood guard outside Carole's house so that only reporters would gain entrance. The press descended early. A buffet was set up in the living room, and Clark and Carole, dressed as they had been at the wedding ceremony at Kingham – she in a gray flannel suit with a gray-and-white polka-dot vest, he in a dark navy-blue suit and dark tie – posed for pictures and were cordial to everyone. They both looked radiant, and easily fielded all the predictable questions.

The next day Clark returned to filming *Gone With the Wind*.

Carole was instrumental in helping him through this difficult period. *GWTW* was running over budget, and everyone was under a great deal of pressure. While Lombard was trying to comfort Gable, he in turn was trying to comfort Fleming. The director finally cracked, and suffered a nervous collapse. For two weeks Sam Wood took over the direction. Then Fleming, at Gable's request, returned to direct the remaining scenes that involved Gable.

Gable's troubles with Leigh continued even after shooting was over. The two stars had been sent notes by Larry Barbier instructing them to report, in full dress and make-up, at eleven in the morning to shoot stills for advertising and publicity. At eleven Gable was there, but not Leigh. After a while, Gable asked Barbier, 'Where's the star?'

Barbier found that Leigh had not even arrived at the studio.

131

'I didn't know what to do. Clark was a man who could overlook almost anything but having you lie to him. But I knew that if I told him the truth he wouldn't wait. So I took a chance. I didn't want to lose him as long as I had him there.'

Hoping that Leigh would arrive any moment, Barbier told Gable, 'She's being made up right now.'

Barbier was in trouble. As he tells it, Gable 'was pretty patient. He waited for another half-hour, then came storming out of his dressing room. "What the hell is this?" he demanded. "You told me she was in make-up. If she was, she would be here by now, wouldn't she?" '

Barbier was forced to agree, and then told Clark that he had lied and explained why.

'Did you put the call through for her yesterday?'

'Yes,' said Barbier.

'In writing?' asked Clark.

'Yes.'

'Time and Gable wait for no actress,' Clark stated as he angrily departed, a few minutes after noon.

Leigh arrived at one. She was furious to learn that Clark hadn't waited.

At the rescheduled photo session, several days later, Clark and Vivien appeared amicable. Clark's only concern was that Barbier wasn't in hot water. He asked Larry, 'What happened the other day didn't get you in any trouble, did it?'

'No,' answered Barbier.

'Okay,' said Clark. 'I just didn't want you holding the bag.'

According to Barbier, 'That was the sort of guy Gable was ... he wouldn't stand your lying to him. But in this case he understood my position, that I'd had little choice. He was always like that, always for the little guy.'

Gable was finished with *Gone With the Wind* the last week of June, 1939. But the problems Selznick and his staff had with him during filming were almost minor compared with the lack of cooperation they'd receive from Gable concerning the picture's promotion and distribution.

CHAPTER NINETEEN

While Clark was in the throes of finishing *Gone With the Wind* Carole had returned to work. She had been 'plenty pissed' at Myron Selznick when he didn't get her the role of Scarlett, and to appease her the agent negotiated a spectacular two-year four-picture deal with RKO at $150,000 per film plus a percentage of the profits.

Her first movie for RKO was *In Name Only*, with Cary Grant, and it was Lombard who personally campaigned for her friend Kay Francis to get the key role of Grant's bitchy, ruthless wife. Miss Francis's career was, to put it mildly, in the doldrums. *In Name Only* temporarily put her back in Hollywood's front ranks, and Lombard even insisted that Kay receive equal billing with her and Grant.

By July Carole had completed *In Name Only* and Gable was through with *Gone With the Wind*, and the newlyweds were ready to move into the new ranch.

A great deal of work had been done on the property. In addition to the fifty thousand Carole had paid Walsh, she had invested thousands more in improvements: irrigation lines, power lines, cesspools, fences, pruning costs. The bids were astronomical, and finally Clark, always frugal, said, 'The hell with it. At least let's leave the trees the way they are.'

They did.

To give the house a New England effect, Carole had the building painted white with dark green shutters. She supervised the interior decoration herself, haunting antiques shops for 'just the right piece'. Her primary aim was to make the place 'a man's home'.

When the work was completed she told Clark, 'Well, old king, you've finally got a castle.'

He was justifiably proud of his 'old lady'.

Clark enjoyed puttering around the ranch. He personally planted many trees, and delighted in buying and using a spray machine for the trees. With the help of Al Menasco, he even built and painted a fence, under his father's supervision.

Carole's and Clark's home was worthy of *House Beautiful*. Clark loved it. Taking guests on what he called the 'fifty-cent tour', he'd say, 'Ma sure knows her stuff', to which Carole would laughingly add, 'Watch him or he'll collect the fifty cents.'

Visitors seeing the living room for the first time loved it immediately. Even men remarked, 'This is a real *home*.' The large room was airy yet warm and cozy, with white and yellow the predominant colors. The paneled woodwork was white, as well as the brick and paneled fireplace. Carpeting, made to order, was canary yellow. Also yellow were two large sofas. Red and green were chosen as accents. Two red wingback chairs and two large green club chairs, one of them Clark's favorite, flanked the sofas. The red and green hues were picked up in the English print drapes on the windows. The star attraction in the room was a Colonial-design staircase which led to the second floor.

The room which received the most 'oohs' and 'ahs' was the dining room, which Carole had designed as a typical Early American tavern. The dominant piece in the room was a long tavern-type table, a reproduction which had been in Clark's home before he married Carole. She wasn't happy with the antiquing job which had been done on it, so she sent it out to be refinished; it was put outdoors to become weathered. The story goes that every so often either Clark or Carole would say, 'Let's go visit our table!' Once there, they would do everything possible to hasten the aging process, including pouring water on the table, stubbing their cigarettes out on it, and even beating it with a heavy chain. Finally it was ready to their satisfaction, and, once polished, 'was a joy to behold'.

The dining room was finished in natural pine. The ceiling had grayish-white beams, and the fireplace was brick. The open bar counter had a game table near it. Captain's chairs were around the dining table. Braided red and beige rugs brightened the room, and the walls were covered with prints of horses and outdoor scenes. And, once again, Carole had added just the right touches to give an air of elegance to the otherwise rustic atmosphere. Behind the bar counter was a gleaming collection of antique and modern glassware, and off to one side of the fireplace was an antique set of pink Staffordshire.

The most popular room on the tour was Clark's gun room, of which he was justifiably proud. It was a real man's room. A huge gun cabinet covered one entire wall. In it Clark kept his prized firearm collection, most of the guns cased in beautiful hand-tooled leather. Old English prints on the walls and deep sofas and lounge chairs gave the necessary comfort to the room.

Gable and Lombard each had a master-bedroom suite. In Clark's bedroom the outdoor colors of brown and green and their various shades and tints predominated. The brown appeared in the antiqued woodwork and an old pine desk which had been given to Gable by nemesis David Selznick when *Gone With the Wind* was completed. The room also contained a brown tufted leather bed, bookcases, and a dictionary stand. Books were everywhere. Clark was always trying to improve his mind, saying, 'I'm just a guy trying to learn.'

Off to one side of the room there was a large green couch. The chintz curtains were green, too. Clark's bathroom, with its collection of antique bottles, was done in beige marble. He had a huge mirrored dressing room large enough to hold his vast wardrobe.

As Clark's room was masculine, so Carole's was the ultimate in femininity. Almost everything was white: the ankle-deep rug, the goatskin throw rugs, the organdy tester and flounce on the four-poster bed, the sofa and chairs, the chintz and organdy curtains. The mahogany in the bedside tables was matched by the mahogany of the bed. Her bathroom was a shimmering vision of mirrors, white rug, white marble tub and lavatory, and silver and crystal fixtures.

The Encino ranch was the setting for Clark's and Carole's happiest moments. An average day would often end with Gable reading mystery novels in bed, soft music playing in the background. Clark was enjoying the rarest of experiences, especially for him: being in love. Carole was determined to keep it that way, despite the fact that their sex life was, for her at least, far from spectacularly fulfilling.

There are dozens of tales about Gable often being impotent, especially with women who expected him to be a great lover. Carole once confided to an intimate group of girlfriends that Gable had reached the point in their marriage at which he sometimes required 'additional stimulation' to perform adequately. A high-class lady of the evening clued Lombard in on the following: 'Gargle with some mint. That will work him up.' Carole tried it one night when she discovered that Gable had fallen asleep before she got into the bedroom. When he felt the sting of mint, he leaped out of bed, and almost broke

135

his ankle. However, their sex life was never the basis for their union. They were happy just being together.

The ranch became Clark's hobby, a way of channeling nervous energy in a positive manner. A small yellow tractor was the 'farm toy' he enjoyed most, even more than the road scraper he occasionally operated.

Carole was that *rara avis* who could excel both indoors and out. She owned a suitable, usable sports wardrobe. She didn't mind braiding her hair, pigtail-style, and roughing it with Clark on his beloved hunting-fishing-camping expeditions. Their vehicle on such jaunts was a custom-built Dodge station wagon complete with sleeping compartment.

Carole and Clark both became interested in horseback riding. Two of their best friends and frequent visitors to their home were 'Val' and 'Mrs Val'. They were old friends of Clark's who owned the Valdez Riding Stables in Coldwater Canyon. With the assistance of the Valdezes, who also took care of the Gables' horses, both Carole and Clark bought beautiful handmade saddles.

They each had favorite riding horses. Carole's was named Melody, Clark's Sonny. But Carole really didn't enjoy riding. She did it to please her husband. She liked to agree with him on everything. There was only one touchy subject in their marriage. The Gables tried to avoid arguments over Carole's brothers.

Lombard liked to tell her friends about her brothers' gag when she and Gable returned from their elopement. Fred and Stuart had hung a shotgun over the connubial bed.

Even after her marriage, Carole retained close ties with her brothers and mother. Bessie had been set up in nearby Brentwood. Clark liked Bessie, but had no use for 'those two hangers-on'. But the family was drawn close together late one evening in the fall of 1939. Clark anxiously phoned them: 'Ma is in Cedars of Lebanon. They say it's her appendix. I've got a room next door, and I'm staying right with her.'

There was no need to worry. Carole's appendectomy was routine, and she was soon her old self, clowning and playing practical jokes on the doctors and nurses. Visitors and flowers were everywhere; the doctor soon curtailed the number of well-wishers, and Carole had the flowers sent to the wards and the children's wing.

Clark, meanwhile, sleeping at the hospital every night, was

136

the target for the starstruck nurses, who tried every trick in the book, including overtime work, to get near him. Carole laughed and teased Clark quite a bit, but she noted to friends: 'He's so shy and uncomfortable with them!'

Her health in fine shape again, Lombard returned to work. The film was *Vigil in the Night*, in which *she* played a nurse.

At RKO, as at Paramount, Lombard was Queen of the lot. Whatever studio she worked at, she always had the best dressing room. The scene around her often resembled a three-ring circus: noise, people, activity, laughter, music blaring, phones ringing, general confusion. Carole liked to be surrounded by people. She still used her trusty motor scooter to travel from dressing room to set, and cheerily greeted everyone along the way.

Carole's contract, in addition to giving her an enormous salary, had clauses which gave her the right to select her own crew members. For her hairdresser, she had Loretta Francel, a free-lancer known as 'Bucket', who appeared on the set every morning at seven to give Carole her shampoo. Other regular favorites included Peggy Mercer, a manicurist, Betty, Carole's stand-in, and Irene, the famous dress designer, who created all of Lombard's professional and personal wardrobe after Carole left Paramount. Irene says, 'Whenever I'm asked to name the most exciting woman I've ever dressed, I say Carole. She was a real clothes horse. Everything looked good on that beautiful figure. She knew clothes, and she knew how to wear them.'

Carole always insisted that Pat Drew, an electrician who had lost a leg in a plane accident, be employed on her pictures. But she refused all publicity about such gestures, and once warned a gathering of reporters who wanted to write about her helping Drew, 'I'll break your heads if you use one word about this.'

When *Vigil in the Night* was finished, Carole, as was her custom, staged a party for cast and crew. First she showered them with gag gifts, like crutches and bedpans. The real gifts followed, and each person received an item indicating Carole's genuine thoughtfulness.

'Strike-the-set' or 'wrap' parties were a regular practice on the last day of shooting a film. At such parties, stars would give gifts to the director, crew members, and sometimes even to other people in the cast. Gable, however, eschewed this custom: 'A man does a day's work and gets paid for it. He shouldn't expect anything more. I never got anything I didn't work for.'

MGM re-teamed Clark with Joan Crawford for *Strange Cargo*. Her career at Metro was finally on the wane, but contractually Joan still received top billing. Meanwhile, elaborate preparations were being made for the Atlanta premiere of *Gone With the Wind*.

Clark wasn't interested in having anything more to do with the film. Lombard, along with Strickling and Mannix, talked to him. Clark finally agreed to go to the premiere, but only if Carole went too. MGM thought Carole might steal some of the limelight, and they were reluctant to agree. But then Gable learned Laurence Olivier was accompanying Vivien Leigh.

'They aren't even married!' he bellowed.

Lombard would accompany Clark to Atlanta, and Selznick was thrilled. But he cautioned his staff, 'Clark is a very nice fellow, but a very suspicious one, and very quickly and not infrequently gets the notion in his head that people are taking advantage of him. All we have to do is to have this happen through trying to get too much, and anything can happen, from not having him show up at all to having him very difficult when he does get there.'

Strickling assured Selznick that Clark would be in Atlanta and would attend the charity ball, even though, as Selznick put it, Gable was 'still squawking about the ball, claiming that going to the opening is bad enough, but that selling thousands of tickets because of a personal appearance by him at a ball is a little thick.'

Selznick was aware of the favor Clark was doing him and the picture by appearing in Atlanta. He said at the time, 'In Clark's case I feel that whatever he does for us is in the nature of a great favor, and that we should regard it as such. He doesn't need Atlanta and he doesn't need us and he doesn't need these idiotic festivities. He is the biggest star in the world, and any time he wants to show his face for three minutes, he can get a fortune for it.'

But as the plans for Gable in Atlanta became more and more demanding, in late November Strickling warned Selznick, 'Make one more request of Gable and he won't show at all.' Selznick and his staff proceeded cautiously.

Victor Fleming was furious with Selznick too, and now he refused to go to Atlanta. Drunk one night, Fleming told his

138

friend John Lee Mahin, 'You were right, he's a son of a bitch.' Fleming had been outraged when he'd found a press release stating 'There were three directors on *Gone With the Wind*, all supervised by David O. Selznick.'

Since Gable shared Fleming's dislike for David O., Clark used this incident as a basis for announcing that he wouldn't join the star contingent flying to Atlanta either. MGM brass went to work quickly. C. R. Smith, who was anxious to promote his fledgling American Airlines, offered the studio free use of a DC-3. 'You won't have to go with the others,' Mannix told Gable. 'You and Carole will have a plane all to yourselves.'

Gable agreed. While Selznick, Leigh, Olivier, and de Havilland flew on one plane, Gable and Lombard, along with Strickling and Otto Winkler, flew on another. Winkler was deathly afraid of flying. But he couldn't refuse.

Carole had a clever plan in mind to promote Clark. Before she left, she told Russell Birdwell: 'I'll make that fat-assed Dutchman the biggest man in America. I'm not going as a movie star but as Mrs Clark Gable. From the minute the plane lands, I'm going to cling to his arm and do nothing but gaze into his eyes. He'll end up being an absolute hero.'

And Carole stuck to her word, from the time their plane landed and throughout the entire three days of celebration.

Gable's arrival was planned meticulously. He was purposely late. All the others had been gathered for a huge parade. But the parade had been delayed while Gable's plane circled the field. Though he was tacitly cooperative, for the entire three days of festivities Clark and his party remained distant from the others.

Carole sat quietly in a box at the charity dress ball while Clark – along with Vivien Leigh and Olivia de Havilland – made grand entrances dressed in their costumes from the film. Carole tried to be as inconspicuous as possible, and Gable remained aloof. Margaret Mitchell also wanted little part of the hoopla and promotion going on throughout the city. But she did appear at the premiere, and she and her husband, John Marsh, sat with the Gables.

Carole befriended the frightened and rather awed Mrs Marsh. 'C'mon, honey,' she said to the famous author at the premiere, taking her by the hand after the film was over, 'I'll help you.' Lombard led her up to the stage to the wild cheers of the audience, and Margaret Mitchell told the crowd, 'Thank you – for me and my poor Scarlett.'

Gable and Lombard liked Mrs Marsh, and as a favor were guests at a luncheon she held at her club. The Gables were relieved, however, when the three days of continuous activities were over and they could return to Los Angeles.

The famous Clark Gable hotel room story originated with this trip to Atlanta but has been told about every hotel at which Gable ever registered.

A woman wanted the room Clark had just vacated.

'We haven't had time to change the sheets, madam.'

'No – no – don't change the sheets. I want it exactly as it is.'

Everyone wanted Clark Gable.

Selznick wanted to repeat the famous premiere in Hollywood, and once again the problems exploded. Clark refused to attend.

'I'll go with Lew,' Carole teased. She referred to Gable's stand-in, Lew Smith.

Clark finally relented. He'd go to the theater, but under no circumstances would he go to Selznick's party after the film. Gable felt Selznick and MGM were continuing to exploit him.

The second premiere was as gala as the Atlanta one had been. Jean Garceau and her husband, Russ, were very excited to be the Gables' guests at the event. Gable, Sr., and his wife were also present.

The crowds in front of the Carthay Circle Theatre were enormous. Giant klieg lights flashed through the dark sky. The fans went absolutely wild when the Gables arrived. Women swooned and fainted at the sight of Rhett Butler in person. Carole looked stunning in a gold lamé evening gown and cape designed by Irene. Cameramen mobbed the couple to get as many pictures as possible.

As soon as the film started, Clark, Carole, and Marion Davies escaped to the manager's office, where champagne was conveniently waiting.

Gable was adamant about *not* attending Selznick's bash at the Trocadero. Lombard pleaded, but this time in vain. They went home, and Selznick was hurt and offended by their absence.

In ensuing years the producer had only flattering comments to make about Gable, despite countless opportunities to do otherwise. In the final analysis, it had cost Selznick millions to use Gable in *Gone With the Wind*, but he never regretted it:

'It was worth every penny. I don't know of any actor who could have played Rhett Butler as well as he did. Clark made you believe whatever he was playing. He had that God-given thing: a theatrical personality, the ability to communicate with the audience, something all the training in the world cannot give you. Without this quality, there is no such thing as a star. It is not just being photogenic. It is an indefinable thing,' Selznick boasted, 'which I like to think I can spot immediately in a person.'

Of Gable's performance as Rhett, Selznick glowed:

'Rhett will probably remain among the most memorable roles Clark's ever created on the screen. It was a difficult and frightening role for him to tackle only because of the unprecedented public interest in the character.'

Even at the height of their unhappy association, Selznick had thought that once Gable saw the film he would forget any differences they'd had during production. The producer felt he'd gone out of his way to satisfy Gable but the actor had been very ungrateful. (As things turned out, they would never work together again.)

Meanwhile, Selznick and Carole Lombard had one picture to go on their two-picture deal. Myron Selznick had arranged a meeting for them to discuss a possible comedy script. David contacted Carole and let her off the hook. He wrote her a letter in which he stated, 'I shall always look back on our past associations as among the most pleasant of my career. Certainly I have always held you up as the shining example of what a joy it can be to work with a star when that star appreciates a producer's problems and cooperates in their solution. But I must face the fact that you are married to Clark, and that Clark obviously feels quite differently about me.'

It was obvious that Gable hated Selznick's guts. They had even had a fist fight at a Hollywood garden party. If Carole made another film for Selznick, it would put her under a terrible strain. Lombard and Selznick had made a top-drawer professional team. Their two films together had both been hits, and if she wanted to hold him to the contract, she could.

'The decision is entirely yours,' Selznick wrote her. 'You would suffer much more from the repercussions in your personal life than would I; and I can stand it if you can.'

Carole saw the wisdom of Selznick's thinking. By mutual consent, their contract was canceled.

141

CHAPTER TWENTY

If a marriage is to be successful, mates – even celebrated ones – must be willing to make certain concessions along the way. In the case of Gable and Lombard, it was she who compromised. Her liberal attitudes concerning her husband's extracurricular sex life made her a woman decades ahead of her time. Lombard knew it would be foolish to expect Gable to be physically faithful; this was impossible. She accepted this, and settled for emotional fidelity.

Now that the *Gone With the Wind* ordeal was over, Clark could relax, and they could concentrate on having a family. Carole wanted a child. They already had everything else.

Fate had other plans.

Meanwhile, their seemingly charmed lives glided along.

Christmas at the Gables' in 1939 was a happy one. At a small dinner party, which included Carole's mother and brothers and Clark's father, stepmother, and Aunt Pinkie, Clark surprised Carole with a ruby heart, lots of feminine wearing apparel, and her favorite perfume: Chanel No. 5. Carole gave him monogrammed pyjamas, with a matching robe, of heavy off-white silk from Hong Kong, which had been designed by Bob Von Cliff of Bullock's Wilshire. Clark liked them so much that he had them copied each year after that.

Lombard, the inveterate gift giver, never stopped at one gift. She did all her own gift wrapping and was extremely organized. Each gift was marked and checked against her list, and arrangements were made for its delivery. She was noted for her beautiful papers, ribbons, professional wrapping jobs. And Carole was thoughtful.

Al Menasco once complained to her that he couldn't get any shopping done in New York. The stores were always closed when he had free time, and there were a couple of items he would have loved to buy.

'What sort of things, Al?' she asked.

A small tool kit, for one, very compact and made to fit into an automobile glove compartment. And a set of road maps that compressed into a tiny box.

'In what store did you see those things?' she wondered.

'Some store with a funny name,' he answered.

'On Fifty-seventh Street?'

'That's it.'

'Hammacher Schlemmer?'

'That's the one!'

To Al's astonishment, months later the two items were surprise gifts from Carole. Obviously she had purchased them after their talk and waited for an appropriate occasion to surprise him.

Carole was generous to a fault. Her largesse extended so far as to bestow an expensive fur coat on her secretary. This trait of generosity rubbed off, somewhat, on Clark. The previous year, in addition to a gag gift – a huge plaster statue of himself – he had given Carole a yellow Cadillac convertible. The Caddy was one of her prize possessions.

While Carole was content with one car, Clark had to have many. He had a fascination for automobiles, and often could be found in the garage tinkering with them. At various times he owned Fords, Chryslers and Lincolns, and later Jaguars and a Mercedes-Benz.

In addition to cars, Clark loved clothes. His fastidious dress habits had been with him since the early days when, although poor, he always managed to look perfectly groomed. Now he could afford anything, even English handmade shoes. His valet, Martin, kept the shoes and all of Clark's clothes, including blue jeans, in the magnificent condition Clark demanded. The only exception was in the area of hats. Gable had a penchant for favorite old ones, and never would allow them to be cleaned.

Carole always dressed to please Clark, wearing his favorite colors, the neutrals. Her wardrobe was filled with white, gray, beige, and black outfits, all of which she knew how to wear to advantage, adding exactly the right accessory.

She, too, was mad about hats, sometimes buying as many as a dozen at a time. 'I'll probably never wear them. I just want to take them home to make Pa laugh.'

Carole loved scrapbooks and pictures. She had a small Brownie camera, and adored snapping away to mark the Gables' activities together. She kept her own career scrapbook, and started one on Clark as well.

Thanks to Carole, it was a happy household: gag gifts, joking, laughing. Clark was the center of everything, just as Carole planned it. If Clark was depressed, she joked around until he came out of it. He adored her, and felt that Carole was the most wonderful, sexy woman in the world.

When Carole made up her mind that she wanted a baby, she discontinued horseback riding. She felt it might interfere in some way with her ability to conceive. But other activities continued. The Gables loved their Dodge station wagon. They still liked to get away from Hollywood by driving off on hunting and fishing trips, sometimes alone, other times with close friends who weren't in the movie industry. Carole liked roughing it, but in the Hollywood manner: She'd used one of her old mink coats to line her sleeping bag.

In the early winter of 1940 the Gables went off to Baja California on a duck-hunting expedition. It was Clark's thirty-ninth birthday, so Carole and the people at the Mexican lodge whipped up a handsome birthday cake for Gable. On the way home, Clark and Carole were driving on the muddy roads toward Ensenada when their car skidded and they got stuck in the mud.

Later they loved telling friends how they had to spend the night in the back of the Dodge bundled up in their sleeping bags and eating 'that rotten cake'. Years before Carole might have referred to it as 'that fucking cake'. But the 'profane angel', as she was dubbed by Mitchell Leisen ('because she looked like an angel and swore like a sailor – the only woman I ever knew who could tell a dirty story without losing her femininity'), had changed her ways.

Gable didn't like to hear Carole use dirty language. After their marriage he very calmly told her: 'I'm the man of this household, and if there's going to be any swearing done, I will do it.' Carole was stunned but impressed. She seldom uttered four-letter words in front of 'Pa' after that.

Not everyone could comprehend Carole's infatuation with Clark. Mitchell Leisen said he could never understand why Carole was so devoted to Gable, and was amused when she used to insist on leaving promptly at six each day 'to get home to her man'.

Meantime, the Baja trip had created headaches and head-lines: GABLE AND LOMBARD MISSING IN MEXICO! The stars hadn't checked in with MGM, and the studio was frantic. It was Otto Winkler who had blundered by releasing the story

144

that the Gables were missing. At great expense, the Mexican government sent out cars, planes, and searching parties, only to discover that the Gables were safe and sound. The Mexican government was irate. Mayer fired Winkler, but Gable intervened, and he was rehired.

Carole and Clark celebrated their first wedding anniversary ('They said it wouldn't last!') on March 29, 1940, by going to the races at Santa Anita. Placing only two-dollar bets, Clark finished the day thirty-six dollars ahead, and Carole was out ten. Clark kidded, 'I try to pick 'em by studying the racing sheet. Ma bets on a horse if she likes the color of the jockey's silks.'

All bets had been on Clark's winning the Oscar for his portrayal of Rhett Butler. Ironically, he was the only principal in the film who did not win the famed statuette.

At the Academy Award ceremonies that year, at the Coconut Grove of the Ambassador Hotel, Bob Hope quipped, 'What a wonderful thing – this benefit for David Selznick.'

Gone With the Wind won eight Oscars, and the Thalberg Award for Selznick.

On the way to the party afterward, Selznick was silent. Then he yelled at Russell Birdwell, 'I don't know why we didn't get the "Best Actor" award for Gable. Somewhere you failed.'

Birwell was stunned. He didn't go to work for days. Finally Selznick telephoned him and apologized.

Gable hadn't won the Oscar because his own studio really had, in this instance, sold him down the river. MGM knew *Gone With the Wind* needed no box-office push, but another of their films, *Goodbye Mr Chips*, did. So they swung all their votes to Robert Donat.

But Gable was unfazed. He revealed later that he had given the Oscar he had won for *It Happened One Night* to Filedsie's son. 'It meant little to me,' said Gable, 'and the boy seemed to want it.'

In 1940 the world had more to concern itself with than Oscars. Europe was at war, and it was certain that eventually the U.S. would be involved. But Hollywood was an insulated town. Clark and Carole returned to work. He filmed *Boom Town*, co-starring Spencer Tracy, Claudette Colbert, and the alluring new sex symbol, Hedy Lamarr. According to accounts by observers on the scene, Miss Lamarr and Gable '*almost* made it' together. Hedy was very available, but things 'just didn't work out'. People were always 'bursting into the dressing room', and the necessary privacy eluded them.

At home Clark and Carole attempted seriously to make the farm self-sustaining. Gable joined the Citrus Association, under whose program workers were sent in to pick the fruit, after which it was graded and marketed. The Gables eagerly awaited the check from the Association for the first season's yield, which had been very large. Finally the check came. It was for six dollars and twenty-eight cents. The fruit had been graded 'culls', more commonly known as rejects.

Clark, very disappointed, was determined to make a go of it. He saw to it that more care and attention were given to the citrus trees. He carefully regulated the irrigation system, and did much of the work personally.

An infestation of red spiders ruined most of the second season's yield, and the third season's crop was destroyed by an unexpected freeze. Clark was forced to admit that the citrus growing wasn't going to be a commercially profitable venture, and so he dropped it.

Next Clark tried to make a go of the ranch with chickens. 'We'll sell the eggs, and the chickens will pay for themselves,' he said.

The Howard Stricklings, who had a very successful chicken business, gave Gable and Lombard invaluable aid in setting up the operation, and Carole even designed an egg carton which had a picture of an egg and a chicken wearing a tiny crown. Naturally, they were called 'The King's Eggs'.

But, for some unknown reason, the hens didn't produce the expected output. Everything was tried, including changes in feed and lighting, but to no avail. The few eggs produced were bought by the Gables themselves, the farm help, and close friends. Finally, when Clark's secretary–business manager pointed out that the eggs were in reality costing them nearly a dollar each, the venture was abandoned.

Clark's next project was raising beef cattle, which did prove successful – until the time came to butcher them. Fred, the ranch hand assigned the task, finally confessed to Clark, 'I just can't kill them.' So Clark had to call in a professional butcher to do the job. Finally the time came when they all sat down to eat their first home-grown beef. No one could touch it. Carole summed up the feelings of all who had grown so attached to the animals: 'I can't help it. I keep thinking about those big sad eyes!'

The rest of the meat was sent to the Children's Hospital – another project abandoned.

The only undertaking at the ranch that did prove successful was the raising of two dairy cows. Clark had a milk room with the latest and best equipment, and for some time they enjoyed a plentiful supply of milk, buttermilk, butter, and cream.

On the ranch Clark took great pride in the Gable doves. He loved hearing them coo in the mornings and evenings. And, of course, they had great sentimental value: The original doves had been the famous present from Carole. When the Gables had moved to Encino, the doves had been installed in a special pen, where they continually multiplied.

White doves – and orange blossoms, too – were the order of the day for William Powell in 1940. He'd recovered from his dread disease and found new happiness.

By the end of May, 1939, he had been well enough to socialize at his usual pace. In August he had gone before the cameras again, filming *Another Thin Man*.

The change in his outlook which had begun with Harlow's death and continued through his illness became more pronounced. 'I've come to one conclusion about this town,' he observed. 'A lot of youngsters are needlessly sacrificed. When you read that a husky youngster like Don Ameche has to take a rest cure because of overwork, and you know of other cases not so widely publicized, you sort of make up your mind that the effort is hardly worth the risk. Jean Harlow died only because she had worked herself to a point of nervous exhaustion. You see, we get caught up in the swing of doing things, and we don't know where to call a halt. It's not the money involved that makes you keep going – after all, you can ride in only one car, eat only one meal at a time, live in only one house at a time.'

Powell had bought a modest new home in the city, abandoning the sprawling mansions he had lived in previously. He had no desire to acquire a ranch or a large piece of property, as was the custom of so many stars. He said, 'It's amazing to learn, on a visit to Myrna Loy's ranch, that limes can be picked from trees as well as lifted from a sack. I can see how Myrna can be happy on her ranch, how Clark Gable, Spencer Tracy, and Robert Taylor can get a kick out of farm life, but I'm just a city fellow, I'm afraid. I can find plenty of exercise in my pool and on my badminton court. Since I'm not cut out to retire to the soil, I've got to keep on working in pictures. But I'm not shedding any tears because of it.'

On January 5, 1940, Powell, forty-seven, surprised all of Hollywood when he married Diana Lewis, a twenty-one-year-old starlet. He had apparently known her only a short time. She said, 'I had been out with him several times. Then, one night in the upstairs room at Chasen's, someone was playing the piano. All old songs. I started to sing them. This sorta got Bill. He said, "I didn't think a young kid like you knew those oldies." '

Two days later they were wed.

The ceremony took place at a dude ranch in Warm Springs, Nevada, near Las Vegas. Justice of the Peace B. D. Hickman performed the single-ring ceremony. Diana wore a blue flowered-print dress with a matching turban. Powell was attired in a gray suit with a blue sweater. Carole Lombard's agent from Selznick office, Nat Wolff, and his wife, Edne Best, were among the witnesses.

Diana had begun her career in the chorus of a local show. Paramount had signed her shortly afterward. The Monday after her wedding to Powell, Diana had to return to the cameras to do *Forty Little Mothers,* in which she had the lead. But one of the conditions Powell insisted on was that Diana give up her career and devote herself to their marriage.

While Lombard hadn't given up her career for Gable, she couldn't have been a more devoted wife. When Clark was unhappy because Carole had to go on location and he was between pictures, she said, 'Come with me, Pa. It'll be like a vacation.'

She was going up to the Napa Valley to shoot scenes for *They Knew What They Wanted.* It was a difficult picture to make. Neither director Garson Kanin nor Lombard got along with Charles Laughton. Carole even had a clause in her contract that she wouldn't have to kiss Laughton on the lips. Carole reverted to some of her saltiest language in dealing with the Britisher.

Clark busied himself with hunting and fishing. During the year the Gables spent much time with their hunting friends, Harry and Nan Fleischmann. The Fleischmanns owned a duck club near Bakersfield, and they had built a cabin to be used jointly by the Gables and the Kenny Watterses of Santa Barbara. Carole described the comfortable decor: 'We furnished it in Early Sears Roebuck.'

One evening, as the three couples sat around the living room, Clark said to Fleischmann, 'Harry, why don't you give us a half acre of land here?'

Harry turned to his wife. 'Nan, I think maybe we should. How about it?'

'I'm not giving a half acre to anyone, especially Gable. Let him buy his own land.'

Carole, collapsing in laughter over Nan's reply, said to Clark, 'That'll teach you to open your big mouth.'

In addition to the Fleischmanns, the Menascos, and Walter and Fieldsie Lang, some of the close friends who shared time with Clark and Carole were Howard Strickling and his wife, Mr and Mrs Andy Devine, and Mr and Mrs Buster Collier.

Clark hated any type of entertaining which involved huge crowds and formal dress. His idea of a good time was a quiet evening at home, enjoying dinner and conversation with these few close friends.

If the Gables didn't entertain at home, Clark's idea of just as good a time was an evening visiting someone else's home. One night they were entertained by Fred and Lily MacMurray. Carole was decked out in a long white 'soufflé' evening gown. The expensive costume had, of course, been designed by Irene. Lombard was wearing it for the first time. While cavorting around the swimming pool, she fell in. She spent the rest of the evening in one of Fred MacMurray's dressing gowns.

The next day Carole told Irene what had happened. Irene recalls: 'Anyone else would have been disturbed over ruining the dress, but not Carole. She thought it was a big joke on herself. I told her to bring it in and let me look at it, but it was beyond repair. Carole laughed and ordered another.'

One subject Carole couldn't joke about, however, was her inability to get pregnant. She was determined to take a year off after her remaining commitment at RKO.

Clark was back at MGM filming *Comrade X*, with Hedy Lamarr. Once again gossip circulated, but if Clark and Hedy were 'making it', Carole didn't care. She knew he might bed down with the raven-haired beauty, but that was as far as it would go.

149

Lombard began *Mr and Mrs Smith*. It was a rather dull comedy, and today film buffs are surprised that it was directed by Alfred Hitchcock. The explanation is simple. For years Carole had been considered one of Hollywood's social leaders. Hitchcock was always impressed by such things, and when Lombard personally asked him to direct her, he could hardly refuse.

At the time Hitchcock had given an interview in which he said actors were 'merely cattle'. On the first day's shooting of *Mr and Mrs Smith*, the director discovered a small corral, complete with three calves, on the set. They were labeled: 'Carole Lombard', 'Robert Montgomery', 'Gene Raymond'.

Carole continued her antics. While she was making *Mr and Mrs Smith*, she persuaded Hitchcock to let her direct the small scene in which he, following his usual practice, appeared.

Hitchcock should have known better. Carole was in her element. She pretended to take everything seriously, criticized everything he did, and shot the scene many times before she finally said, 'Cut and print.' The newspapers got wind of the incident, as did the wire services. *Life* magazine used it for a pictorial story.

On the home front, the Gables appeared so happily married that others in their circle of friends sometimes asked for marital advice. Alfred Hitchcock's wife, Alma, approached Carole one evening at a dinner party. She explained that she and 'Hitch' were quarreling after twelve happy years. Carole, always a sympathetic listener, told Alma an outrageous story:

Before she married Clark, he had given her a good-luck charm, a shrunken head. Soon afterward Carole felt that the head was in some way responsible for the frequent quarrels she and Gable began to have. One night Carole and Clark went for a drive. As they drove up a winding mountain road, she said, 'Stop the car.'

Carole went to the roadside and tossed the head into the canyon. 'The goddamn head must have some curse on it,' she explained to the surprised Gable, 'that's why we're quarreling.'

'But,' Carole explained to Mrs Hitchcock, continuing her story, 'Clark was worried. He was afraid the police might find the head, with our fingerprints on it.' So they drove back to the canyon and, on their hands and knees with a flashlight, tried to retrieve the head. Police were astonished to find the two celebrated actors engaged in a deadly earnest search in the dark canyon. 'I explained what we were doing, and the cops offered to help. One of them found it.'

Carole concluded her tale by relating that she and Gable then decided to bury the head. 'We put a curse on your marriage by burying it in your yard,' she told Alma, straight-faced.

Carole and Clark were forever joking, delighting in putting people on. But they were not delighted by their increasing lack of privacy. Encino was far from Hollywood, but not far enough. Many fans tried to enter their property. Sightseeing buses regularly rolled up to the front door to let tourists gawk at their home.

Consequently, Clark had to install fences to keep intruders out. An electric gate was controlled from the main house. When fans (mostly women) managed to scale the split-rail fences, he had to resort to a chain-link fence. Gable even had roses planted along the fence, hoping that the thorns would make the fence more difficult to climb.

One day, Clark, obviously alarmed, tore into his secretary's office, shouting, 'There's a woman behind me!'

Jean Garceau flew out to waylay the intruder, a sloppy blonde, who promptly settled herself in one of the patio chairs, lit a cigarette, and said: 'I'm not leaving until I see Clark Gable.' Mrs Garceau phoned Howard Strickling, who arranged to have studio police sent out. The MGM policemen chased the interloper in and out of the trees before they caught her. Then she was persuaded to leave.

Clark deplored such invasions of his privacy. However, in public he was always delighted by his fans' attention, and happy to give them autographs.

In their desire for privacy, Clark and Carole thought it might be a good idea to buy a larger ranch, farther away from Hollywood and Los Angeles, where they wouldn't be so accessible. Al Menasco offered some advice: 'Why not look over some of the Arizona ranches, see how they operate? You might like that country.'

So the Gables and the Menascos took off for a weekend at the O-W Ranch, in the high Mogollon Mesa area of Arizona. It was an actual ranch, not a weekend tourist retreat. They pitched in to help with the ranch's regular activities. Al recalled:

'Clark and I helped with the haying, and I wish you could have seen the girls doing the washing. The only piece of modern equipment was a hand wringer, and Carole tangled with that. She got herself soaked as she wrung out the Levis. When the clothes were dry, Clark loaded them into a basket, placed it on his head, and carried it to the house.'

While going about the ranch, Carole was unlucky enough to step on a rattlesnake. She let out a horrified scream and jumped away not a second too soon.

'Clark and I began banging away at point-blank range,' remembered Al, 'but it took twenty-two shots to kill it. This was pretty bad shooting, and we both felt terrible. We were using Frontier forty-fives, and just the day before had demonstrated that we could hit anything in sight, deadeye. Clark had hit a rattler at fifty yards' range with just one shot.'

The rattlesnake incident didn't deter Carole from continuing to join Clark on these woodsy outings.

It had become a custom for the Gables to go on a hunting trip with friends each fall. In 1940 the party consisted of the Fleischmanns, the Buster Colliers, the Phil Bergs, and Eddie Mannix. Everyone came in cars, except the Bergs, who arrived in a small rented plane which Phil was testing before buying. Berg called it the *Puddle Jumper*.

When the hunting proved poor at La Grulla (the group's gun club), they decided to go to Laguna Hanson, a lake high in the mountains. Berg's plane was too small to carry everyone plus all the equipment. Carole wouldn't let Clark get in it anyway, because she had seen Phil narrowly miss some treetops on his arrival. Clark thought of his old friend Paul Mantz. 'Let's get Paul down here. He'll take us to the lake.'

Mantz arrived with his Sikorsky S-38 twin-engine amphibian, which they promptly dubbed *Nellie the Goon*. He flew the group to Laguna Hanson, where they commandeered an old hunting cabin and happily settled in. Mantz, who stayed with them, recalled:

'Clark and Carole were down-to-earth people. I was glad to be a part of their gang. They didn't act like movie stars. I loved being with them.'

On the last day of the expedition, Carole was horrified when she was surrounded by a horde of bees. According to Nan Fleischmann:

'Everyone stood around advising her to keep still, not to slap them and they'd go away. Poor Carole did her best, but she was wearing short hunting pants and socks, and one of

152

the yellowjackets zeroed in on her bare leg, and she got a bad sting.'

Leaving Laguna Hanson proved difficult. There wasn't much space for the amphibian plane to maneuver. Mantz described the scene at the lake:

· 'It was as smooth as a mirror, so I taxied in a circle in order to rough it up and create a few waves. We were carrying two cases of ammunition and a heavy battery, however, and when I'd reached the point of no return, I aborted the takeoff, and we had to start over again.

'This time we unloaded the ammunition and the battery, and Clark said, "I'll send a jeep back for them." I guess I'm ultra-conservative, but maybe that's why I'm still flying. We made it the second time.'

Mrs Fleischmann noted:

'It was very exciting, for *Nellie the Goon* just barely missed the treetops. Carole, who was never afraid of anything, turned pale and said to Clark, "Please, let's never travel in separate planes. Whenever I fly, I want you with me." '

The Gables had spent almost the entire year together. Each had had a marvelous effect on the other. Carole was more serious and found less of a need to garner attention by wacky stunts and 'colorful' language. Clark was loosening up, learning to enjoy life and spend money.

As Christmas of 1940 neared, Gable spent much time tinkering with his car. He seemed to find something different wrong with it each day. Carole, wise to his ways, told her secretary, 'My old man tickles me. He thinks he's fooling us, but what he's really doing is building up to a new car. The 1941 models are out, and he won't rest until he has one.'

She knew her man. Before the week was out, Clark told Carole that he thought it would be best to trade his car in for a new one. Carole just smiled and told him, 'That's a good idea.'

To an intimate she observed, 'You know, it's ingrained in Clark's nature – a sort of guilt about spending money, a fear that he's going to be without it. To justify buying the new car, he had to convince *himself* that he *needed* it.'

Christmas was a happy time, with the usual overabundance of gifts. But hovering over the joy of the season was an anguishing doubt in Carole's mind. Was it her fault they hadn't had children? The Gables decided on a trip east for medical advice. Did Lombard need medical help to conceive, or did the problem lie with Gable?

CHAPTER TWENTY-ONE

One of the most fascinating rumors about Clark Gable is that he was sterile. There is absolutely no proof that he was. But it is understandable that such stories evolved. Gable did, of course, have a son with his last wife, dispelling most of the nasty innuendoes. And Anita Loos unequivocally states that there is an illegitimate child, a daughter born to an actress with whom Gable was on location for a film in the thirties. Others, however, point to the fact that Gable slept with literally hundreds of secretaries, waitresses, chambermaids, starlets, and others throughout his life. And, except for the Norton paternity suit, which was sheer nonsense, there is no record of any woman's ever claiming Gable fathered her child. Nor were there any stories of abortions hushed up by MGM brass.

The Gable-sterility theory is given some validity by an incident which occurred early in Clark's adult life. In the 1920s, prior to his marriage to Josephine Dillon, while he was living in boardinghouses and doing bits in stock, Clark suffered a terrible accident.

A now famous character actor, who was then in the same play, describes the incident: 'I went into Clark's room to wake him. He was a tough character to rouse. Finally, he threw the covers off and sat on the edge of the Murphy bed. He always slept in the raw – who could afford pajamas in those days? He was still sitting on the edge of the bed, crouched down, his head in his hands, when I passed the room a few minutes later. "C'mon," I said.

'You know how those old beds were. The mattresses used to depress, and the bedsprings, which were paper thin, were visible. Clark jumped up and then let out a fierce howl. His balls had gotten caught in the springs.'

Doctors contend that any severe accident to the testicles can cut down a man's sperm production. It is reasonable to assume

154

that a man with a low sperm count would have difficulty producing a child, and that there would be periods when he would be sterile.

Though it was reported that Lombard had been pregnant but miscarried, Carole had made the rounds of Hollywood's leading doctors to check her ability to conceive. Now she decided to undergo rigid examinations by gynecologists at Baltimore's Johns Hopkins University. The hospital staff found nothing wrong with Carole. They did concede that minor corrective surgery could be performed, but insisted that Mrs Gable wait until it could be determined that the inability to conceive was hers. The doctors suggested that the problem might rest with Clark's and Carole's sexual relations.

Whether Gable's potency was tested on this trip to Johns Hopkins is undocumented. MGM's official statement was that the actor was there because he was suffering from the shoulder injury received four years before on the set of *San Francisco*. Naturally, the studio could under no circumstances reveal that the virility of the country's leading sex symbol was in question – not to mention the effect of such an announcement on Gable's own ego. Besides, such topics were hardly discussed in family newspapers in those days.

After the Johns Hopkins jaunt, Clark and Carole were so close to Washington that they decided to visit the capital. MGM representatives arranged for a grand tour of the city.

The Gables stayed at the Shoreham Hotel. Their host was Carter Barron, a Loew's-theaters division manager. Barron arranged sightseeing tours for the couple, and tried to keep publicity down to a minimum. But wherever Clark and Carole went, throngs of onlookers appeared.

What could be more spectacular to top off the trip than a visit to President and Mrs Roosevelt, who were both Gable–Lombard fans? The President had particularly admired Carole since her highly publicized income-tax story. And, of course, both Franklin and Eleanor were like other millions of Americans who had seen and loved Gable as Rhett Butler.

Not only were the Gables invited to the White House, they were given the privilege of being present at one of President Roosevelt's famous fireside-chat broadcasts. Clark and Carole couldn't help being impressed on meeting the Roosevelts, Sara Delano Roosevelt, the President's mother, and Cordell Hull, the Secretary of State.

155

Since Carole and Clark were both extremely patriotic, this memorable evening – and the half-hour they spent chatting with the First Family after the broadcast – would be a story to tell their grandchildren.

For the entire new year – 1941 – Carole Lombard became a 'rancher's wife'. She shopped, fussed with the house, entertained friends. She hoped that by leading a very easygoing life and withdrawing from the inevitable tensions of day-to-day moviemaking, the chances of her becoming pregnant would improve.

In terms of excitement, the thoroughly unglamorous off-screen existence led by Mr and Mrs Clark Gable during the year would have shocked the average fan-magazine reader.

Advised that exercise was good for a potential mama, Lombard resumed her interest in tennis, and often played with her friend, tennis champion Alice Marble.

Carole saw a great deal of her family. She and Fieldsie were close as ever, and the girls were thrilled that Bill Powell had regained his health and married Diana and was settled back into the Hollywood scene. Carole also indulged herself by playing elaborate gags and pranks. One of her classics was when she had a photo of Gable on a rocking horse blown up life-size and sent to him with some real horse manure to strew around the bottom.

Hollywood's most glittering couple apparently liked to think of themselves as farmers. Standing one evening on the porch, 'Pa' turned to 'Ma': 'Look at that beauty, look at those flowers and trees. They're all ours. What else could two people want? What else do we need?'

'Another load of manure for the alfalfa field,' replied Carole.

But life at the Gables' had its elegant side, too. Theirs was not an average Middle America type of existence. For all the homeyness, at dinner Carole would have only formal service, even when they dined alone. Fabulous Waterford crystal and Spode adorned the table, which was lit by costly antique kerosene lamps. The silverware was antique, too, including extremely valuable pistol-handled knives whose blades received a daily polishing and sharpening.

The food, however, could accurately be described as 'regular'. It was 'he-man' grub, featuring the edibles Clark loved best: meat, potatoes, baked beans, spare-ribs, corn bread, chicken, hamburgers (with onions), chocolate cake, homemade ice cream.

The Gables often delighted in what could be described as infantile behavior. They liked to team up and play practical jokes on people usually *not* their close friends. There are many stories about Clark and Carole staging mock arguments in front of visitors, then sitting down to dinner and casually throwing around vulgarities:

'Pass the fucking salt.'

'Where's the fucking potatoes?'

'Where's my fucking salad?'

Janet Gaynor, who did not consider herself a prude, was a guest at one of these dinners. She and her husband, MGM designer Adrian, later told Russell Birdwell, 'It was strange. So childish.'

Though Janet failed to appreciate Carole's sense of humor on this occasion, they were friends. Carole was instrumental in helping Miss Gaynor unload a novel to which she had bought the screen rights. The novel had been ballyhooed to Miss Gaynor as a 'can't miss' vehicle for her talents. But after the deal was signed, it became apparent that the book was in fact all wrong for Janet, and badly written.

'Don't worry about it,' Carole advised. 'I'll get you twice what you paid for it.' She proceeded to call several producers, casually dropping into the conversations the fact that 'Janet has bought the rights to a fabulous novel that's perfect for you. But don't try to get it for under forty thousand.'

Carole drummed up enough interest so that Miss Gaynor was able to sell the book and make a tidy profit.

Although she was taking a year off from work, Lombard wasn't losing sight of her career. She was unhappy with Myron Selznick's handling of her. Even though he'd gotten the deal at RKO, she wanted a release from her contract. He refused. Clark's attorney, W. I. Gilbert, who had handled Clark's divorce from Ria, was also unsuccessful in trying to get Myron to agree on an out-of-court settlement, so they had to go to arbitration court.

The hearing lasted several weeks, the tedium broken only once. It was discovered that when she had signed the contract, Carole, in her usual clowning way, had inserted a clause which gave *her* 10 percent of Myron's earnings.

The Gables often said they enjoyed watching lawyer Gilbert 'operate'. He would appear to be nodding off and unaware of what was going on, but when a critical moment arrived, Gilbert was instantly alert, heatedly challenging the opposing lawyer.

Eventually Carole won the case, agreeing only to give Myron a percentage of the films he had helped negotiate. Free to choose another agent, she decided on Nat Wolff, who had now set up his own business. She admired Wolff's 'get up and go' attitude. Furthermore, she and Clark both liked Nat and his wife.

Carole's inability to become pregnant was so frustrating that she became upset over situations she ordinarily would have shrugged off. Lombard had, according to a reliable source, actually beaten one blonde beauty who had bedded Clark Gable.

Since Lombard spent Sundays with her mother, Clark took to frequenting a Hollywood bar that was popular with celebrities. On one particular Sunday, Carole Landis, a beautiful young blonde actress, and Clark made contact. Gable made the mistake of taking Landis home to the ranch, since he assumed that Lombard would, as always, be with her mother. However, Lombard returned early, and when she discovered Clark and Carole Landis together, she became violent. Although she didn't lay a finger on Gable, she directed her considerable anger at Landis. Talk in Hollywood was that 'Carole Landis has been hit by a Mack truck – named Carole Lombard.'

Lombard no longer found Gable's infidelities amusing. While Carole looked the other way when it came to bit players and secretaries, there now appeared to be a more serious threat on the scene: Clark had been cast opposite twenty-one-year-old Lana Turner in *Honky Tonk*.

Lana was startlingly beautiful, blonde (Gable always preferred blondes), and unashamedly available. She was the hottest new star at MGM, a girl who knew what she wanted and went after it. It was no secret that she was after Clark Gable. And, at forty, Clark couldn't have been riper for a fling with this dazzling new sexpot. When Carole got wind of Lana's dallying with Gable, she was furious: 'That little cunt! That soft ass of hers is gonna get quite a beating.'

Carole dropped in on the set of *Honky Tonk* many times to

158

observe Metro's nymphet in action. When Lana, during a love scene with Clark, saw Carole hanging around, she 'retired' to her dressing room. Talk was that Lombard even told Eddie Mannix that unless Lana was curtailed, Gable might have to stay home several days, and 'wouldn't it be too bad for the film's budget!'

The Lana episode blew over when *Honky Tonk* wrapped and Lombard had Gable back home. Theirs was almost an exclusively 'at home' marriage. Carole's closeness with her family prompted Clark to try to get closer to his father. He succeeded somewhat, and Carole was proud to note that a good rapport had developed between Clark and Gable, Sr. 'Pa had such a bad time of it with Father Gable when he was a boy. It's a joy for him to be on good terms with his dad now.'

Clark even had a house built for the elder Gable, where the old man lived until his death in the late forties. Gable, Sr., was a temperamental old codger, and some of his temper obviously had been inherited by Clark. Carole told her friends how Clark 'threw a fit' the time she suggested, 'Let's enlarge the dining room.'

'No! Absolutely *no*.'

Gable was furious, and Carole couldn't understand why. He was so angry that they didn't speak for three days. Finally:

'Listen, you son of a bitch,' Carole exploded, 'I want you to hear me out. What the hell is wrong with you? Why do you go off your rocker when I merely mention that I'd like having something changed?'

'I can't stand carpenters. That's why.'

'What do you mean by *that*?'

'They're the only workmen who don't clean up when they're through on a job. Painters clean up, plasterers clean up – but not carpenters. I won't have them in the house. I don't want to be here and see the mess they make.'

Carole didn't argue. She bided her time, and when, six months after their argument, Gable had to go on location for three weeks, she brought in the carpenters to enlarge the dining room.

When Clark returned and saw the room, his only comment was: 'All right, Carole. It looks fine.' Later Carole confided, 'The day before he came home I went to town and bought a magnifying glass. You're crazy if you don't think I got down on my hands and knees and went over every inch of the place with that thing in my hand.'

Lombard's painstaking efforts to keep Gable happy were obviously what made the marriage work. She went to any lengths necessary.

Gable was of the old school, and certainly would not have cared for today's women's liberation movement. Although women were important in his life, they were strictly sex objects. His 'manly pursuits' and his career came first. When women did enter the picture, he believed they belonged at home, doing all the wifely and motherly chores women were expected to do.

Even when he married Carole, one of the most successful career women of her day, he insisted that in their private life he be head of the family.

As the fall of 1941 approached, still with no child in sight, Carole began to lose her lightheartedness. Bessie encouraged her daughter to try religion as a source of some inner peace. Clark and Bessie both encouraged Carole to return to making films. She would be happier, and they could always 'keep trying'.

Lombard's old friend from Paramount, Ernst Lubitsch, was preparing a new film for Alexander Korda, a comedy with Jack Benny. Benny was to co-star with Miriam Hopkins, but when he heard that Lombard might be available, he suggested her for the part.

'It sounds marvelous!' Bessie told her daughter. 'Why not take it?'

To Be or Not to Be was an anti-Nazi film set within the framework of a satire, not unlike Chaplin's *The Great Dictator*. If Carole couldn't serve the cause for peace in any other way, at least she could make anti-Nazi films. But, of course, business first. Lombard insisted on a percentage of the profits, and star billing over Benny. She got both. And she would start work after the annual Gable fall hunting party.

The Gables' party, with the Fleischmanns as their guests, was what youngsters today would call 'a bad scene'. As Clark said, 'Everything that could happen, happened.'

It began well enough, with Carole eager to wear her new Irene-designed mink-lined hunting jacket and Clark giving both girls corsages.

The first mishap occurred when their flight from Albuquerque was grounded due to bad weather. The flight was

160

replaced by a train to Kansas City, which arrived too late to make another plane connection. Settling for the night in the Muehlebach Hotel in Kansas City, somehow unrecognized by the hotel clerk, they were given two cramped rooms. When the hotel manager realized who the arrivals were, he made new room assignments, giving the Gables the bridal suite and the Fleischmanns a similar setup. He even sent up a beautiful dinner, which Carole laughed about: 'We had a waiter standing behind each of our chairs at dinner, and you know how Pa hates formality.'

Clark, determined that they not miss the opening of the season in Watertown, South Dakota, called the airline and insisted, 'You've got to get us out of here tonight.'

The four of them departed on the only plane available. It was a large transcontinental model, and they were the only passengers on it. According to Carole, they flew to Omaha 'rattling around like mad'. Changing planes in Omaha, they arrived in Watertown at two in the morning, went straight to the private house where they were to stay, changed into their hunting clothes, and, after being driven sixty miles, were at the duck blinds in time for the opening of the season. They got their full quota of ducks.

Early in the afternoon of the same day, they were on hand to greet the start of the pheasant season. Clark suggested they not go: 'It's pouring.'

Carole insisted otherwise: 'We came here to shoot pheasants, and that's what we'll do.' She was delighted whenever she hit one, calling to the others, 'Did you see that?'

Nan recalled, 'She could hit and retrieve like a pro.'

Clark was overjoyed. 'What a girl!'

On this trip they constantly had to evade the public. The couple was starved for privacy. So, when they returned home, they decided to sell their dream ranch for a place yet farther away from Hollywood. 'Let's put the ranch up for sale and take our chances on finding the place we want by the time we sell it.' The move precipitated a lot of gossip that Gable and Lombard might be calling it a day.

But when the war broke out, the Gables withdrew the ranch from the market.

The Day of Infamy. December 7, 1941. The Pearl Harbor attack upset Carole much more than Clark. They had a number of arguments for many weeks. Lombard, always the idealist

161

and activist, thought they should each enlist at once.

'*You* a *WAC*?' laughed Clark.

'Maybe the WAVES. The Red Cross.'

'Oh, come on.'

'Pa, you should join up too.'

Gable would have none of it, but Carole coerced him into writing to President Roosevelt to offer their services. Gable was relieved – after all, he was making $7,500 a week and was forty-one years old – when the President wrote back that the Gables would serve their country best by continuing to appear in films and building the public's morale in time of war.

Lombard disagreed with the President. She wanted Gable and herself to play a more active role. To quiet her, Gable had the studio arrange a meeting with Lowell Mellet, Roosevelt's liaison to the movie industry. Mellet reconfirmed the President's opinion.

Carole was annoyed when MGM re-teamed Gable with Lana Turner for *Somewhere I'll Find You*. Lombard signed to do another film, Columbia's *They All Kissed the Bride*.

Christmas, 1941, was a solemn time throughout the country. Carole's last day of shooting *To Be or Not To Be* was on Christmas Eve. 'So long, you guys. It's been swell!' she shouted after doling out gifts to cast and crew. She was off to the Metro lot, where she and Clark were hosting a party for servicemen.

Gable and Lombard decided it would not be appropriate during wartime to do their usual extensive gift-giving to family and friends. 'We'll just send out cards,' said Carole, 'notifying people that we're making a gift to the Red Cross and other charities in their names. We won't do any Christmas shopping this year.'

They did, of course, exchange gifts with each other. Clark surprised Carole with a pair of diamond-and-ruby clips. They matched the ruby heart he'd given her the previous Christmas. Carole gave Clark a slim, solid gold cigarette case, inscribed: 'Pa Dear – I love you – Ma.' It was the same inscription she'd scrawled on the back of his favorite photo of her.

She had less than a month to live.

CHAPTER TWENTY-TWO

Three days after Pearl Harbor, the Hollywood Victory Committee was formed. The movie industry wanted to organize itself to help entertain the armed forces. Gable was named chairman of the talent-coordinating division of the Hollywood Victory Canteen. Actually, it was a nominal post. Any services called for were performed for Clark by MGM. When he was asked to recommend a star to launch the nation's first Victory Rally in Indiana – it would also be that state's first bond drive – Gable nominated his wife. He thought of her instantly, since she was a native of Indiana, and he also knew that this might satisfy her itch to do something for the war effort.

Carole was thrilled, and threw herself wholeheartedly into the project. She wanted Clark to accompany her. He wasn't enthusiastic, and countered with 'Bessie's a Hoosier too. Why not take *her* along?'

It wasn't exactly the same as going with Clark, but Carole knew her mother would get a kick out of the trip. She contacted Irene, to design traveling wardrobes: black daytime dresses, black evening gowns, fox capes, and jackets. The only jewelry Carole planned to take were the ruby-and-diamond clips and pendant Clark had given her.

At first Corney Jackson was set to accompany Lombard and Mrs Peters on the tour. But when Corney couldn't make the trip, Clark said, 'I'll ask Otto Winkler to go with you in my place. Just to keep an eye on you dames.' He told Winkler, 'You know how hard Carole works at everything. She'll kill herself if she gets the chance. Watch out for her. There will be people swarming all over, tugging at her; luggage to be taken care of.'

Otto and his wife, Jill, had become close friends of Clark's and Carole's and Clark trusted him implicitly.

Winkler wasn't anxious to take the trip, but he agreed out of deference to Clark and Howard Strickling. Jean Garceau wanted to accompany Carole too, but Carole said, 'No, I'm sorry, Jeanie, but it's unfair to take an entourage.' It was wartime, and since Carole was off on official government business, she wanted to keep the group as small as possible. 'Wait, Jeanie, and we'll take a trip together later. We'll go to New York, see all the shows, buy clothes, and have a grand time.'

Carole was still insisting that Clark join the service, and though MGM opposed the idea, the studio knew better than to voice that opinion. Of course, if he did join Clark would undoubtedly receive a commission. Though some say Lombard wanted him to enlist as a private, this is pure fiction. She thought he should be made a commissioned officer immediately. 'She won't settle for anything less than a colonel,' quipped Clark.

Gable was not there the day Carole left on her fateful trip. According to the official version released by MGM, and erroneously reiterated through the years by various Gable biographers, Gable was in Washington, D.C., conferring with his good friend Air Force General 'Hap' Arnold, 'concerning the possibility of getting into the service in some useful capacity'. The studio said Clark was due to return to Los Angeles the day after Carole was scheduled to leave.

However, today the accepted truth is that Gable was in Hollywood the day Carole left. Clark did not see her off at Union Station because he and she had quarreled violently. After he repeatedly refused to change plans and accompany her on the tour, claiming he had to make the Washington, D.C., trip and be back at MGM for the start of *Somewhere I'll Find You*, Carole countered that it wasn't the film but his interest in Lana Turner and others that was keeping him in town. Lana had made no secret that she was out to steal Clark from Carole. But, as Carole knew, Lana was only one of several on the lot with whom Gable was sleeping. In addition to Virginia Grey, Gable was also carrying on with Ann Rutherford, the sweet young brunette who played Mickey Rooney's upper-crust girlfriend Polly Benedict in the *Andy Hardy* films.

These girls were more than ten years younger than Carole. Clark had gone for older women when he was young, but now that he was over forty his interest in very young women had obviously intensified.

Carole was hurt and humiliated, and wasn't going to stand for any more of these indiscriminate sexual flings. Their bitter quarrel ended when Clark stormed out of the house. Quick to anger, Carole was equally quick to forgive. Since they were to be separated, she wanted to leave on a happy note. As she, her

164

mother, and Otto Winkler were leaving for Union Station, Carole left a series of notes for Clark with Jean Garceau. There was one for each day she expected to be away. She told Jean, 'Be sure to give him one each morning.' In addition, to make amends, Carole played what would be her final practical joke. She had gotten a department-store mannequin, put a blonde wig on it, and stuck it in Gable's bed. She knew he'd roar when he read the note she attached: 'I'm Lana Turner's stand-in. I'm just as good a lay, and you won't feel guilty about it later.'

Mrs Garceau says that although Carole was never overly affectionate or demonstrative with any women, and though she never hugged or kissed her, as she was leaving for the station Carole hugged her hard and long, kissed her, and said, 'Take care of my old man for me, will you, Jennie? You know you'll be working with him more and more now.'

Usually lighthearted and gay, Carole left the house depressed. But by the time her train arrived in Salt Lake City the following day, she had thought out her argument with Clark and telephoned him.

Clark and Carole always kept in touch by phone when they were apart. He had cooled off, and they made up, and she delighted in telling Clark about the huge crowd that had waited for her in Salt Lake City, despite the ten-below-zero temperature. She called again from Ogden, Utah, and again from Chicago. And she sent her husband the now famous one-sentence wire: HEY PAPPY, YOU'D BETTER GET INTO THIS MAN'S ARMY.

Carole Lombard's last day was frenetic. She, Bessie, and Winkler arrived in Indianapolis in the early morning and were rushed, with screaming motorcycle escorts, from the train station to a flag-raising ceremony in front of the State House. On the platform with Carole was Will H. Hays, head of the Motion Picture Association, the mayor of Indianapolis, Reginald H. Sullivan, and the governor of Indiana, Henry F. Schricker.

'Here's the little Hoosier girl who went to Hollywood and made good!' exclaimed the Governor, introducing Carole.

Carole made the speech she'd memorized and had delivered in the several cities prior to Indianapolis. The MGM publicity department had prepared it for her, and she'd rehearsed it until it was letter perfect. Like the expert actress she was, she

165

made it sound spontaneous, ending it stirringly:

'Heads up – hands up, America,' she screamed. 'Let's give a cheer that will be heard in Tokyo and Berlin.'

Then, in the crowded rotunda of the State House, Carole began what was to be the nation's first war rally and what would become the most famous Hollywood-star bond sale of the war. 'Let's go!' she cried. And hundreds of men, women, and children came forward to meet Carole Lombard and help the war effort. Not one bond was sold without a personal word from Carole: 'Hello, how are you?'; 'Glad to see you!'; 'Nice of you!'; 'No, I'm not tired, thank you.'

By noon over one million dollars in bonds had been sold. The goal had been set at half that sum.

'Let's keep going,' said Carole. 'Let's pass the two-million-dollar mark.' The eventual sale was $2,100,000.

In the late afternoon Carole, still remarkably fresh and charming, was guest of honor at a tea for various women's organizations. Then she changed into a black evening gown and long black gloves and rushed to the Cadle Tabernacle to hear the chairman of the Indiana Defense Savings staff introduce her as 'Indiana's Number One Saleslady' and announce the sale of over two million dollars' worth of bonds and stamps.

The bands from Indiana and Purdue Universities played, and there were speeches, songs, and victory cheers. To end the evening, Lombard led the group in singing 'The Star-Spangled Banner'.

The tour was over. Carole was exhausted. Will Hays was so impressed by Carole's performance and selling abilities that he wired Gable: GREAT DAY HERE. CAROLE PERFECT. MAGNIFICENT. SOLD IN ONE DAY $2 MILLION WORTH OF BONDS. EVERYONE DEEPLY GRATEFUL.

Lombard was anxious to start for home immediately, by plane. Her mother and Winkler, equally exhausted, tried to dissuade her.

'No,' said Carole. 'I want to leave *tonight*.'

Bessie objected. She was afraid of flying, and had never flown before. Besides, she'd been warned by her astrologer to 'stay off planes'. Furthermore, she had consulted her astrology charts and, using her knowledge of numerology, decided it would be unsafe to fly. It was the 16th, and that number forecast danger.

Otto Winkler agreed. Not that he was superstitious, but he was tired, and knew that the long trek by plane would probably make him sick. 'Why not take the train as we planned?' he suggested. 'We can rest and be fresh when we get to L.A.'

'I won't have any trouble sleeping on a plane. Not the way I feel,' Carole insisted. But, always fair, she said they would flip for it.

'Heads, train. Tails, plane.'

'I won!' she squealed, and Winkler dejectedly went about making arrangements for the flight home. He found they could get a flight out of Indianapolis at four that morning.

'It's the milk run, Carole – we'll stop a hundred times.'

'I don't care. Let's go.'

The trip from Indiana to Los Angeles would take fifteen or sixteen hours. But that was fast travel in 1941.

'Oh, no!' cried Bessie when they arrived at the airport. The flight number was 3.

The plane was a DC-3.

And Carole was thirty-three years old.

'Three's an unlucky number, dear. Please, let's not do it.'

'Oh, mother, there'll be a straitjacket waiting for you if you keep this up.'

Carole was also an astrology and numerology buff, but this was carrying things too far. Though it was early in the morning, Lombard was now wide awake. She started studying her script for *They All Kissed the Bride*.

'You try to get some sleep,' she urged her mother and Winkler. But Otto was too nervous, and afraid he'd be airsick, so he sat near the lavatory.

The plane stopped in Kansas City.

From there Carole wired Jean: I'M DEAD TIRED. EAGER TO GET HOME. HAVE PEGGY AND BUCKET READY. Carole wanted Peggy and Bucket, her hairdresser and manicurist, at the ranch the next morning to do her hair and nails.

The plane stopped in Wichita.

Among the newly boarded passengers was concert violinist Joseph Szigeti, a Hungarian refugee. He was working up his courage to talk to Carole. Everyone on the plane knew who she was, but they were trying to retain their 'cool' and not bother her, because she was obviously tired.

The plane stopped in Albuquerque.

Szigeti and three other civilians were bumped off the flight, because the transport plane was going to be filled to capacity with pilots returning from the Army Ferrying Command to their base in California.

It was the afternoon of the following day. Carole was eager to get home, and she, her mother, and Winkler were hot and tired.

'Mr Winkler,' asked a TWA executive. 'Would you give up your seats for three officers?'

'Carole,' Winkler said, 'they want us to get off and give our seats to three Army pilots.' Winkler wouldn't have minded staying in Albuqerque, resting up and then taking the train home.

'No,' said Carole. She told TWA that she had priority because she'd been on a government mission. Her mother's nervousness was rubbing off, and they were all irritable, since they hadn't got any sleep.

Normally the flight flew nonstop from Albuquerque to the Burbank airport. But TWA announced they'd have to make a stop for fuel in Las Vegas.

'Oh no,' moaned Bessie, clutching Carole's hand. It was the landings and the takeoffs she feared most.

'Now, Mother, we'll be home soon,' soothed Carole.

The plane landed in Vegas at six-thirty P.M. It was fueled and ready to take off a little after seven. It was a clear, starry night.

Meanwhile, back in Encino, Clark, though tired after the first day's shooting on *Somewhere I'll Find You*, was planning a big welcome-home party. Carole's brothers, Stuart and Frederick, Freddie's wife, Virginia, and Otto's wife, Jill, had all been invited for dinner. There were fresh flowers everywhere. The house was cheerful and beautiful. Clark had gone to great lengths to replay the practical joke Carole had played. He'd had the boys from the studio make up a male dummy, much more lifelike than the mannequin she'd used. It had a glorious twelve-inch erection. He knew Carole would appreciate the joke and make a few choice remarks about Pa not being in the same league.

Clark wondered why Larry Barbier hadn't phoned yet. Barbier was meeting Carole's plane, and when the phone did ring Clark figured the flight had landed.

'Larry?'

'No, Eddie.'

It was Eddie Mannix.

'Can I call you back? I'm expecting Larry to call any minute.'

'I know,' said Mannix. 'Larry phoned me.' The burly Irishman didn't mince words. Clark always appreciated directness. 'Carole's plane went down a few minutes after it left Vegas.'

There was a silence. Then Clark asked, 'How bad is it?'

'We don't know yet.'

Mannix told Clark he was sending a car for him. Gable phoned Fieldsie. 'I'm afraid something has happened to Ma,' he told her. 'Her plane is down.'

Fieldsie soothed him. She reminded him that Carole had been in several plane incidents. One plane had been drowned, and another had caught fire while in the air.

There was hope.

Clark phoned Jean Garceau. 'Ma's plane is down. Howard Strickling and Ralph Wheelwright are picking us up, and Jill and I are going out to the airport to check on it. I'll call you later.'

In the car on the way to the airport, Clark sensed the worst. Each new bit of information on the radio was ominous. No word from the plane. Workers at the Blue Diamond Mine in Vegas reporting a flaring light and the sound of an explosion. But, of course, it could be a forest fire ...

Both Carole's brothers phoned Mrs Garceau, wondering if she had any news. Stuart rushed to the airport to join Gable.

Clark phoned Jean from the airport. 'The plane's down near Las Vegas. Howard has chartered a plane, and we're all flying over there. I'll keep in touch with you at the ranch.'

Jean and her husband went to the Encino ranch. They were joined by Fieldsie and Walter Lang, Phil Berg, and Ivan Goff and his wife. They kept a quiet vigil, waiting for word from Clark.

Clark, Jill, Stuart, Strickling, and Wheelwright flew to Vegas. Freddie and Virginia Peters began making the six-hour drive there.

When Clark and the group arrived, they sped directly to the sheriff's office. The place was swarming with deputies, state police, military police. They were looking at maps, plotting routes in preparation for rescue parties to head into the mountains. They'd located the approximate area of the crash.

'How do you know the plane is there?' asked Clark.

'Because it's on fire,' the deputy answered. 'The flames shot up two or three hundred feet.'

'My wife's on that plane,' Clark muttered quietly.

'Clark's face whitened,' remembered Ralph Wheelwright. 'I think he knew then.'

The wreckage had been spotted by a Western Airlines pilot, Art Cheyney, and he'd radioed the information back to Vegas. As soon as possible, the rescue parties were organized and dispatched. Clark wanted to go along, but Strickling and Mannix talked him out of it. 'We'll come back for you when we locate the plane,' Mannix argued.

Clark, Jill, Stuart, and Strickling checked into the El Rancho Vegas hotel, and from his bungalow Clark could see a glow in the distance – probably the burning wreckage. Strickling stood close by as Gable paced the floor, chain smoking. Crowds of reporters were buzzing around the hotel, and scores of curiosity seekers began gathering.

Two rescue parties of deputies, miners, ranchmen, and Army recruits started up the barren, snow-covered mountain with a pack of horses and mules. A seventy-year-old Indian guide was leading the expedition. The snow was hip-deep, and the guide said it might take twenty-four hours to reach the scene of the crash.

These were the days before helicopters, and if there were any survivors it would be a long trek down the mountainside to a hospital. When a second rescue party was organized, Clark again insisted on going. 'Suppose the first party brings Carole back and you're not here to greet her?' argued Strickling. The veteran publicity man knew nothing could be gained by Gable's accompanying them.

Neither Eddie Mannix, chunky and over fifty, nor Ralph Wheelwright, not a youth either, was dressed for this kind of expedition. They tore their shoes to bits in their seven-mile climb up the cliff. The plane, which was seven miles off course, had crashed into Table Rock Mountain, about two hundred feet below the crest, and then fallen into a steep ravine. The flames had melted the snow and set the trees afire.

There were no survivors. The crew and all twenty-two passengers were dead.

The air smelled of burning flesh. There was blood everywhere. It was impossible for Mannix to identify Carole's body immediately. Later, remains thought to be hers would have to be identified via dental records.

It has been mistakenly reported that Mannix found 'a wisp of Carole's blonde hair and her diamond-and-rub clips'. He

170

found nothing on the scene except carnage.

Wheelwright and Mannix started back down the mountain. Halfway down, they spotted a telegraph station. Wheelwright wired Gable: NO SURVIVORS. ALL KILLED INSTANTLY.

'I knew I had to make it plain to Clark immediately that Carole and her mother and Otto had not suffered,' Ralph said.

When the message arrived, Clark was out on the balcony of his room, alone. Strickling handed him the wire. It was bright daylight by now. He watched Clark as he read the message and then crushed the paper in his hand. A heavy mantle of guilt, which Gable would not shake off for many years, fell over him.

'Why did Ma have to go?' he asked Strickling.

Soon afterward, Clark phoned Jean Garceau, and the retinue of Gable–Lombard friends gathered at the ranch. They had been up all night, keeping up a steady stream of small talk, reassuring each other that Carole, Bessie, and Otto would be all right.

The Gable phone call was brief. 'Ma's gone,' he said. 'I'll have to stay here a day or so until the rescue parties come down the mountain.'

When Mannix and Wheelwright got to the hotel, they were surprised to find Clark more composed than anyone. 'Jill was hysterical, and Clark really stood by her,' remembered Wheelwright. Both Mannix and Wheelwright again reassured Clark that Carole had suffered no pain. 'She never knew what happened.'

Mannix told Gable that the trail from the accident was narrow and treacherous and it would be two or three days before the bodies could be brought down. They could no nothing but sit and wait.

Gable's other close friends had heard the news on the radio and phoned Clark to see if they could be of help. Al Menasco was urged by Howard Strickling to join Gable in Las Vegas.

'Strickling said Clark wasn't eating or sleeping and would talk to no one,' recalled Menasco. Buster Collier had also driven from California to be with Gable. Not only wouldn't Clark eat, he even refused a drink: 'I'm numb enough without it.'

Although some have glamorized the tragedy by reporting that Mannix found Lombard's diamond-and-ruby clips when he visited the wreckage, and brought them back to Gable, this

171

is untrue. Only a portion of one of the clips was ever found. It was badly damaged but identifiable. A looter at the site of the wreck had found it, and a day later tried to sell it to Ralph Wheelwright.

'It's a cruel thing,' Wheelwright admonished the boy, 'trying to sell Mr Gable his wife's clip.'

'But I thought I oughta get somethin' for it,' protested the youth.

'A jail term,' countered Wheelwright angrily. He took the fragment from the boy and threw him out of the room.

Many items from the wreck had been stolen, but were later recovered by the military police. One of these was Otto Winkler's watch, which had been a present to him from Clark. Never found was the diamond-and-ruby heart-shaped pendant Gable had given Lombard.

CHAPTER TWENTY-THREE

When Al Menasco arrived in Vegas, Clark was in his room, alone, unshaven, eyes red.

'Why did this happen, Al?' Gable wanted his friend to help him find out how the crash occurred.

'I was hard put to answer,' recalled Menasco. 'I took him for a drive in my car and let him talk. He wanted me to show him where the plane had crashed, so we drove to a point at the foot of the mountain where we could see the plane wreck from afar. I tried to explain from a technical standpoint what I thought *might* have happened. This seemed to satisfy him. We drove around for a couple of hours and then returned to the hotel. Clark ate his first meal then.'

Buster Collier also tried to comfort Gable. He suggested they go for a walk in the desert behind the hotel. When they returned from their walk, Clark took his first drink since the ordeal had begun.

Other friends rallied to Gable's side in Vegas. Everyone reports that when the exhausted men from the search parties returned, Clark met them personally. He was calm and restrained. He saw to it that the men were taken care of with steaks and coffee. He even helped serve the food.

'Grief usually makes men completely self-centered,' said Ralph Wheelwright. 'Clark was just the opposite in his agony. He was so kind, so solicitous of everyone. And so grateful to the soldiers from the air base for the way they had helped out.'

One tireless worker, a small man who was a deputy coroner, was having difficulty eating. He had no teeth. Clark gave Ralph a hundred-dollar bill: 'Give it to that little guy and tell him to get himself some teeth.'

Although Carole's remains were among the first to be brought down, Clark refused to leave Las Vegas until the bodies of Bessie and Otto also had been turned over to him.

The ghastly job of recovering the bodies and bringing them down the mountain took many hours. A coroner's inquest was held at once so that Gable could take the bodies back to Los Angeles. Strickling and Mannix refused to allow Clark to go to the inquest. It was Ralph Wheelwright who made the official identifications.

Ralph cut a lock of Carole's blonde hair and put it in an envelope in case there would be further questions. He later gave the lock of hair to Jean Garceau, who gave it to Clark.

Clark personally selected the caskets, and decided on a double funeral for Carole and her mother.

The MGM contingent accompanied Gable on his sad mission back to Los Angeles. They sneaked him into a drawing room on the train to avoid reporters in Las Vegas. As the train was speeding to California, Clark went to Wheelwright's compartment. 'I understand you have something of Carole's,' he said.

'I had cleaned up the clip as best I could,' Ralph recalled. 'I handed it to him. Clark took it in his hand, stood looking down at it for a moment; then, without saying a word, he went back to his own compartment.'

MGM representatives took care of everything. Newsmen were on to the fact that arriving celebrities usually stopped in Pasadena, one stop ahead of Los Angeles, if they wanted to avoid publicity. Strickling outsmarted them and arranged to have his MGM crew waiting at Colton, one stop ahead of Pasadena. The bodies were taken to Forest Lawn. Gable, too grief-stricken to return home, went to San Gabriel with Al Menasco to await the funeral arrangements.

Clark had called Jean Garceau from Las Vegas, asking her to meet him at Forest Lawn. According to Mrs. Garceau, 'This was one of the saddest moments of my life. I was shocked to see the change in him. He seemed to have aged years, was hollow-eyed with grief and loss of sleep.'

Jean knew the stipulations of Carole's will and outlined them to Clark. He quickly vetoed all other funeral suggestions and ordered things as Carole had wanted them. She'd even specified the Bible text to be read and the order of the service.

Clark selected simple crypts for Carole and her mother. And one for himself.

The funeral was held on January 22, 1942. Clark remembered that at Jean Harlow's funeral Carole had said she wanted no spectacle 'when I go'. With MGM's help, Gable saw to it that her wishes were followed. It was a quiet, dignified affair. The public and photographers were barred. Only a few select reporters were admitted. Just members of the family and a few close friends were in attendance. In addition to the Gables' closest friends and William Powell, others included Spencer Tracy, Myrna Loy, the Fred MacMurrays, Jack Benny.

Fieldsie, the only person who could have made up a list of all Carole's friends, had been too grief-stricken to do so. Many of Carole's pals who were not invited were hurt. But director Mitchell Leisen later called Fieldsie and said, 'You forgot to call me, Fieldsie, but I'm not hurt. I just went ahead and held services of my own.'

At the funeral, there were no ritual prayers, no hymns or songs. Clark sat solemnly but composed through the service. More visibly shaken were Stuart and Frederick Peters. They had lost their beloved sister and mother, and theirs had been no ordinary family relationship.

The service ended with a four-line poem which both Bessie and Carole had loved:

> The dark threads are as needful
> In the Weaver's skillful hand,
> As the threads of gold and silver
> In the pattern He has planned.

This was followed by a simple affirmation of faith in the words of a Persian philosopher:

I have made death even as glad tidings unto thee.
Why doest thou mourn at its approach?

But mourn Clark Gable did. For the rest of his life.

After the simple funeral, most of the group went back to the ranch with Clark. It was his first return there since the evening Carole's plane was reported missing. Strickling, Mannix, Harry Fleischmann, Nat Wolff and his wife, Jean Garceau and her husband, and a few other intimate friends spent the evening with him. Fleischmann planned on staying with Gable for several days.

Jean Garceau still had one more note in the series Carole had left for Clark. This was the note she was to deliver if Carole did not arrive on schedule. In the privacy of her office at the ranch, Jean handed Clark the letter and watched as he read it. He broke down completely.

In Mrs Garceau's words: 'It's a dreadful thing to see and hear a strong man cry. My own heart was so full, I felt it would be cruel to witness his agony. To spare him embarrassment, I turned to leave, but he caught my hand and held it. All I could do was stand by his side, lending what strength and comfort I could muster until he was calm again.'

Mrs Garceau has added that after this, Gable was in perfect control. He masked his grief, sought and wanted no sympathy, and was 'unapproachable'. The following day, Gable accompanied Jill Winkler to the funeral of her husband. In addition to his guilt over Carole's death, Clark felt that he was responsible for Winkler's death.

Although many reports have stated that Gable waived his right to sue the airline and 'wanted nothing for himself but felt there should be equitable settlements for Mrs Winkler and Carole's brothers', the facts belie this. He did not waive his rights to sue the airline. Jill Winkler was persuaded to waive *her* rights, and Clark arranged for her to build a house at his expense across the street from the Stricklings' on property she and Otto already owned.

Studio publicity releases claimed that Clark had waived his rights to sue on the condition that Jill be paid $100,000 by TWA. However, many years later, after Clark's death, Jill, since re-married, sued Clark's estate for $100,000. She claimed that he had promised to establish an annuity for her in that amount and hadn't done so. And the house he had built for

175

her had cost only $7,500.

Another disturbing report surfaced. It is said that Carole's brothers confronted Gable and charged that he was responsible for Carole's and Bessie's deaths. If Clark and Carole had not argued, Bessie would not have gone on the tour, and Carole wouldn't have been in such a rush to get home.

It is true that after the plane crash, Gable, who never really had liked Stuart or Fred Peters to begin with, refused to associate with him. He had always considered them leeches, which was unfair. Carole was a generous person and enjoyed lavishing gifts on her family and helping them financially. In contrast, Gable's frugality always stood in the way of gestures like these. His only living relative, his father, received five hundred dollars a month in support from Clark. But an ex-business manager states, 'It often took weeks to get Gable to sign that monthly check.'

Not only had Stuart and Fred lost the two women they loved, but they were financially cut off from their sister's estate. Gable inherited everything. The estate was appraised at almost three hundred thousand dollars, a considerable sum in 1942. They did not include the ranch, which was in Gable's name already. Nor did it include the percentages Lombard owned in her last five films. This amount was eventually estimated at seventy-five thousand dollars.

In her will, however, there were provisions for two small annuities. They amounted to less than thirty thousand dollars. One was for Fieldsie, the other for Bessie. As Bessie's heirs, Stuart and Freddie inherited this modest annuity.

Gable's compulsive frugality was apparent even through his grief. He returned some expensive clothes that Carole had bought from United Artists, outfits which she had worn in *To Be or Not to Be*. He got a full refund.

At first Clark supposedly considered getting rid of the ranch and moving back to Beverly Hills or Bel-Air. He almost bought Garbo's old house in Brentwood. But he could never bring himself to move.

Actually, since Carole's will was in probate for many years, Gable touched nothing at the ranch. This led to the erroneous legend that he had made a shrine of Lombard's bedroom. In fact, after the estate was settled, Clark disposed of her clothing and gave away many personal possessions to friends. He gave her riding outfits and saddle to Mrs Valdez.

176

But he did leave the rest of the house intact.

MGM had shut down production on *Somewhere I'll Find You*. All of Hollywood had mourned Carole's death. On the day prior to the funeral, activities at all studios were stopped at noon and taps were sounded for Lombard. President Roosevelt sent Clark a cable: 'Mrs Roosevelt and I are deeply distressed. Carole was our friend, our guest in happier days. She brought great joy to all who knew her and to millions who knew her only as a great artist. She gave unselfishly of her time and talent to serve her government in peace and in war. She loved her country. She is and always will be a star, one we shall never forget nor cease to be grateful to. Deepest sympathy.'

Lombard was posthumously awarded a medal from the President. It read: 'The first woman to be killed in action in the defense of her country in its war against the Axis powers.'

There was talk that the plane had been sabotaged, since there were fifteen pilots aboard. The Civil Aeronautical Board investigated and ruled that the crash was due to pilot error. But disbelievers scoffed, saying that it *was* sabotage but the government didn't dare admit it. The country was suffering such severe losses in the early days of the war that public morale would have been seriously affected by the admission of such a successful plot.

Lombard's death caused United Artists to delay release of *To Be or Not to Be*. Director Lubitsch cut out a line of dialogue in which Carole asks Jack Benny, 'What can happen in a plane?'

Production on *Somewhere I'll Find You* remained shut down while Gable and Harry Fleischmann traveled up to the Rogue River in Oregon for several weeks. On his return, Clark looked and behaved as his friends had always remembered him. He was courteous, cheerful, smiled a lot, and seemed happy to see everyone. However, he had lost twenty pounds, and had been drinking so heavily that doctors now limited him to white wine. From this time on, Clark always drank a great deal, and cared little about his physical appearance.

Clark wouldn't go back to work until MGM changed the title of *Somewhere I'll Find You*. During the remainder of filming the picture was called *Red Light*, but on its release the studio reverted to the original title.

On the set, Clark appeared to be the same man the cast and crew had known before the tragedy. 'The only difference,' says

177

an ex-publicist, 'was that at lunchtime he ate alone in his dressing room. He used to like to eat with the crew, or at the directors' and writers' table in the commissary.'

Ironically, *Somewhere I'll Find You* was directed by Wesley Ruggles, the man who had directed Clark and Carole in their only film together. And the cameraman was Hal Rosson, whose talents were now engaged in photographing Jean Harlow's blonde successor at MGM.

'Let's not baby Clark, he's not that kind of man,' Ruggles told Lana and the rest of the cast and crew. Lana soft-pedalled her usual fun-filled, spunky-on-the-set attitude, and any chance for a romance between her and Clark Gable was over.

Instead of quitting at five, Clark would tell Ruggles, 'Don't lay off so early. I want to work.'

Though seemingly his old self at the studio, Gable went home every night, drank, and watched Lombard's old movies on a projector which had been a Christmas gift from her. He leafed through her old scrapbooks of their life together.

His friends thought he should keep working, and naturally MGM was eager to rush him into another film. But Gable was now determined to join the Army.

Clark's pal Vic Fleming pleaded with him to do a film biography of World War I flying ace Eddie Rickenbacker. After all, Gary Cooper had just won an Oscar for his portrayal of World War I hero Sergeant York. One night, Fleming asked Al Menasco, 'How can Gable make better use of himself, by trying to do something any healthy twenty-one-year-old kid can do better or by telling the story of our greatest flyer?'

MGM executives kept talking Gable out of joining up. He was, after all, forty-one, and even President Roosevelt had told him he could do more for homefront morale by making movies than by joining the service.

Though Clark was in mourning, there was the usual bevy of women eager to console him. One was Joan Crawford. The film Lombard had signed for, Columbia's *They All Kissed the Bride*, had gone into production as planned, with Crawford as Lombard's replacement. Joan announced that she would donate her $112,000 salary to wartime charities, notably the Red Cross. Crawford went so far as to fire her agent when he attempted to deduct his 10 percent before the donation. Nonsensical publicity of the day hinted that Miss Crawford had stepped into

178

the film to show Gable she could not only replace Lombard on screen but she could do so in private life as well.

Joan, now over thirty-five and nearing the end of her MGM contract, sent Clark a note inviting him to stop at her house on his way home from the studio. He did, and, according to Miss Crawford, they talked for hours. The visits continued for four or five months, and Hollywood wags said Joan Crawford was finally going to nail Clark Gable. Joan discounted this and claims simply, 'He was a moody man who needed friendship.' She noted Clark had helped her through a difficult period in the early thirties, and now she was returning the favor.

Gable tried to pull himself out of his depression, but he couldn't. He would wander desultorily about the ranch, going to spots which he and Carole had shared. In the garden he would stare for hours at trees which Lombard had planted. At the stables he tried to comfort Melody, her horse, who had become very skittish since Carole's death. Sometimes he went to the garage and stared at the station wagon they had used on their hunting trips. He never drove the Dodge again. Everywhere he went on the ranch, Clark was followed by Commissioner, Carole's dachshund. When Carole was alive the dog would never go near him. Now the dog had attached himself to him.

Memories of Carole were everywhere. The release of *To Be or Not to Be* brought a flurry of articles lamenting her premature death. Adela Rogers St John wrote, 'Carole can symbolize to a nation which just happened to know and love her, better than some of the other heroes who have already fallen, the first great personal chance to catch the stride of the martial music to which all must march now.'

A Navy air squadron had as its insignia a profile of Lombard over the outline of Indiana, her native state.

An anonymously authorized magazine called *Carole Lombard's Life Story* appeared, giving an account of Clark's seeing Lombard off on the tour with 'a kiss of which the Hays Office would not have approved'. Clark wished that such a scene had taken place.

Memories of Lombard's death were stirred anew when later that year Gable attended the funerals of John Barrymore and Buck Jones, two men who had helped Carole in her career.

Mrs St John summed it up:

'For months after her death, Clark was almost out of his

179

mind with grief. I'd go to his house and he'd be having dinner alone in the dining room with Carole's dog and Siamese cats at the table. He refused to touch her room, and left it just the way it was when she left. I asked, "Why don't you go out? Why don't you call your old friends like Vic Fleming?" And he'd say, "Carole used to make the calls when we wanted to go out." '

In April, *Somewhere I'll Find You* wound up production. Gable told the studio: 'That's it. No more films.' He'd met an Army Air Force colonel, Luke Smith, who suggested that Gable become a gunner. Smith told him, 'Everyone wants to be a pilot. But you'd be doing a real service as a gunner. It would help glorify the crews and the grease monkeys.'

The MGM hierarchy, realizing it was now impossible to dissuade Gable, set their machinery to work. Though the official announcement said Clark was going to be an ordinary recruit enrolled in Officers Candidate School in Miami and earning $66 a month (as opposed to his $7,500 weekly salary), the facts were not quite that spartan.

MGM had arranged with the government to have Andy McIntyre, a studio cameraman, inducted at the same time as Gable and sent with the actor to help Clark 'adjust to Army life.' In addition, the always money-conscious Gable couldn't refuse MGM's offer of $150,000 a year while in the service. It would enable him to meet comfortably all his financial obligation without dipping into capital. And the studio considered it was getting a bargain, since this arrangement guaranteed them a new contract on Gable's services after the war.

CHAPTER TWENTY-FOUR

When Clark entered the service, he made it clear that 'I don't want to sell bonds. I don't want to make speeches and I don't want to entertain. I just want to be sent where the going is tough.'

Before he left for training, Gable made extensive arrangements for his ranch and staff. Other jobs were found for the valet and cook, with the understanding that they would return to the ranch when Clark did. Roy, the caretaker, Juanita, the maid, and Mrs Garceau were to remain. Gable gave farewell gifts of gold identification bracelets to the Stricklings, Jill Winkler, and the Garceaus.

At Clark's request, Jean and Russ made good use of Gable's horses. Clark told the Garceaus, 'For goodness sake, use the good saddles.' Clark also told Jean she could have the five new tires he had purchased for his Dodge. With the tires, the Garceaus were able to use their car for the war's duration.

It hadn't been a simple matter for forty-one-year old Gable to pass the Army physical. He failed the first time. The Army wanted additional work done on his teeth. He easily passed the Government Intelligence Test, which called for an IQ score of 120.

Gable entered the service as a buck private on August 12, 1942, and, along with Andy McIntyre, left for Miami to enter Officers Candidate School. About Andy, Gable quipped, 'I enlist as a private and find myself in charge of a two-man contingent.'

All along the way Gable was besieged by fans. Although his itinerary had not been announced, they managed to find him. In New Orelans, he was so swamped by admirers that he was delayed a full day.

The first thing Clark faced was an Army crew cut and having his mustache shaved off. Then he and Andy were assigned to scrubbing the lobby floor in the Collins Park Hotel. It was a rainy day, and people constantly tracked mud across it.

At OCS, Gable was subjected to a strict regimen. Reveille was at 4:15 A.M., fall-in time at 4:30. Then there was a march of a mile or two before breakfast. John Lee Mahin, Clark's friend, who had an Army commission, saw Clark puffing his way around the race track one day, trying to keep pace with men half his age. As an enlisted man, Clark couldn't speak with Mahin, but when Gable spotted him Clark broke out into a grin and shot the writer a glance which clearly said, 'Oh, Christ!'

Clark found the classroom work hardest. He had never been a good student, and had never developed good study habits. He finally resolved his dilemma by treating the material like a movie script and memorizing every page. Unfortunately, the early lights-out call precluded any studying in the barracks.

181

Gable resorted to going into the john, sitting on the toilet, and memorizing far into the night.

In letters to his secretary, Clark described the training camp as a 'complete madhouse', and asked Jean, 'Could you send me some of Jessie's gingerbread?'

Clark took much ribbing from the younger men. One fellow, in particular, liked to pick on him. McIntyre recalled, 'A little guy. For inspection you have to have your shoes polished, clothes as immaculate as you can have them. But the brass is the main thing. You polish your brass and you polish it. It's unforgivably low for someone to touch your brass. This little officer came along and wet his thumb and drew it across Clark's belt buckle. Clark just stood there. And the guy said, "Gig that man, give him a demerit." Clark had to take plenty of that from jerky kid officers for months.'

The other rookies began to feel more kindly and friendly toward Clark after an incident in the washroom. Taking out his upper denture, he waved it and said laughingly, 'Look at the King, the King of Hollywood. Sure looks like the Jack now, doesn't he?'

McIntyre, summing up Clark's first six months in the service, said, 'Greatest guy I ever met. Many, many times we had fun. Gable did not like people to paw him or "yes" him. But he would do anything for you. Once I was sick and he saw that I was fed. When we went out together, he did not grab the check. But you knew this was out of consideration for your pride. If we'd go out, it was fifty-fifty. We borrowed from each other, and always paid back. The Army didn't give him a damned thing. I never saw him mad. But I saw him assert himself.'

Even in the service Clark was pursued by women. At one point the Army issued a press release: 'Lieutenant Gable will appreciate it if the public will not interfere with his training. He wishes to be treated like every other member of the Service.'

Clark graduated from OCS on October 29, 1942, finishing in the top third of his class. He received his diploma from his pal, Air Force chief Hap Arnold. Chosen by his classmates to deliver the comments following General Arnold's address, Clark said, 'I've worked with you, scrubbed with you, marched with you, worried with you over whether this day would ever come. The important thing, the proud thing I've learned about us is that we are men.... Soon we will wear the uniforms of officers. How we look in them is not very important. How we *wear* them is a lot more important. . . .'

Unable to get home after graduation – he had to report immediately to Gunnery School at Tyndall Field, Panama City, Florida – Clark mailed everyone at home invitations to the dance which preceded graduation, for which he was a member of the Entertainment Committee.

At Tyndall Field Clark was subjected to more classroom work, but by then he had grown philosophical. And he also got a chance to do a lot of flying, which he enjoyed.

Clark became good friends with Lieutenant Norman Price and his wife, Loulie, with whom he spent much of his free time. And in his letters home to Jean he constantly requested cookies and candies for his friends. He let his mustache grow back and ordered some custom-made uniforms, which, because they were tailored by MGM, made him one of the sharpest-looking officers around.

After six months of training, Clark got his first leave. He arrived at the ranch in time for Christmas, and spent a great deal of time with Virginia Grey. But his remorse over Carole's death had not disappeared completely. He told his secretary, 'Jeanie, you know I have everything in the world anyone could want but one thing. All I really need and want is Ma.'

Clark graduated from Gunnery School on January 7, 1943. He received his silver wings, qualifying him to fly at the thirty-thousand-foot level. Then he received a special assignment from General Arnold to produce films about aerial gunners which would be used for recruitment purposes.

Before Gable left for England to make these films, he traveled around the United States to a number of bases, gathering together equipment and crew. Andy McIntyre, of course, was assigned as cameraman. Also on Clark's crew were Sergeants Mario Toti and Robert Boles, cameraman, Lieutenant Howard Voss, a sound man, and Lieutenant John Lee Mahin, his MGM scriptwriter friend. This troop of six referred to themselves as the 'Little Hollywood Group'.

Gable managed to return home twice before departing for England. Then he didn't contact the ranch for a long time, and Mrs Garceau became worried. Gable, Sr, assured her, 'You don't need to expect to hear from Clark. He left me in Oklahoma in 1922 and I didn't hear one word from him until 1928.'

Clark was now stationed at Peterborough Air Base, eighty miles outside London, with the 351st Bomber Group. Due to heavy losses within the group, promotion came rapidly. Clark, Mahin, and McIntyre soon were captains, with Clark's promotion, of course, receiving wide publicity.

In England Clark spent much of his time working on the film assignment. But he also saw combat action. Serving as a cameraman, he flew in many dangerous missions, including a raid into Germany in August, 1943, aboard a Flying Fortress called *Ain't It Gruesome?* For seven hours he sat behind the chief aerial gunner, taking pictures of the action. Their plane sustained heavy damage but managed to return to the base even with fifteen holes in the fuselage. Clark had escaped serious injury when a twenty-millimeter shell entered the plane, deflected off Clark's boot, and ripped out through the plane only a dozen inches from Clark's head. Gable dismissed the incident, saying to reporters later, 'I didn't know anything about it until we had dropped eleven thousand feet. Only then did I see the hole in the turret.'

Mario Toti said, 'Clark worked very hard and was all business. He had his whole heart and soul in it, and said he was going to get the pictures he wanted even if Jerry dropped a bomb down the back of his neck.'

Toti also recalled Clark's affection for the men and his concern the day Andy's plane had to make a crash landing. 'As they hit the runways, the plane broke in two. Clark and I were on the field waiting for them, and we raced over. Fortunately, the crew had all gone forward in the plane, and none of them was hurt except the pilot, who got a clip on the jaw. They took them all to the hospital anyway, but found they were just shook up. By the time they lifted a few Scotches, they were feeling no pain.

'Clark really loved those boys on the base,' said Toti, 'and when one of them he'd been using in the film was killed on a mission, he gave up a few hours' leave to stay behind and write the man's widow a letter of condolence.'

At the base Clark refused special living quarters and lived in the barracks with the men. The only pictures he ever kept were those of Carole. The fragment of Carole's diamond clip was kept in a little box which he wore around his neck, under his shirt. He had had his identification tag altered so that in addition to containing his serial number and his blood type, it

184

also held a picture of Carole.

Never one to miss an opportunity for sex, Clark dated at whatever base he was on. John Lee Mahin recalls that one time Gable was dating the daughter of one of their commanding officers, a particularly unattractive girl, who wore thick glasses and had a girth larger than Clark's. Mahin asked him, 'For God's sake, how can you bother with her, Clark, with every other woman in the world dreaming of you at night?'

Clark, with an almost embarrassed look, said, 'She *is* kind of homely, isn't she? But she makes no trouble. And sometimes the homely ones are the best, easy to please, and they sure are grateful afterward.'

Clark received even more attention when his name was put on the list of Americans whom Hermann Goering, Hitler's Air Minister, wanted dead or alive. Gable was the Fuehrer's favorite American screen actor. A pirated print of *Gone With the Wind* was constantly screened at Hitler's Bavarian retreat.

Goering promised five thousand dollars, a promotion, and a furlough to the flyer who downed Gable, dead or alive. Gable had one fear while in the service: that of being captured by the Germans. He told Mahin, 'There is one thing I'll never do. I'll never bail out. If I ever fall into Hitler's hands the son of a bitch will put me in a cage like a big gorilla. He'd exhibit me all over Germany.'

Clark's fears were not completely unfounded. The group he was serving with was under the command of Colonel William Hatcher and was known as 'Hatcher's Chickens'. One day, over the radio, Lord Haw Haw, the German propagandist with a British accent, said, 'Welcome to England, Hatcher's Chickens, among whom is the famous American cinema star, Clark Gable. We'll be seeing you soon in Germany, Clark. You will be welcome there, too.'

On another combat mission, over France, Clark, still taking pictures, took over the nosegun while they were over the target. After this mission he received the Air Medal, for 'exceptionally meritorious achievement while participating in five separate combat bomber missions'. The citation also said that 'his courage, coolness and skill in five missions reflected great credit on him and the Armed Forces'. Clark, speaking of his latest mission, said, 'I could see the German pilot's features.'

Frank Capra saw Gable one night in the lobby of London's Grosvenor House. Capra remembered that Gable wasn't happy to see him, 'or anyone else, for that matter'. The director chatted with Clark's commanding officer, and the General responded to Capra's question. 'How's he doing? He's scaring the hell out of us, that's how he's doing. The damn fool insists on being a rear gunner on every bombing mission. Public relations, my eye! He's a hot potato! And I'm pulling every string to get him out of my command, tell you that. Guy gives me the willies. Know what I think? Gable's *trying* to get himself killed. Yeah! So he can join up with his wife.'

Clark always insisted on not receiving preferential treatment. Every couple of weeks he had to go to London for two days to have film processed. On these occasions Mario Toti went with him, and recalled, 'As a sergeant I expected to have to carry Captain Gable's bags, but Clark would never let me do it. He carried his own.'

Busy as he was with his wartime activities, Clark still found time to brood about Carole. One night, lying in his bunk, Clark said to Mahin, 'You don't believe all of that shit, John, do you?'

Mahin queried, 'About what?'

Clark, after a long pause, said, 'All that shit about religion.'

'Well, I was raised in a religious family. I don't go to church now, but I believe in God. Is that what you mean, Clark, that you don't believe in God?'

'What I believe in,' Clark emphatically said, 'is the love of a good woman for a good man. That's what I believe in.'

Mahin, very sagely, stated, 'If you believe in that, we've been talking about the same thing. You believe in God whether you realize it or not.'

Army life had a few lighter moments. Clark managed to find an old English motorcycle, which he used to travel around the base. Toti recalled an incident when a man named Pool, who was not an experienced driver, was assigned to drive Clark in a jeep. Toti said, 'Clark usually rode with his right leg over the side of the jeep. They were en route to the bomber area when Pool lost control of the jeep, and almost took Clark's leg off as he scraped against a tree. Clark's only remark was "That's the last time I'll ride with Pool." '

By October, 1943, when Clark and his crew had shot fifty thousand feet of color film, they were ordered home. Instructions were to report to Washington to give the Pentagon a first-hand report. On the flight to the United States Clark gave

186

his berth to a sick man and sat up all the way.

He created havoc when he appeared at the Pentagon. Secretaries and stenographers fought to get a glimpse of their hero. Clark was annoyed to find that a press conference had been arranged. He was being treated like a hero, and stated frankly, 'Other men have done so much more.'

He also received a hero's welcome when he returned, by train, to California. At MGM, in the commissary, he received a standing ovation. Publicist Eddie Lawrence described it: 'Richard the Lion-Hearted didn't get a better reception when he came back from the Crusades.' All these receptions embarrassed him. He was delighted to escape to the peace and quiet of his ranch.

Gable now received a new MGM contract, for seven years, at a salary of $7,500 a week, starting immediately, although he wasn't yet out of the service. In the new contract was a clause he had long fought for: He could quit shooting at five o'clock. In addition, the contract gave him four months' vacation after each film.

Gable's visit home was upset by the death of his good friend Harry Fleischmann. An unhappy Clark stayed close to home, awaiting the arrival of his film. Then he had to report to 'Fort Roach', the Hal Roach Studios in Culver City, which were being used as headquarters for the photographic division of the Air Corps.

Reminiscing about his wartime experiences, Gable told friends, 'I saw so much in the way of death and destruction. I realized that I hadn't been singled out for grief – that others were suffering and losing their loved ones just as I lost Ma.' He also said, 'I love the quiet at the ranch. The only thing I really want now is peace – peace, and a quiet life in my own home with those I trust and love around me.'

Early in the new year Clark reported to Fort Roach, where old pal Paul Mantz, now a lieutenant colonel, was his commanding officer. When he tried to salute, Mantz said, 'Na-a-ah, sit down and relax.'

Most of the film editing and cutting was actually done at MGM, where Gable had complete access to facilities. Even Blanche Sewell, the famous film editor, was assigned to him. An observer at the time recalled, 'There was a wonderful feeling about Clark at the studio. Everyone wanted to be of service to him.'

187

In January, 1944, grief came back to Clark anew when he was asked to participate in a ceremony to christen and launch the Liberty Ship *Carole Lombard*. Louis B. Mayer served as master of ceremonies, and an emotional Fieldsie Lang was matron of honor. As Irene Dunne smashed the bottle of champagne against the ship, Clark saluted, tears streaming down his cheeks.

Clark spent the next several months working hard on the combat footage, and put together five films. The films eventually became part of the Army's training-and-recruitment program.

Gable was promoted to major, and in June, 1944, he was discharged from the service. His discharge papers were signed by Captain Ronald Reagan of the Air Corps Personnel Office, Culver City. Clark continued to work on his Army films, periodically delivering them to the Pentagon. Then he went to New York for a brief vacation, and saw a great deal of Dolly O'Brien.

Dolly was a lovely, blue-eyed blonde socialite with tons of money and an unerring sense of style. Her clothes, jewels, and finese were very Lombard-like, and friends felt that Clark was searching for Carole's replacement. However, so far as Dolly O'Brien was concerned, 'We live in two different worlds.' She told Clark, 'You like the outdoors, and I love luxury. Your life, frankly, would bore me to death.'

The fall found him spending much time hunting and visiting with the widowed Nan Fleischmann, a woman who understood Clark's situation. Then Gable went to Palm Beach for two weeks to attend Dolly O'Brien's pre-Christmas party. He returned to the ranch in time to celebrate Christmas with the Stricklings.

When the new year rolled around, MGM still hadn't found the proper vehicle to herald Clark's return. He had a lot of time on his hands, and began to drink heavily. He dated Kay Williams, a blonde divorcee under contract to MGM, Virginia Grey, Anita Colby, Marilyn Maxwell, Audrey Totter, and socialite Millicent Rogers.

Three-times-married Millicent, a Standard Oil heiress, had a twelve-month fling with Clark. She fell madly in love with him, and even followed him when he went on dates with others. In a letter she wrote Clark, after they had broken up, she said, 'I'm sorry I failed you ... failed because of ... my own desire

... my own inability to be patient and wait like a lady ...'

Gable re-activated his membership in the Bel-Air Golf Club, and played with Eddie Mannix, Howard Strickling, MGM casting director Billy Grady, and Adolphe Menjou. Joe Novak, the club pro, recalled, 'Gable was not an aggressive player, but had great potentialities as a star player. He was powerful in build and loved to "play the big ball".' Joe also recalled a time when Clark, playing with Menjou, who was coaching him, overplayed the cup. Menjou screamed, 'For Christ's sake, Clark. This is a matter of mind and judgement, *not* a matter of muscle and force!'

Gable's drinking led to the infamous automobile accident that night in Brentwood in 1945 when he lost control of his car and smashed into a large tree. Fortunately, the owner of a house nearby was Harry Friedman, an executive with the Music Corporation of America. Knowing how adverse publicity could affect Gable's image, the MCA agent called Strickling, who in turn called Ralph Wheelwright, who lived nearby. By the time the police and press arrived, the story was that Gable, in trying to avoid a drunken driver, had crashed onto Friedman's lawn in order to avoid a head-on collision. Strickling and Wheelwright took Clark to Cedars of Lebanon Hospital, ostensibly for 'observation', but actually so the actor could dry out.

Clark's acquaintances have described his drinking habits:

'He drank like a man with twenty pounds of blotting paper in his stomach.'

'He *had* to be drunk because of the enormous quantities he'd put away in a night. But his tongue did not fuzz words. His speech did not become erratic. He did not become bad-tempered. The only way I could tell when he was stoned was when he would try to get through a doorway. He would always walk sideways then.'

Al Menasco has described Clark's drinking: 'I never saw a man who could drink as he did. I'd bought cases of Old Rarity Scotch whiskey some years before. I'd got it at a good price. He liked that twelve-year-old-or-more stuff. He also very much liked Black Label whiskey. Clark could put away three-quarters of a fifth or a whole bottle of Scotch before dinner without showing any effects. We would join my wife. His eyes would light up on seeing Julie. He would comment on the dress she was wearing or some little new thing she had done to the house. Or he'd talk to her about our boys.

'He never had to pretend or put it on with Mrs Menasco. But he was like that with most of the women who were wives of his friends. However, the point I'm trying to make is how little that whiskey affected him when he could talk to her like that.'

MGM came up with *Adventure* as the film to bring Gable back to the screen. At the start, the project seemed very promising. Greer Garson, then at her peak, was to be Clark's co-star. Joan Blondell and Thomas Mitchell had supporting roles. Sam Zimbalist was producing, Victor Fleming directing, and Joseph Ruttenberg heading the camera crew.

Clark asked Don Robertson, Jean Harlow's cousin, who had worked his way up through the MGM ranks, to be his make-up man. Robertson recalled, 'Clark was jittery the first few days of shooting, but finally settled down. He never complained, just kept his feelings to himself. He'd be a little moody for a day or so – then suddenly it would pass and he'd be the same old Clark again.'

Gable found he did not like the picture or working with Greer Garson. He knew early on the film was 'lousy ... I could tell because I had to work so hard. A picture that is going to turn out well is easy to do. It just seems to flow along by itself. Everybody on it has a great time. Nobody strains, because he doesn't have to. And it all comes out fine. When you are on a bad picture you find everybody working like hell, and nothing comes of it.'

On one occasion, Howard Strickling had out-of-town friends visiting the studio and sent them over to the set of *Adventure*. But Greer Garson had barred visitors from the set that day. Larry Barbier talked to Gable, who stepped outside the sound stage to meet Strickling's friends. He spent a half-hour with them, and even sent for a photographer so they could be photographed with him. When a frantic assistant director came out a second time and repeated, 'Miss Garson's waiting', Gable replied, 'Let 'er wait.'

Clark was particularly incensed by the advertising adopted for the picture: GABLE'S BACK AND GARSON'S GOT HIM. One critic, after seeing the picture, added to the slogan, 'And they deserve each other.'

The picture wasn't good. But Clark's box office was solid, and *Adventure* was one of the highest-grossing films of the year.

A series of undistinguished films followed. One, *Home-coming*, re-teamed him with old flame Lana Turner. Another, *Key to the City*, co-starred him with Loretta Young.

In his personal life, Clark wandered from woman to woman, 'still living with Carole's ghost'. Determined to fill the void in his life, he finally settled on another sophisticated, sexy vivacious blonde. Like Clark, she had already been married three times.

CHAPTER TWENTY-FIVE

'Do you actually want to go through with this?' Strickling asked Gable that December day in 1949.

'Of course he wants to!' snapped the blonde.

'I wasn't talking to you,' retorted Strickling. He repeated his question to Clark.

'It will be all right. Don't worry about it,' a drunk Gable replied.

Clark Gable had met Lady Sylvia Ashley that summer, at a dinner party given by Minna Wallis. He had known Sylvia earlier, when she was married to Douglas Fairbanks, Sr. Sylvia had been responsible for breaking up 'the marriage made in heaven' between the legendary Fairbanks and Mary Pickford.

Sylvia was ten years younger than Clark. Born Sylvia Hawkes in England, she had been a lingerie model, then a London chorus girl. Her first marriage was to Anthony, Lord Ashley, son of the Earl of Shaftesbury. It ended in divorce when Sylvia had an affair with the senior Fairbanks. She later married Fairbanks, who died in 1939. Her third marriage was to Baron Stanley of Alderly, another Britisher. After their divorce, in 1948, she reverted to using the title from her first marriage.

Clark found the gay blonde divorcée charming. She was full of fun and laughter, and when he had a lot to drink, she seemed a perfect replacement for Carole.

191

Gable ignored the warnings of many and married Sylvia on December 20, at a ranch near Santa Barbara. Three days later, the couple sailed aboard the *Lurline* for a honeymoon in Hawaii. Everywhere they went, they were swamped by fans.

When they returned to Clark's Encino ranch, Sylvia proceeded to make a number of changes which angered Clark. She transformed the gun room so completely that Larry Barbier later said, 'She made that room look like the reception hall of a French whorehouse.' She claimed that she needed a sitting room, so she commandeered Jean Garceau's office.

Clark also objected to Sylvia's taking her Chihuahua, Minnie, everywhere they went. Surprisingly, however, he did buy a diamond collar for the dog. He was particularly annoyed that Sylvia's relatives – her sister and brother-in-law, and their children – spent so much time at the ranch. A final source of irritation was that Sylvia continued to maintain an active social calendar for them. Clark, who preferred being a homebody, found himself attending numerous dinner parties and socializing constantly with the Continental set: the Ronald Colmans, the David Nivens, the Fred Astaires, the Douglas Fairbanks, Jr's, the Tyrone Powers, the Gary Coopers – not to mention Charles Boyer, Louis Jourdan, Gloria Swanson, Clifton Webb, Cole Porter, Joan Fontaine, the Ray Millands, and Pat Kennedy. It was like life with Ria again!

Clark's next picture was *To Please a Lady*. Old pal Hal Rosson was the cameraman. Barbara Stanwyck co-starred, and the picture was shot on location in Indianapolis. Sylvia went with Clark, and cooked on a hot plate in their suite at the Hotel Mariott. When the film was completed, Sylvia left for Europe 'to tend to some business'. Clark refused to accompany her. 'It won't be any fun for me.'

When Sylvia returned, preparations for Clark's next film, *Across the Wide Missouri*, which was to filmed in Durango, Colorado, had already begun. Again Sylvia trailed along. They stayed in guest cabins at El Rancho Encantado. Sylvia had grass turf and flowers planted around the Gable cabin. She also brought twenty-seven pieces of luggage, including high-heeled shoes for trekking in the desert. She insisted on bringing Minnie to the communal dining table, which caused Clark much embarrassment. She attempted to try fishing with Gable, but soon realized it was not her cup of tea.

There began to be 'subtle hints' that all was not well with

192

the marriage. Friends started to hear and see things at the ranch which set them to thinking. Al Menasco first suspected that things were going wrong when Clark asked him to look at some property for him, telling him to buy it if he could get it for seventy-five thousand dollars. Menasco said, 'Do you think Sylvia will like this quiet country life?'

To which Clark simply said, 'That won't make any difference.'

The straw that broke the camel's back came on Clark's fiftieth birthday. Sylvia planned a special party at which Clark's favorite meal, chicken and dumplings, was to be served. Unfortunately, a new cook, preparing the dish a day in advance, didn't refrigerate it properly, and rancid food was served. Clark left the table, and didn't return.

Sylvia planned a trip to Nassau, and Clark refused to go. She was furious. 'All right then,' she said, 'I'll go alone.'

When she returned, she filed for divorce, on May 31, 1951, and then sailed for Hawaii.

Clark, meanwhile, began work on *Lone Star*, with Ava Gardner, a good friend, and Broderick Crawford. They appeared to have a lot of fun on the set, playing prankster gags on each other. But it wasn't like the old days.

Wary of Sylvia's financial demands, Clark filed his own divorce action in Las Vegas in early October. He established residence in Nevada, transferring all his assets and going to live there to avoid California's community-property law. Eventually an out-of-court settlement was agreed upon. Clark paid Sylvia $250,000. When the divorce was granted on April 21, 1952, Gable lied to reporters: 'She's a fine woman. It is too bad that we couldn't get along.'

It's almost unbelievable, but the women in Gable's life, whether his wives or lovers, never said unkind words about him when the relationships ended. Russell Birdwell explains: 'Gable knew how to pick 'em. He picked champions except in one case, and champions don't cry or make scandals for the newspapers.'

Clark continued drinking heavily, and started to put on weight. And, because he had forked over so much money to Sylvia, he began to worry once more about financial security. He worked out a deal with MGM to do his next three pictures abroad. Since they would be filmed out of the country over an eighteen-month period, his salary would be exempt from income taxes.

Next came a memorable picture for Clark, MGM had decided to do a remake of *Red Dust*, with Gable in the same role he had played twenty years earlier opposite Jean Harlow. Now his co-stars would be Ava Gardner, in the Harlow role, and Grace Kelly, in the Mary Astor part.

Mogambo was being shot in Kenya, and was the most prestigious Gable film in years. John Ford was the director, and the studio had allocated a top budget for production. The picture received quite a bit of publicity, because Frank Sinatra had also gone on location, to attempt a reconciliation with his estranged wife, Ava.

Gable loved doing the film, because he had many opportunities to go on hunting safaris. He didn't shoot big game, however, a practice he despised; he shot game only for meals.

Frequently Clark was accompanied on the safaris by Grace Kelly, who reminded him somewhat of Lombard. Miss Kelly got up at four in the morning to go with the men, and never complained about the jungle conditions or the oppressive heat. Clark asked her, 'What is there about this that you like?'

She replied, 'It's the excitement and the strangeness of it all. I want to be able to tell my children about it someday.'

Grace and Clark developed a close rapport, she calling him 'Ba', the Swahili word for 'father'. They saw quite a bit of each other, even after their return to Hollywood. Many predicted that Grace would become the next Mrs Gable. Though she told friends, 'His false teeth were just too much', this was press-agentry. Actually, she was quite broken up over Gable. During one of her visits to the MGM home office in New York, she spent hours crying her eyes out and moaning, 'He thinks I'm too young for him. He doesn't want to marry me ...'

Gable was nearing the end of his long stay at Metro. Although *Mogambo* was a hit, his next, *Betrayed,* with Lana Turner, was a dud. Like all the studios, MGM was undergoing hard times financially. They couldn't afford Gable's whopping $7,500-a-week salary. In March, 1954, they dropped him.

Gable still harbored a grudge toward MGM because it had never given him a share of the huge profits from *Gone With the Wind*. He said to a friend, 'I bet those bastards in the front office won't even give me a goodbye lunch. And after all the millions of bucks they've made with me.'

Of course, MGM did give the lunch, and when Gable got up

to speak, all he would say was: 'I wish to pay tribute to my friends and associates who are no longer alive.'

Mogambo had been such a box-office success that MGM tried to lure Clark back on a free-lance basis. But he would have none of it. He told his agent, 'See how high you can get those sons of bitches to go. And when you get their best offer, tell them to take the money, their studios, their cameras, and lighting equipment and shove it all up their ass!'

Gable was now able to free-lance, and he took his time choosing his next picture, although he could not understand why he was still in such great demand. 'By rights, I should be playing character parts at my age, or thinking of retirement.'

Gable knew he was getting old. His most unforgettable snub occurred around this time. He was staying at a plush New York hotel. A chambermaid came into the room while Gable was still in bed.

'Take off your clothes and join me,' he said, flashing that Rhett Butler half smile. But it was almost two decades later.

'How much will you pay?'

Astonished, Gable replied: 'I'd think you'd want to sleep with me just to be able to say you did so.'

If it had been two decades earlier, she probably would have leaped into Gable's bed. But now the girl insisted on cold cash. Clark refused, and the maid waited outside until he left.

Back in Hollywood, Gable pondered his career. He began to date again, and it soon became obvious that the front runner was blonde Kay Williams, whom Clark had seen something of in the forties when he came out of the service. While waiting for Gable, Kay had married and divorced Adolph Spreckels, the sugar heir. Clark was very fond of Kay and her two children by Spreckels, Bunker, six, and Joanie, four.

Then Gable signed a two-picture deal with Twentieth Century–Fox. His salary was to be 10 percent of the box-office gross. Rumour had it that he was guaranteed five hundred thousand dollars for each film. After these movies – *Soldiers of Fortune* and *The Tall Men* – Gable decided, for the fifth time, to try marriage. On July 11, 1955, Kay and Clark were married in a private ceremony carefully arranged by Al Menasco. Then they left for an eight-day honeymoon at the Menasco ranch.

A comparison between Kay and Lombard was inevitable. Kay and Clark called each other 'Ma' and 'Pa'. Kay dressed like Carole, swore like Carole, and gave in, as Carole had, to every one of Gable's wishes. They moved into the Encino ranch, and Kay left it as it had been furnished. 'Kathleen', as Clark called her, was a great companion, and provided Clark with a ready-made family.

For Gable, life finally settled into a pleasant routine. He stayed at home much of the time and was truly a family man. He was ecstatic in the early fall when Kay became pregnant, and very despondent when, after eleven weeks, she miscarried. The doctors told them to try again, but Gable was pessimistic. He told Al Menasco, 'The combined ages of Kay and myself amount to almost one hundred years. I don't know. I sure don't know.'

Gable's next film was *The King and Four Queens*, the first production of Gabco–Russfield, the independent company formed by Gable with Jane Russell and her husband, Bob Waterfield. Kay accompanied Clark to the location shooting in St George, Utah. She stayed away from the set, but had a comfortable home waiting for Clark each evening.

On their return to Encino, Kay fell ill: a heart condition. She was in the hospital for three weeks. Clark spent the next several months tending to her.

The Gable career kept up its pace: *Teacher's Pet,* with Doris Day; *Run Silent, Run Deep*, with Burt Lancaster.

As he had with Carole Lombard, Gable and Kay visited Washington and had a meeting with the President. This time it was President Eisenhower, and afterward the Gables lunched in the Senate dining room.

Clark next made *But Not for Me*, directed by Fieldsie's husband, Walter Lang. Then he went to Rome to shoot *It Started in Naples* with Sophie Loren. Kay accompanied him everywhere.

Meanwhile, in New York, a publisher, Frank Taylor, was about to become a movie producer. Taylor, Arthur Miller's Amagansett neighbor, had decided to produce a film which Miller was writing, *The Misfits*. John Huston was set to direct. Montgomery Clift would co-star. And Gable was offered the fattest fee he had ever received: $750,000 plus a percentage of the profits to star opposite the generation's leading sex symbol, Marilyn Monroe. In addition, Gable would be paid $48,000 a week if the film ran over schedule. It was almost certain that the film would run over schedule. Monroe was in a pathetic state emotionally, and Miller, her husband, hoped the movie would salvage what was left of her life.

Clark began dieting strenuously, preparing for his role. He told a friend, 'I've got to get in shape. If I'm to play a lean, tough horse wrangler, I need to drop about thirty pounds.'

The friend commented, 'Why knock yourself out? This is going to be a rough picture.' Gable was warned by other friends that *The Misfits* would be trouble from start to finish.

Clark's response showed that he hadn't yet lost his old fear of poverty: 'I know, but I can't turn down that kind of money.'

Work on *The Misfits* began on July 18, 1960, and it *was* a rough experience for Clark. Marilyn was having difficulties with Arthur Miller, and was at the breaking point. The heat was unbearable. Temperatures in the desert sun often rose to 130 degrees. And almost everyone, except Clark, had a tendency to show up late on the set. Clark, remembering his early screen days, said, 'It was a different era. In those days, when stars were late, they were fired.'

Marilyn was thrilled to have Gable as a co-star. He had been a father figure to her, but Clark quickly ran out of patience with Marilyn's unprofessionalism. He had never worked with a co-star whose working habits were so unpredictable, and he found it infuriating, especially when the entire company catered to her.

The picture called for Clark to do strenuous physical scenes, such as roping mustangs from the back of a truck and taming a wild stallion. Although he had lost thirty-five pounds for the role, his age, fifty-nine, was apparent, and these scenes taxed his strength. In addition, with the tension on the set, Clark, had resumed drinking steadily. The only good thing that happened at this time was that Kay told Clark she was pregnant. She promised, 'And this time there will be no accident, Pa. And it will be a boy. I guarantee it.'

Clark was overjoyed. 'Imagine a wonderful thing like this happening to an old guy like me. It's an extra dividend from life, and I want to make the most of it.'

In mid-October the entire group returned to the studio for the indoor scenes. The last day of shooting was November 4. On November 5 Clark suffered a heart attack, and was taken to Hollywood Presbyterian Hospital. Each day his condition improved, and two weeks later his doctor told him that he might go home in several weeks, but only if he promised to watch himself carefully. Clark said, 'Don't worry. I don't intend to do a lick of work until after my son is born. I want to be right there when he arrives, to look after him and watch him grow. You couldn't tear me away.'

But death took Clark Gable that night. He suffered a second, fatal heart attack.

Kay was bereft. She blamed *The Misfits* and, indirectly, Marilyn Monroe, for killing Gable. Kay said it wasn't the physical exertion that had done Gable in. It was the tension. The constant waiting. The fact that when he had to wait he became angry. In addition, she cited the fact that Gable refused to use a stunt man to do the scenes in which he was dragged by horses.

While Kay accused others, some of Gable's close friends accused Kay of bad judgement on Clark's behalf. Supposedly Kay had sneaked her husband's favorite foods into the hospital to please him, even against doctor's orders.

The King was dead. It was almost the final straw for Marilyn Monroe, who was close to the end herself. Having heard Kay Gable's accusation, Marilyn broke down: 'Oh my God, I killed him, I killed him ...'

Gable was accorded a full military funeral. Services were held at the Church of the Recession in Forest Lawn, the church at which Carole Lombard's funeral had been held. Among the pallbearers were Al Menasco, Howard Strickling, Eddie Mannix, James Stewart, Robert Taylor, and Spencer Tracy.

John Clark Gable was born March 20, 1961, four months after the death of his father.

CHAPTER TWENTY-SIX

Because William Powell has been out of the public eye for two decades, many people don't realize that he is still very much alive. As this book goes to press, Powell is eighty-two years old. He lives quietly but comfortably in Palm Springs, California. The actor is still married to Diana Lewis, affectionately known throughout Palm Springs as 'Mousie', Powell's nickname for her.

Although he retired permanently from the screen in 1955, William Powell enjoyed a sporadic but very rewarding and lucrative career up to that time. He played Father in the film of Clarence Day's *Life with Father* in 1947. Powell, then an MGM property, had implored Louis B. Mayer for years to purchase film rights to the play. Mayer kept saying the $500,000 asking price was too high. Powell did the film on loan-out to Warner Brothers, and received his third Oscar nomination. But he lost to his good friend Ronald Colman for *A Double Life*.

During the forties Powell also made his last two *Thin Man* films: *The Thin Man Goes Home* and *Song of the Thin Man*. Off screen he continued to live the simpler life he settled on after his return from Europe a number of years earlier. Powell and Diana appeared completely devoted to each other. 'Mousie' called him 'Mr Poo'. They even had matchboxes with these names printed on them.

True to his screen image, Powell remained a fanatic about neatness, especially in public appearances. He wouldn't carry cigarettes because his pockets would bulge. He was very reserved, avoiding fans as much as possible. He even took to sneaking out back doors and delivery entrances to dodge people.

Close friends say he had become very much like the Nick Charles *Thin Man* character. But now there were no longer any dashing debonair roles for him to play; he had to settle for character parts.

In 1953 Powell made his final film under his MGM contract, *The Girl Who Had Everything* in which he played Elizabeth Taylor's lawyer father. Ironically, the film was a remake of *A Free Soul*, the 1931 vehicle which had established Clark Gable's popularity.

And then, 'I'll just go down to Palm Springs and sit on my patio,' said Powell. 'I guess after forty years a guy rates a little relaxation. If a terrific part comes along, I suppose, like the old fire horse, I'd respond to the call. But for all practical purposes, I'll be gone from the screen.'

Two good parts did come along. He played the supporting role of a rich Texas oil man in *How to Marry a Millionaire*, for Twentieth Century–Fox, and Doc in *Mister Roberts*, for Warner Brothers.

In the 1960s Powell underwent another cancer operation. Again he was lucky, as he had been more than twenty years earlier. But tragedy did strike his son. William David Powell, who had become a television writer, committed suicide. He left a four-page note, saying, in part: 'Things are not good here. I am going where things are better.'

Unhappy memories of the past haunted William Powell throughout the decade. A lurid biography of Jean Harlow became a best-seller. His only comment was a sad 'She wasn't like that at all.' Not one but two movies were made about Harlow, and a publisher was found for *Today Is Tonight*, Jean's novel. Mrs Bello had died in 1958 and left the rights to the book to Mrs Ruth Hamp. The novel was not a success, but the public's interest in Jean Harlow had been revived.

Kay Mulvey has retained fond memories of Jean. For years Kay worked on a documentary film on Harlow's life. But when the Harlow craze peaked, the public wanted only sensationalism. So the documentary was overlooked, and still hasn't been released. Kay also has fond memories of Powell. They keep in touch, and she tries to visit him when she's in Palm Springs.

Today William Powell is largely confined to a wheelchair. Occasionally he talks on the telephone with his old, old friend Myrna Loy. He sees very few friends, but the few who see him report that his mind is alert as ever. 'Mousie' remains at his side.

Only Powell knows if, when he dies, he will be laid to rest in the crypt next to Jean Harlow.

Clark Gable is buried next to his love, Carole Lombard.

Gable. Even though he has been gone for fifteen years, his name remains synonymous with male sex appeal. The reissues of *Gone With the Wind* introduce him to new generations, who react just as their parents did. *Lombard.* Her amazingly contemporary quality and zest for living shine through even her most dated films. *Powell.* The epitome of the suave sophisticate. *Harlow.* What other single name can better conjure up an entire era?

There will never be film stars like them again, because the system that produced them – and the audience that *needed* them – are gone.

CHAPTER TWENTY-SEVEN

THE MAKING OF THE MOVIE *GABLE AND LOMBARD*

Re-creating the fabulous era in which Gable and Lombard lived was no small task. It cost Universal over $4 million to accurately reproduce Hollywood of the 1930s. No expense was spared on costumes, art direction, location shooting.

In winning the roles of Gable and Lombard, James Brolin and Jill Clayburgh took on the challenging assignments with enthusiasm.

With some assistance from the expert Universal makeup department, James Brolin achieved a remarkable resemblance to Clark Gable. But a physical resemblance was only the beginning. Exactly how would Brolin go about playing Clark Gable? Brolin's friend Clint Eastwood gave him a suggestion: 'Find a couple of mannerisms that the public associates with Gable, and use them. But from then on build your own characterization.'

Brolin says: 'After I got the role, I went to see *Gone With the Wind* for the first time, up in San Luis Obispo, where I live. It was a young audience, but when Gable came on the screen, you could hear them gasp.

'I've seen a lot of his movies and I've read books about Gable. I thought of working on the voice with a tape machine, but decided against it. I just wanted to get the rhythm and the feel of his voice. The rest was my own interpretation.'

Brolin, 35, has been an actor since his college days at UCLA. The 6-foot 4-inch 195-pounder is a genuine screen actor. He believes that men like Clark Gable, Gary Cooper, James Cagney, and Humphrey Bogart were basically screen actors, consummate at utilizing a 'bag of tricks' – certain actions, facial expressions, mannerisms which over the years worked for them and were kept in their repertoires. Brolin feels that Gable's facial expressions, particularly the use of his mouth, were probably based on the fact that Gable wore false teeth.

Brolin, like Gable, is an outdoor person. He lives with his wife Jane on a sprawling 230-acre ranch in Northern California, where they are bringing up their two sons. Their hobbies include fishing, scuba diving, boating, and motorcycling. And, like Gable and Lombard, the Brolins operate their ranch on a paying basis.

Over the years, Brolin has won millions of fans throughout the country for his portrayal of 'Dr Steven Kiley' in the hugely successful television series, *Marcus Welby, M.D.* He made the successful transition to the big screen in *Skyjacked*, with Charlton Heston, and *Westworld*.

The role of Clark Gable promises to establish Brolin as the screen's new matinee idol.

When she was cast in *Gable and Lombard*, Jill Clayburgh had never seen any of the Lombard films. She wasn't even born when Carole's plane crashed into the Nevada mountainside in 1942.

'I've seen about all of the films now,' says Jill, 'and some I've seen several times. Carole was extremely good as a dramatic actress, especially in *They Knew What They Wanted*. I'm not as crazy about *My Man Godfrey* as some people are, but I thought she was marvelous in comedies like *20th Century* and *Swing High, Swing Low*.

'At first I tried imitating Lombard's external look and mannerisms, mostly her voice. But that was superficial. She gives me the impression of being sweet on screen. I think there was more acid in her off camera.'

Jill points out that her performance as Lombard is not an imitation but an attempt to capture the spirit of the woman.

No newcomer to films, Jill Clayburgh has appeared in *The Terminal Man*, *Portnoy's Complaint*, and *The Thief Who Came to Dinner*. But the role of Carole Lombard is her first all-out starring part.

Director Sidney Furie spotted Jill when she co-starred with Lee Remick in the highly acclaimed television special, *Hustling*. Jill received an Emmy nomination. Furie tested her for the role of Carole Lombard, and the test was so impressive that the crew burst into applause after the director yelled, 'Cut.'

Like Lombard, Clayburgh comes from a wealthy background. She is intelligent and sophisticated, a graduate of Sarah Lawrence College. At 5 feet 8 inches she is three inches taller than Lombard. Though she is reminiscent of Lombard with a light, breezy manner, the high Lombard cheekbones and the graceful, easy carriage so memorable in Carole, Jill has a style and distinct quality of her own.

202

Jill observes: 'People worship Lombard, which is awesome. It was her personality that intrigued them, and one aspect of Lombard's personality, which had to be captured in the film, was her use of foul language.' But Jill points out that the Lombard language may appear tame today. 'If she said, "Oh, this is a piece of shit" now, people would probably consider that pretty mild.'

Jill was unconcerned with duplicating Lombard's physical appearance except she did bleach her hair for the role, which was an exacting task when it came to getting just the right blonde shading.

But it wasn't the 'Lombard Look' but 'that Lombard *quality*' that Jill sought. 'My performance is an impression of Lombard. Not an impersonation. It's an interpretation of what Carole was like *in real life*, and I had an advantage of Jim Brolin in that respect. People only have the Lombard screen image in mind.'

The assignment to create the fabulous wardrobe for *Gable and Lombard* – and accurately re-create 'The Gable and Lombard Look' – went to internationally famous Academy Award-winning costume designer Edith Head.

No one knows better than Miss Head the importance of costumes to a film. The roster of past-and-present superstars she has dressed comprises a virtual *Who's Who* of Hollywood: Katharine Hepburn, Grace Kelly, Elizabeth Taylor, Ingrid Bergman, Fred Astaire, Bette Davis, Cary Grant, Ginger Rogers, Marlene Dietrich, Audrey Hepburn, Paul Newman, Robert Redford – the list is incredible.

Edith has won more Academy Awards – 8 – and more Academy nominations – 33 – than any other motion-picture designer. She won Oscars for *The Heiress*, *All About Eve*, *Samson and Delilah*, *A Place in the Sun*, *Roman Holiday*, *Sabrina*, *The Facts of Life*, and *The Sting*. Her nominations include *The Greatest Show on Earth*, *To Catch a Thief*, *The Rose Tattoo*, *The Ten Commandments*, *Funny Face*, *Love With the Proper Stranger*, *Sweet Charity*, and *Airport*.

For *Gable and Lombard* Edith Head had an unlimited budget and created a spectacular assortment of costumes – from golf garb to evening gowns, including one of the most expensive gowns made for a film in recent years. Invaluable was Miss Head's first-hand knowledge of Gable and Lombard. Edith designed gowns for Lombard at Paramount in the 1930s and notes: 'Jill Clayburgh has the perfect body for Lombard clothes.'

There are thirty different *Gable and Lombard* outfits in all. The *pièce de resistance* is the breathtaking $7,500 bugle-beaded evening gown. The design was inspired by a gown Lombard actually wore. According to Miss Head, nothing like this new gown has been made for over thirty years – 'not because of the cost', states the designer, 'but because that sort of elegance hasn't been in style'.

Thanks to *Gable and Lombard*, it may come back in style. But not many people will be able to afford it. The gown would have taken eight to ten weeks to make in Lombard's day, and, because everything is done by hand, it took just as long today! A special silk chiffon material had to be located, which took weeks. Then the fabric was hand embroidered with a staggering total of forty thousand silver-lined bugle beads. The pattern was then cut. The entire ensemble cost $7,500, the price of a luxury automobile. In Lombard's day the same gown, according to Miss Head, would have cost around $1,000 to $1,500.

Gable and Lombard director Sidney Furie was born in Toronto, Canada, forty-three years ago. He graduated from Carnegie Tech in Pittsburgh, where he majored in fine arts and drama. Furie's first film success was the British-made *The Ipcress File*, which introduced Michael Caine to American audiences and won the British Academy Award for Best Picture.

When the director moved to Los Angeles in the mid-1960s he made many Hollywood films, including *Little Fauss and Big Halsey*, starring Robert Redford and Michael J. Pollard; *The Lawyer*, which introduced Barry Newman; and *Lady Sings the Blues*, for which Diana Ross won an Academy Award nomination as Best Actress for her performance as Billie Holiday.

Furie had always wanted to do a true love story for the screen. What better background for a love story than the tale of the courtship and marriage of Clark Gable and Carole Lombard.

Furie observes that the film, *Gable and Lombard*, 'is the story of two famous personalities whose love endured the narrow confines of the victorian morality of the thirties'.